RESEARCH ON EDUCATIONAL INNOVATIONS

THIRD EDITION

Arthur K. Ellis

EYE ON EDUCATION
6 DEPOT WAY WEST, SUITE 106
LARCHMONT, NY 10538
(914) 833–0551
(914) 833–0761 fax
www.eyeoneducation.com

Library of Congress Cataloging-in-Publication Data

Ellis, Arthur K.
     Research on educational innovations / Arthur K. Ellis.—3rd ed.
          p.   cm.
     Includes bibliographical references and index.
     ISBN 1-930556-12-8
     1. Education—United States—Experimental methods. 2. Educational innovations—United States. 3. Education—Research—United StatTitle.es. I.

     LB1027.3 .E45 2001
     370'.7'2073—dc21

                                                                              00–049589

10 9 8 7 6 5 4 3 2 1

Editorial and production services provided by
Richard H. Adin Freelance Editorial Services
52 Oakwood Blvd., Poughkeepsie, NY 12603-4112
(845-471-3566)

TABLE OF CONTENTS

ABOUT THE AUTHOR

Arthur K. Ellis is Professor of Education and Director of the International Center for Curriculum Studies at Seattle Pacific University. Previously, he taught in public schools in Oregon and Washington and at the University of Minnesota. He is the author or coauthor of 18 published books and numerous journal articles, book chapters, and scholarly papers. He consults to numerous government and private agencies and foundations and to various school systems in the United States and abroad.

PREFACE

Just as in agriculture the operations that come before the plant-
ing, as well as the planting itself, are certain and easy; but as
soon as the plant comes to life, there are various methods and
great difficulties in raising it; so it is with humans: little in-
dustry is needed to plant them, but it is quite a different bur-
den we assume from the moment of their birth, a burden full of
care and fear—that of training them and bringing them up.

Michel de Montaigne

Welcome to the third edition of *Research on Educational Innovations*.
The favorable reception and many positive reviews, citations, and adoptions given the first two editions is indeed gratifying. The purpose of this
edition remains as it was for the previous editions: to bring to your attention such fundamentals as definitions, descriptions, theoretical and empirical bases, critical analyses, and conclusions. This is done in a spirit of
inquiry in which you are invited to participate. The focus is upon major
educational innovations, by which is meant programs and curriculums
that have achieved widespread influence. Because the influx of new ideas
into our profession is continuous, it is necessary to be selective about the
innovations that can reasonably be included in this book. Specific practices and programs come and go. The criteria for a program's inclusion are
that the program be one of the most dominant in the literature, that it often
appears as a topic of professional meetings, that it is widely used in school
settings, and that it is emphasized in teacher education, both preservice
and inservice. The attempt is to be dispassionate and to avoid either promoting or disparaging any given innovation simply out of hand. Basing
the case on the evidence discovered, the clear prefererence is, to paraphrase Michelangelo (not Buffalo Bill), to let the chips fall.

Since the first two editions were published, major restructuring efforts
have dominated the educational agenda. The call for reform seems as ur-
gent at it ever was, perhaps more so. As a result, interest in innovative
practice remains high.

The emergence of new research and changing perspectives in the field
have made it possible to take a fresh look at many of those innovations
which were examined in the previous edition but which remain in the
forefront today. Some things fade away. New topics appear. Another
change from the first two editions is that my friend and colleague Jeff

Fouts has left university teaching to pursue other interests that make it impossible for him to be involved in this effort. I wish to acknowledge with gratitude the contributions he made to the first two books. His influence continues into this new edition. Thanks also to Naomi Petersen, Greg Firn, and Craig Scheiber for the work they did in finding sources of information.

We are fascinated by the new: new cars, new fashions, new insights, new ideas. There is something exciting and motivating about newness. Think about it: new hope, new beginnings. In recent American political history, we have had both the New Deal and the New Frontier. Our desire to try something new is often based on a wish to break with the past and the present, especially where feelings of discontent exist. In some sense, the new brings to mind utopian images and dreams of a better world.

American schools have become seedbeds of discontent in recent times. We read everywhere about the loss of confidence in our schools on the part of the public. Anyone who follows the story line has heard talk of a golden era in American public education. Our current efforts are placed alongside those of a mythical past and are found wanting. And even for those who don't spend a lot of time longing for the golden days of yesteryear, there is always the desire to improve, to do better. We set our goals not at levels of mediocrity, but at the far reaches of excellence.

So the search for what is new and good continues. The dream of every teacher and administrator is of new heights of achievement, civic participation, and personal fulfillment for the next generation. Much hope exists for the young. We see that hope at the PTA meeting when so many parents of kindergarten and first grade children show up. And we see the hope turn to reality, for better or for worse, as children find their way through the school years.

Like pilgrims in quest of the Holy Grail, we look for the curriculum or method that will get us where we want to go, to the land of excellence. And with great perseverance and unflagging good cheer, we are willing to try this or that innovation, hoping that at last we have something better than we've ever had before. We hear about cooperative learning, and we agree to try it because maybe it will improve the social fabric of classroom life and raise achievement at the same time. We hear about self-esteem programs and wonder what role we could play toward making kids feel better about themselves. And we read an article on brain-based learning and find ourselves agreeing that, of course, the little three-pound organ called the human brain has unlimited capabilities.

So the quest continues. Each year, it seems, new ideas about improving the system are brought to our attention, often with great fanfare. Some of them literally scream for our attention, reminding the more reflective among us of the centuries-old words of the writer Baltasar Gracian, who noted that a brand-new mediocrity is thought more of than accustomed excellence.

A dedicated purpose of this book is to help you separate the "brand-new mediocrities" from that which is excellent, whether old or new. To do this it proved useful to set up a screen, much in the way someone panning for gold in a mountain stream uses a screen to dip into the rushing waters. The screen allows what is not valuable to return to the creek while the rich ore is retained. It's not a perfect system, whether you are seeking gold ore or golden educational ideas. But if you are persistent, you will find some nuggets.

The screen used here is published research. This is so for two reasons. The first is that virtually everyone has access to published research through the readily available journals in education. This is not true of unpublished research. It is often nearly impossible to access. Much of the time we hear about it only because someone touting an innovation refers to certain glowing results without showing us the conditions, the controls, the design, and the analysis.

The second reason for setting this standard is that published research has undergone levels of careful scrutiny to which unpublished research is not subjected. Does this mean that unpublished research is necessarily bad? Perhaps not; it is difficult to say. But you can be assured of this: most of the time unpublished research simply does not meet the standards that you would knowingly demand if you were about to spend much time, energy, and money on a particular innovation. Research published in such journals as the *Review of Educational Research*, the *Journal of Educational Psychology*, and a number of other excellent publications is carefully reviewed by knowledgeable jurors before acceptance, or, in most cases, before rejection. In other words, you should not see the faulty research because it typically doesn't appear in these journals. It is not a perfect system, but it is preferable to the alternatives that come to mind.

It is reasonable to become excited about sound educational innovation. Why shouldn't we be? But there is no point in becoming excited about so-called improvements that really give us no proof of their goodness. Nothing is gained in the name of innovation when we find ourselves in the very same circumstance as that of the ancient King Pyrrhus, who said, "One more such 'victory' and we are undone." In ancient times messengers were often thrown into a well when they brought bad tidings, and merely taken for granted when the news they brought was good. This book contains messges about educational innovations, some favorable, some less so. Let us hope the metaphor of the messenger is not pushed too far. So be prepared—some of the tidings are good and some are less than that.

Let us all agree that we seek progress and not merely change. And let us all have the common sense of the little boy in Hans Christian Anderson's fairy tale, *The Emperor's New Clothes,* who said, "the Emperor is naked, he has no clothes on." When that is the case, we need to say so. The stakes are too high to think otherwise.

> *"It's amazing how little evaluation there is. Since the early 20th century, the people who have peddled the educational reform strategies that we all hear about tend to be successful because they're the best entrepreneurs. It doesn't necessarily have to do with any research credibility."*

Ellen Condliffe Lagemann, President
The National Academy of Education

1

THE NATURE OF
EDUCATIONAL INNOVATION

*One doesn't discover new lands without consenting
to lose sight of the shore for a very long time.*

André Gide

Each generation must answer anew a set of age-old questions. Those questions go to the heart of our existence. They are questions of purpose, of being, of destiny. They are questions of justice, of relationships, of goodness. The fact that previous generations have grappled with the same questions is helpful but not sufficient. The questions are so basic that we must address them; we ignore them at our peril. Others cannot answer them for us, although they can give us insights, and we can benefit from their experience. We must seek our own answers, however different or similar to those arrived at by our predecessors. This is so because the search is as important as the outcome and because situations change over time. It is the process of arriving at answers, however tentative or even deficient, which makes us human.

Just as we seek answers to life's larger questions, we seek answers within the frames of our professional existence, in this case teaching and learning. As teachers and administrators, we seek answers to questions about the nature of knowledge, the nature of learning, and the nature of teaching. We ask ourselves if there is a better way to organize teaching, a better way to present ideas to young people, a better way to assess learning. We grapple with such dualisms as control vs. freedom, cooperation vs. independence, time-on-task vs. creativity. As practical people working in school settings with all the complexities one finds in such socially contrived environments as playgrounds and lunchrooms, and such academically contrived environments as high school physics laboratories and primary reading classes, we wonder what to teach, how best to teach it, and even if what we teach has lasting value. These questions, necessary as they are, can deplete our energy, especially when we are continually reminded by the popular press that American schools are doing a poor job of preparing the nation's young for an increasingly complex future.

At the same time, the educational literature is filled with ideas and strategies for innovation: setting standards, mastery learning, whole language learning, interdisciplinary curriculum, learning styles, developmentally-appropriate practice, cooperative learning, effective teaching, authentic assessment, site-based management, and the list goes on. Each of these innovations is touted by its proponents as the key to an improved school experience for teachers and students. Administrators read about a given innovation and wonder whether it could be the answer for their school. A teacher attends a workshop where the presenter makes a compelling case for some "new paradigm." Like wandering nomads in search of the next oasis, we move from fad to fad in search of the next wellspring with the vague hope that we might find a permanent place to settle. Of course, we never do.

Still, the waves of innovation are received with mixed reactions. What is the source of our ambivalence toward innovation in education? On the one hand, we seem ready, as educational historian Herbert Kliebard (1992) has pointed out, to grasp at anything so long as it is *new*. There is a feeling, almost a fear, that our school could be left behind. On the other hand, those teachers and administrators who have been around for awhile have seen so many "innovations" come and go that a certain degree of cynicism sets in when they are told at fall meetings, "we are going to adopt a site-based management approach," or whatever.

This book represents an attempt to provide you with insights to a carefully selected set of innovations. The innovations chosen to appear in these pages have nationwide (often international) impact. They have application across a range of grade and subject levels. And they have considerable staying power. As you read about them, you should gain knowledge not only of certain specific innovations, but insights into the nature of innovation itself and how and to what extent a particular innovation, perhaps one that is yet to appear, is not merely new, but worthwhile.

At this point a cautionary note must be sounded. No new idea, no matter how well researched, is worthwhile outside a context of purpose. For example, if you were asked, "Is an integrated curriculum a good idea for my school," you really ought to respond by asking, "What is the purpose of my school?" No one can answer that question meaningfully except the people who have a genuine interest in your school. Now this may seem rather simplistic and even obvious to everyone. But the history of failure and disappointment in educational innovation starts with confusion of purpose. It inevitably leads to cynicism and the "we tried that" syndrome.

So somewhere in the matrix of your individual and school goal structures, you must measure any new educational idea's worth. The more meaningful question is not, "Is it the latest trend," but "Is it good for us?" Each educator, each school faculty, and each school community must face the same basic questions:

+ What does our school stand for?
+ What should students learn?
+ What are the best conditions for learning?
+ What experiences enhance learning?
+ How should classes and schools be organized?
+ How can we know if we are attaining our goals?

and so on. The questions are endless because:

+ Teaching is as much an art as a science.
+ Learning is a poorly understood process.
+ Students are diverse and they respond differentially.
+ Societal needs and demands change.
+ Local and site-specific needs differ considerably.

WHAT IS AN INNOVATION?

Innovation and *novelty* come from the same Latin root. They both imply something that is new. The idea that something is "new" is dear to our hearts. We have been conditioned by advertisers and promoters to associate "new" with "improved," whether the product is a detergent or a curriculum. The *Oxford English Dictionary* defines *innovation* as "the introduction of novelties." "Innovation" is a noun related to the verb "to innovate," first found in print in 1561 in T. Norton's *Calvin's Instructions*, in which the sentence appears, "A desire to innovate all things moveth troublesome men." So, the term appears to have reached through to the emotions, negative and positive, from that time to this day.

In the school-based world of teaching and learning, innovation seems to be all-important. School people often express a desire to be on the "cutting edge" of things, to know the latest trends, to avoid being old-fashioned or out-of-date. The teacher workshop/inservice training business, which employs educational innovations as its stock-in-trade, is a multi-million-dollar industry in the United States and Canada and increasingly around the world.

WHERE ARE THEY NOW?

A generation ago, a series of innovations entered the world of education. Depending on your age or your powers of recollection, you may recognize some of them. They included outcome-based education, career education, values clarification, multicultural education, structure of the disciplines, human relations training, open schools, competency-based education, peace education, back to the basics, bilingual education, and a few others. Where are they now? The answers vary. Some disappeared without a trace. Some are the forerunners of present-day reform efforts. Some are still around in one form or another. This will always be the case. Today's trend is often tomorrow's forgotten dream. Some of the innovations that sweep through the school scene are nothing more than fads. Some have greater staying power. Let's look at why this might be so.

RESEARCH-BASED?

A common claim of most educational innovations is that they are "research-based." The intent, apparently, is to give school personnel cause to think that a particular program is valid and reasonable for them to use because it will yield improved results. The term *research-based* lends almost mystical qualities to the innovation, making it difficult if not impossible for the average teacher, administrator, or school board member to challenge the claims made in behalf of the innovation. Who among us, after all, is going to challenge RESEARCH? The fact is that many school personnel simply do not understand the arcane procedures of educational research with its language of statistical analysis, control groups, experimental designs, and so on. As a result, they are left to the mercy of persuasive arguments by "experts" who tell them what the research says and what they should therefore do. The purpose here is to demystify the process.

To begin, it is useful to consider examples of research from the field of natural science because science has served as the paradigm for most social science research, of which educational research is a subset. We begin with the idea of theory. Theories are *tentative* ways of explaining and predicting phenomena. A theory represents a carefully considered set of ideas about something. The development of a theoretical model is often the quest of persons doing pure or basic (as opposed to applied) research. While working in the field of physics, Albert Einstein developed his theory of relativity, a theory that stated that all motion must be defined relative to a frame of reference. In other words, space and time are relative, not absolute, concepts. They take on meaning in relation to their context. Einstein proposed his ideas as a theoretical model to be tested, not as a fact. Other physicists have conducted research on the theory, finding much supportive evidence for it. Today, the theory of relativity serves as a useful model for the explanation and prediction of the behavior of matter and energy. However, as a theory it is subject to new interpretation, and in time it may well be modified considerably in the light of new knowledge.

Most often, scientific theory emerges as the result of some preliminary research in a particular field. When Charles Darwin sailed aboard H.M.S. *Beagle* to the Galapagos Islands and to the South Pacific in the nineteenth century, he made careful, systematic observations of certain animals and their unique characteristics. From his data collecting, he advanced the hypothesis that changes in the physical characteristics of animals were the result of an ongoing, evolutionary process. More than a century later, his theory of evolution remains the object of scientific study, although it has itself evolved considerably over time. Many questions have been answered, but far more questions, remain so research on the topic continues.

These first two examples are about the behavior of matter and energy and adaptive changes in the physical characteristics of animals. As complex as those issues are, they seem pure and uncomplicated when compared to theories advanced within the frame of the social sciences. The theories of Sigmund Freud and Karl Marx, for example, were social theories. Freud developed a theory of personality based on research with patients who were mainly institutionalized, sexually abused women. In time, he built a huge amount of scaffolding around his observations, and his ideas became so pervasive that whole terminologies entered the vocabulary of the middle class (e.g., "Freudian slip," "ego") as a result of his work. To many, his ideas seemed more like solid findings than theories, and they found their way into literature, film, and everyday life, not to mention introduction to psychology classes. Today, many of his ideas seem rather quaint, and unlike Darwin's or Einstein's, they are not really the basis for emerging advancements in the field of psychological research.

The theories of Karl Marx were tried out on about half the world's population under the name of communism. They still prevail in one form or another in certain countries. Marx theorized a leadership of the working class and a utopian society unfettered by religion, private ownership, competition, and other traditional forms of thought and practice. One might argue whether Marx's pure theory was in fact what was institutionalized in the former USSR, its satellites, and so forth. As bizarre and ugly as the socialist "experiment" called Marxism was, it does serve to make a point to consumers of educational research: Theories of human behavior have real, lasting consequences when we try them out on human beings, so we had better be careful when we consider applying them to our classrooms and schools. The leap from theory to practice is often quite a jump and one fraught with imminent peril.

How Educational Theories Develop

Basic or pure research findings from psychology and other fields are often used to develop theoretical models of teaching and learning. Those theoretical models are then used to derive implications for education. In most cases, this process takes many years. A specific school program emerges when certain educational implications are in turn developed into a coherent set of teaching strategies, materials, learner activities, and classroom or school structural changes. Therefore, the developer exhorts us, change what you are doing presently and adopt this innovation. Why? Because it is better, and the "research" shows that to be true or we would not ask you to do it.

Three steps are involved along the way to your classroom or school: (1) pure research; (2) educational implications; and (3) suggested classroom or school practice. Let's examine the steps one at a time using a specific example, *cooperative learning*.

LEVEL I

In the 1940s and 1950s, social psychologist Morton Deutsch used his research findings to develop a theory of social interdependence. Like most good scientific researchers, Deutsch was familiar with prior research, especially, in this case, the work of Kurt Lewin in the 1930s and 1940s. Lewin had developed an idea called field theory which said in essence that a group is actually a "dynamic whole" rather than a mere collection of individuals. What Lewin meant by "dynamic whole" is that the behaviors of members in a group are interactive, thereby creating the potential for greater outcomes than one might get merely by adding the sum of the parts of a group. Deutsch had theorized that social interdependence exists only when the goals of individuals in a group are affected, for better or worse, by the others. It was the "better" that intrigued him. Building on Lewin's insights to motivation, inclusion, and democratic processes, Deutsch theorized that when people with common goals worked with each other in cooperative fashion, something better happened than when they either worked alone or competed with each other. Deutsch went on to hypothesize that the process is enhanced when individuals *perceive* that they can reach their goals only if other members of their group can also reach their goals. In repeated experiments, Deutsch found that his theory seemed to hold up. He published his results, thus allowing others to support, extend, or challenge his findings in the free marketplace of intellectual endeavor. Others, of course, contributed to the theoretical construct. One can, for example, readily trace its origins to Gestalt theory which emerged in nineteenth-century Austria and which became noted for its pioneering studies in perception. Gestalt theory took issue with reductionist, atomistic processes popular at the time. The Gestalt theorem that "the whole of anything is greater than the sum of its parts" is fundamental to cooperative learning.

LEVEL II

In time, educational researchers began to show interest in the theory of social interdependence. They reasoned that what worked in small groups and workplace settings where the theory had originally been field-tested might also work in classrooms. School classrooms seemed like a logical place to apply the theory of social interdependence because a typical room has about 30 kids who traditionally each work alone, often in de facto competitive environments, or who, even when placed in groups, might not have the skills or inclination to identify and achieve a common goal. Also, because of tradition, amongst other things, most students (and often their parents) probably do not *perceive* that they can better attain their academic goals if other students improve as well. It almost seems contrary to common sense. The research studies in classrooms, of which there have been hundreds, were driven by questions of increased achievement, increased motivation to learn, attitude toward school, and attitude toward fellow students, as well as by other outcomes. Among the leading Level II researchers are Robert Slavin of Johns Hopkins University, and David and Roger Johnson of the University of Minnesota, who, in collaboration with their associates, have conducted numerous empirical studies of the effects of cooperative learning in school settings. As the efficacy of cooperative learning became increasingly clear, especially its beneficial effects in conceptual and problem-solving tasks, the argument for teachers and administrators to use it in classrooms became compelling.

LEVEL III

Efficacious outcomes for cooperative learning were increasingly reported at professional meetings and in research in education journals throughout the 1970s, 1980s, and 1990s and on into the present century. Many of the reported studies had been conducted in school classrooms across a range of grade and subject matter levels. The word began to spread. It was at this point that schools of education began to incorporate cooperative learning methods into teacher education courses, and workshops, sometimes conducted by the researchers themselves, sprang up around the country. Any teacher or administrator interested in applying cooperative learning in the classroom or school had little trouble finding workshops, institutes, retreats, classes, or "practical" articles in such magazines as *Instructor* and *Learning*. In short, cooperative learning was sweeping through the educational community like wildfire. The workshops, institutes, retreats, classes, and articles were mainly focused on practical applications of the theory and were available in both initial and advanced forms. Teachers and parents wanted answers to such questions as, "How do I know the slower students won't just copy the ideas of better students?" "How do I measure individual achievement?" "What do I do if a kid won't cooperate with other members of the group?" "How is this different from just assigning kids to committees?" "Won't this slow down higher achievers?" Out of these excellent, practical questions came new educational research studies, journal articles, and books such as David and Roger Johnson's *Learning Together and Alone* (1999).

Thus, more than 50 years after the theory of social interdependence began to crystallize, and more than a century since the origins of Gestalt psychology, the ongoing refinement of school and classroom applications of cooperative learning continues. At this point, more than 900 research studies conducted in classroom settings and school districts have been conducted. Literally thousands of policy articles can be found on the topic. And all of this is completely necessary simply because it's a long leap from a theory of social interdependence formulated by social psychologists in the 1930s and 1940s to a third-grade science class in the twenty-first century.

A final note is in order. A theory exists in relatively pure form. Its empirical test comes when researchers try it out under controlled conditions. These tests make it possible to accept, modify, or reject the theory in specific settings. However, the fact that a theory tests well under controlled conditions does not guarantee that it will survive the inevitable distortions that come with real-world applications by individuals and groups who choose it or are told to use it. These insights have been enriched through the rise of the qualitative research movement where life in classrooms is chronicled on the basis of careful observations, interviews, and interpretations.

In summary, Level I is theory building, or pure research, or both; Level II is empirical research, either quantitative, qualitative, or a combination thereof; and Level III is program evaluation where it becomes possible to learn the extent to which a program or curriculum is successful when its implementation becomes widespread in schools or entire districts.

Cooperative learning as a case study in the nature of educational innovation represents a positive example of the gradual unfolding of the process of how a theory germinates and how it ultimately finds its way to classroom practice. If the theory has real promise, it will interact with classroom practice in such a way as to cause further refinement of the theory. Thus, the process is cyclical rather than linear. If it were linear, we would simply impose the finished product on a classroom. This has been done with disastrous consequences. The exciting aspect of the teacher's role or that of the administrator is that they can be a fundamental part of the process. This is so because they are key figures in the ongoing *refinement* of an idea, not merely because they grabbed on to the latest fad. The practical application of ideas by teachers and students in real-world educational settings represents the best test of an idea's staying power.

CONCLUSION

Each of the educational innovations examined in this book began as a theory far removed from classroom life. Each has found its way into the classrooms and schools of America. Let us examine how that happened. An analysis of each raises a basic set of questions including:

- How sound was the original theory on which the idea is based?
- How appropriate is the research that employs the use of this theory in school settings?
- What does this theory purport to do that will improve life in schools and classrooms?
- What claims are made in behalf of the theory as a necessary component of the school curriculum?
- What are the requisite conditions of the theory for school success?
- Why would someone want to use the ideas that flow from this theory in school settings?

Classroom life unfolds within a complex set of conditions. The list of human and material variables is endless. No two individuals and no two classrooms are the same, just as no two schools or communities are the same. The presence or absence of one student in a classroom changes the circumstances. Each teacher's personal, practical sense of teaching and learning is different. Leadership is variable from one school to the next, ranging from dynamic to nil. The public's perception and support of schools in each community has much to do with a school's success or failure. And, of course, what happens in families matters even more than what happens at school.

As teachers and administrators, we are always trying to improve ourselves. We want our efforts to help young people to learn to be productive. Therefore, we seek the help of others who also care and who can help us. And that is what this book is about.

REFERENCES

Kliebard, H. (1992). Constructing a history of the american curriculum, in Jackson, P. (Ed.), *Handbook of research on curriculum*. New York: Macmillan Publishing Company.

Johnson, D., and Johnson, R. (1999). *Learning together and alone*. Boston: Allyn and Bacon.

2

THE STRUCTURE OF EDUCATIONAL INNOVATION

*Out of every ten innovations attempted, all very
splendid, nine will end up in silliness.*

Antonio Machado

It can be argued that there is very little that is new in education. It can
be argued, and was rather eloquently in the book of *Ecclesiastes*, that there
is nothing new under the sun. Most things have been tried before in some
form. But our experiences are different from those of the previous generation because they are *our* experiences. As we consider the many problems
of teaching and learning, new perspectives emerge and compete for our
attention. In these times of sustained criticism of the educational system,
new ideas, new terminology, and new reform programs are abundant
simply because people sincerely want to improve things. It is as simple as
supply and demand. People demand reform, and someone tries to supply
it. In fact, the proliferation of new programs, which range from the well
researched to something less than that, has reached a level of staggering
proportions.

At this point it will serve us well to return to some of the ideas presented in Chapter 1. The chart presented in Figure 2.1 illustrates how innovative programs emerge and are developed. Early on someone identifies an idea or research which suggests the possibility of a theory about
human behavior. The theory might emerge from insight into human behavior, thinking processes, personality, or perceptions of reality, just to
name a few examples. In any event, the theory may have implications for
how teachers teach and under what conditions students learn best. Jean
Piaget's theory of the development of the intellect, for example, clearly
identified age-related stages through which one progresses. Further, the
theory stated that persons in a particular stage of development are capable of certain intellectual activities and not capable of others, which must
happen later. This theory intrigued quite a number of educational researchers who wished to apply Piaget's ideas to school settings, something Piaget had never done. Some researchers hypothesized that intellec-

11

tual development could be accelerated with enriched programs. This line of thinking amused Piaget; he called it the "American question."

FIGURE 2.1. DEVELOPMENT OF INNOVATIVE PROGRAMS

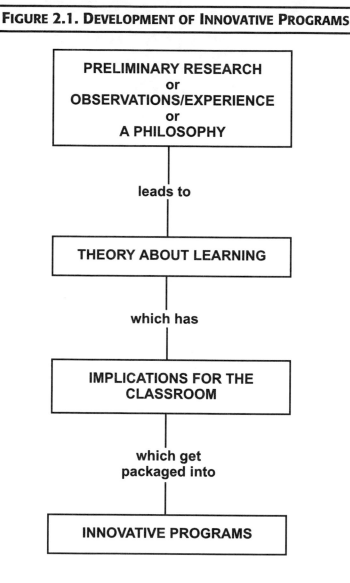

In any event, at some point someone in the education field thinks through the implications of a given theory and develops the ideas into a program or curriculum suitable for use in educational research. This does-n't always happen over night, for one reason or another. An example of this is the Russian psychologist Lev Vygotsky's theory of social and environmental factors in learning, developed in the early decades of the twentieth century. Only recently has it had much impact on American education. A particular program derived from theory might be designed to change teacher behaviors, student behaviors, or classroom environments to conform to the ideal set of conditions on which the theory is predicated.

REAPING THE WHIRLWIND

What is the role of educational research in all of this? How is educational research different from systematic program evaluation? The claims are that many of these innovative programs are research-based. However, it should be pointed out that there is a difference between saying that a program is research-based, and that research has shown a program to be effective under certain conditions. Unfortunately, many educators do not make this crucial distinction. *In fact, the best that many developers can claim is that the theory and resulting programs are developed from basic research, often in psychology, into programs for teaching and learning. Often, however, innovative programs are questionably based on theoretical models, with scant evidence to support or justify exactly how the program is truly a practical application of the theory.* This is the initial realm of question posing that educators should enter with those who tout a particular program.

Ideally, before expenditures of time and money are spent on the widespread implementation of educational innovations, those programs should be subjected to careful, unbiased investigation through the evaluation of pilot programs. Unfortunately, as educational researcher Robert Slavin has pointed out, this generally tends to happen *toward the end* of the cycle of the innovation, after the rush has died down, and educators have cynically moved on to some other new activity or program. Thus, we reap the whirlwind.

How did our profession get caught up in this succession of fad-driven spirals of innovation based not on goodness, but on newness? Slavin (1989), one of the most careful researchers in the educational community, has observed and examined this phenomenon over the years. His insights into the process are rather revealing. Slavin writes that:

> Generational progress does occur in education, but it is usually a product of changes in society, rather than changes in educational techniques themselves. For example, the clearly beneficial trend toward desegregation and more equal treatment of minorities represents true generational progress, but it arose from social and legal changes, not from educational innovation. More often, education resembles such fields as fashion and design, in which change mirrors shifts in taste and social climate, and is not usually thought of as true progress. (p. 752)

Slavin states further that:

One of the most important reasons for the continuing existence of the educational pendulum is that educators rarely wait for or demand hard evidence before adopting new practices on a wide scale. Of course, every innovator claims research support for his or her methods; at a minimum, there is usually a "gee whiz" story or two about a school or district that was "turned around" by the innovation. Alternatively, a developer may claim that, while the program itself has not been formally evaluated, the principles on which it is based are supported by research. (p. 753)

ONE MORE SUCH VICTORY AND WE ARE UNDONE

Pyrrhus, king of ancient Epirus, left us the term *Pyrrhic Victory*, an allusion to his battlefield triumphs, which were often accompanied by horrendous causalities among his own troops. He became famous for his statement: "One more such victory and I am undone." There are many such "victories" in the annals of education, but here is a recent example. Slavin examines in detail the Madeline Hunter model. He calls Hunter "perhaps the most popular educational trainer of our time" (p. 754). This book does not contain a chapter on Hunter's program because the movement itself has faded to the point that many newer teachers have not even heard of it. But it can serve as an excellent example of what happens in the name of educational innovation. Perhaps we can learn from history, perhaps not.

It seems almost inconceivable that there are educators today who have not heard of the Hunter program or model, but there are. So let us give it a brief overview here. The model was sometimes called Instructional Theory into Practice (ITIP) or Program for Effective Teaching (PET). It emerged in the early 1970s, promoted through a series of books and workshops by Madeline Hunter. One of her books is titled *Teach More—Faster!* (1995); another is titled *Improved Instruction* (1995). Throughout the 1970s and well into the 1980s, schools, and oftentimes entire districts and states, provided inservice training in the Hunter model. Entire staff development programs and faculty evaluation procedures were based on it. District personnel officers would routinely quiz prospective teachers on their knowledge of the Hunter model. Courses for preservice and inservice teachers, where people actually got college credit for studying ITIP "theory," were offered throughout the land. Student teachers and students in undergraduate methods classes were expected to develop lesson plans and units that used the ITIP steps to effective teaching as a template. Teachers themselves were often divided over the program. Many became advocates and some were themselves trained as ITIP trainers, creating a multiplying effect. Some teachers shrugged it off as one more fad they had to endure. A few brave souls openly questioned the validity of the entire thing, but that took some courage in light of its overwhelming popularity and near-complete dominance. The amazing thing is that as it disappeared, there were no apologies, seemingly no regrets. But the lesson to be learned by those who wish to profit from it is enormous. It draws out the danger present in what the philosopher Francis Bacon called, "The Idol of the Tribe." When the Idol of the Tribe is worshipped, few dare question events because, after all, everyone is doing it. It's the "in" thing to do. Basically, a mentality is created where criticism is not welcome, to say the least.

The ITIP or PET program itself is a method for thinking through and acting on the key elements of a lesson with suggested procedures for lesson development. Purportedly based on educational and psychological theory and research, it focused on four elements:

1. Teaching to an objective (generally a behavioral objective);
2. Teaching at the correct level of (cognitive) difficulty;
3. Monitoring and adjusting instruction (i.e., formative evaluation and reteaching, mastery learning); and
4. Using established principles of learning (e.g., reinforcement, motivation, and transfer).

In this regard, it could be considered a technical or means/ends tool, designed to help teachers with the "science of teaching."

The ITIP movement followed the "pendulum" swing described by Slavin. It serves as a classic example. The program was proposed in the early 1970s and implemented in a few school districts. Anecdotal claims of great success were made. The word spread rapidly that here at last was a research-based program that worked in real-world school settings. ITIP became *de rigueur* among staff developers. Schools of education incorporated it into their teacher training programs. By the late 1970s and early 1980s the movement had begun to sweep the country, even though there were no quality studies that showed the program was at all effective in increasing student learning. Complaints by researchers and other critics were either ignored or thought of as sour grapes. Anecdotal stories proliferated to verify the program's success.

The program's originator, Madeline Hunter, appeared at conventions, wrote books and articles, and consulted with school districts directly. Where she was unavailable, surrogates took her place. Thousands of teachers and administrators attended workshops at beginning and advanced levels. It became generally expected that anyone who was "current" knew the ITIP protocols. At its peak, the Hunter program was being used, and in many cases enforced by district officers, in all 50 states, and in other countries as well. Its popularity exceeded any phenomenon in modern school practice history.

By the mid-to-late 1980s interest in ITIP began to wane as staff developers moved on to other innovations such as Outcome-Based Education (OBE), itself more recently a victim of changing tastes and times. They did this not because OBE had been proven to be any better, but because it had become "the latest trend." At about this time, evaluation results of ITIP programs showed that the program had impact that was no more positive on student learning than random efforts by teachers. The research results mattered little because by the time they weighed in, ITIP had pretty much run its course. New fads had taken its place.

IN RETROSPECT

What was touted as an educational program based on "research" was actually a classic example of the process of implementation described earlier. Many of the elements of ITIP *were* based on psychological research and learning theory, but the implementation of the program itself had not been evaluated with quality research to determine its effectiveness in increasing student learning. For example, reinforcement was identified as one of the key components of ITIP. Psychological research has, in fact, clearly shown that positive reinforcement of learning predictably results in increased learning. Similarly, psychological research has also shown that the immediacy of feedback, another ITIP protocol, can serve as a highly supportive factor in learning. Both of these are elements of ITIP that have a substantiated research base. Other elements of ITIP, such as teaching to the correct level of difficulty, were based on theoretical models, in this instance, Benjamin Bloom's taxonomy of educational objectives in the cognitive domain, a model the very vocabulary of which raises fundamental questions.

In this manner, then, ITIP was presented as a research-based model of teaching and learning, and in one sense it was. Certain individual elements were based on psychological research in the area of learning. In other words, specific elements of the program may have been sound in and of themselves under given conditions. But when the entire package was put together as a unified model, that is, when individual research findings and theories were combined to form one unified construct (usually in the form of lesson plans) called ITIP, it was no longer actually correct to say that ITIP was research-based. The very act of conceptualizing ITIP resulted in a new construct consisting of many divergent research findings and theories. It was, therefore, a new entity that as such had not been researched at all. In retrospect, that may be giving ITIP too much credit. Actually, the German educator Johann Herbart had conceptualized an almost identical scheme in the nineteenth century, one that identified five points in effective teaching. It, too, swept across our landscape like a prairie fire. Today, only a handful of educators have even heard of it or of Herbart. As the poet and philosopher George Santayana noted, "Those who cannot remember the past are condemned to repeat it."

THE LONG AND WINDING ROAD FROM THEORY TO PRACTICE

Perhaps an analogy will serve us well in explaining the complex issue of validating an educational innovation, even one "based" on sound theories. We know from the laws of physics that a billiard ball struck at a certain angle by another billiard ball will behave in a predictable fashion, at least on a flat, well-made, felt-covered billiard table where there are no competing, interfering variables such as an imperfectly shaped ball, a gale-force wind, a table with uneven legs, molasses poured on the surface, and so forth. But what happens to our billiard ball, even under optimum conditions, if the table is littered with a dozen other billiard balls? The answer is that the laws of physics still work, but the situation is quite complex because of the probable interactions of the other balls with the ball that is initially struck. So now we have balls going in all directions. Actually, a billiard table littered with billiard balls is a fairly simple situation compared to a classroom filled with 30 students. Thus, a theory about motivation developed under controlled conditions during psychological experiments has only limited predictive validity in the seemingly random, infinitely complex world of classroom life. In other words, the conditions of the billiard table in the laboratory may be rather pristine compared to the rather messy billiard table in the form of the typical classroom. The theory itself may indeed be valid, but now the theory no longer stands in the splendid isolation of controlled laboratory conditions. It interacts with and becomes a mere part of an infinitely more complex situation. The point is not to disparage educational or psychological research. On the contrary, it is quite helpful and needed when it is done well. It is the misapplication and over-reaching of research findings that should bother all of us. The claims made by someone who says, "the research shows..." should be carefully considered before we enter into wholesale policy or curriculum change.

The business of teaching and learning in school settings is a very serious trust. All of us involved in the work of schools must do our best to honor that trust. We know that all is not well in the world of teaching and learning in America. As educators, we are very vulnerable to new nostrums and fixes that will make things right at last. Change is a necessary condition of progress, and it behooves us to make the most meaningful changes possible. The best hope is that as you examine the various attempts at innovation found in this book, you will learn to ask the right questions and that you will find useful answers.

REFERENCES

Hunter, M. (1995). *Teach more—faster!* New York: Corwin Press.

Hunter, M. (1995). *Improved instruction.* New York: Corwin Press.

Slavin, R. (1989). PET and the pendulum: Fadism in education and how to stop it. *Phi Delta Kappan, 70,* 752–758.

3

"THE RESEARCH SAYS..."

There aren't any embarrassing questions—
just embarrassing answers.

Carl Rowan

Have you ever found yourself at a meeting or conference listening to a speaker who pauses dramatically and states in august tones, "Well, the research says…?" Everyone, including you, quickly puts pen to paper in anticipation of some significant pronouncement that will change school life forevermore. If we only had a nickel for each time an education hustler has used such a phrase! If only it were as significant a statement as it appears to be to the uninitiated. The only appropriate response that comes to mind in the midst of such confusion is, "What research?"

In fact, the claim of virtually all innovators or purveyors of innovation is that research has in some strategic way played an important part in the evolution and development of their ideas, programs, or materials. And in some sense, the claim is generally true, but often misleading. For example, if someone claims that his or her program for elementary children is based in part on learning transfer, we may be impressed. After all, the concept of transfer of learning is well documented in the annals of psychological research. But the leap from research in a laboratory setting to classroom application is long and difficult.

WHAT "KIND" OF RESEARCH?

The following pages describe a classification system that should prove helpful as you attempt to sort out different kinds of research. With this knowledge you will be able to determine for yourself what is behind the statement, "the research says.…"

The term "research" has become so generic that it can and does refer to a wide range of activities. For example, you may "research" the cost of an airline ticket by checking on prices from five different airlines. To a freshman, a "research" paper is often little more than a collection of what other people have said about a topic. There is the old story of the student who searched the library for ideas before reaching the insight that, to make his term paper truly meaningful, he needed to "research" the topic, so he searched and researched until he got it right. To a geneticist or an engineer, research may mean mainly experimental studies conducted under controlled conditions. On the other hand, we have "the teacher as researcher" model, often referred to as action research, which is typically a narrative of classroom events. So, we use the same term to imply rather different pursuits under rather different conditions.

Currently, there is the ongoing debate over the relative value of two research paradigms—quantitative and qualitative. The origins of the debate are profoundly philosophical, and the nature of the debate is at times quite heated, with each side claiming to do research that is more valid. Others, searching perhaps for the golden mean, cite the necessity of doing both.

In spite of these problems of definition, it is helpful to conceptualize educational research by thinking of a model of research with three levels, each of which has different, but related, implications for educational innovation. The first is basic or pure research done theoretically and in "laboratory" settings; the second is applied research done under reasonably controlled conditions in school settings; and the third is evaluation research applied to school programs once they have been implemented. Each is quite different from the others, and each yields its own unique types of conclusions (see Figure 3.1).

LEVEL I RESEARCH

Level I research is basic or pure research on learning and behavior. It is most commonly conducted in experimental or laboratory settings by psychologists, learning theorists, linguists, and others. Its purpose is to establish a theoretical construct or idea as having some validity. For example, Jean Piaget constructed a theory of stages of intellectual development through which children pass on their way to adult thought (Piaget, 1960). Jerome Bruner constructed a theory of the structure of knowledge that included alternative ways by which knowledge of some reality could be represented to learners (Bruner, 1966, 1996). And Howard Gardner has constructed a theory of multiple intelligences that essentially broadens the definition of the term "intelligence" (Gardner, 1986). There are many such examples in a field that certainly has no shortage of theories.

The research from which a theory emerges may come from controlled studies employing traditional empirical methods, or from qualitative, subjective observations, or from both. Invariably, it also takes into account prior contributions to the topic, modifying or possibly even rejecting them. This type of theory development is referred to as "grounded theory." It is a process of deriving constructs and theories directly from immediate data that the researcher has collected. However, the usefulness of the constructs and theories grounded in the specific data must be validated with further research.

FIGURE 3.1. THE THREE LEVELS OF EDUCATIONAL RESEARCH

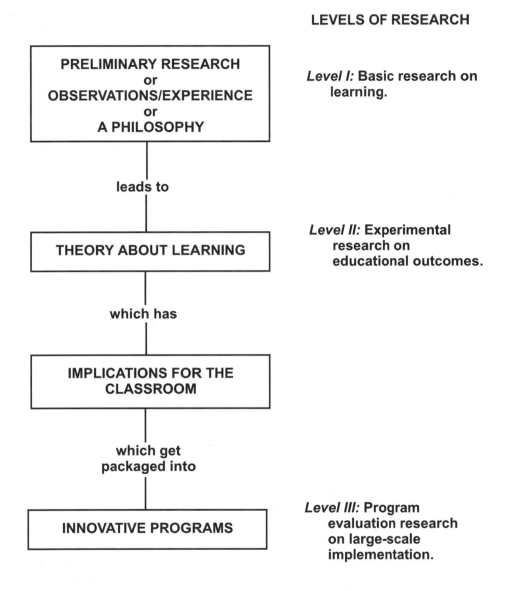

LEVELS OF RESEARCH

PRELIMINARY RESEARCH
or
OBSERVATIONS/EXPERIENCE
or
A PHILOSOPHY

Level I: Basic research on learning.

leads to

THEORY ABOUT LEARNING

Level II: Experimental research on educational outcomes.

which has

IMPLICATIONS FOR THE CLASSROOM

which get packaged into

INNOVATIVE PROGRAMS

Level III: Program evaluation research on large-scale implementation.

It is important to note that not all educational theories are derived from such research. It is possible for a learning theory to emerge out of a philosophical perspective or world view which may or may not have empirical support. For example, if a person is convinced of the inherent goodness of human beings, that person may quite readily propose that children's learning and their accompanying desire to learn would increase in a supportive, nonrestrictive, open environment. For the theory to be taken seriously, of course, it would need to have a well-established rationale. Such examples of theory building based on philosophical positions probably account for as many or more theories than do theories grounded in empirical data. More often, a significant theory contains elements of both.

Although Level I research can serve as a foundation for curriculum development, it is not designed to answer applied educational questions directly. Piaget claimed on the basis of his research that most 8-year-olds are in a stage of concrete operations, leading many builders of innovative curriculum packages to put together mathematics and science activities that involved manipulative materials. And, rightly or wrongly, they did that on the assumption that the message from pure research could be applied to groups of 25 or 30 children learning together in a classroom setting. The extent to which it is reasonable to make such assumptions becomes a function of Level II research.

LEVEL II RESEARCH

Level II research involves studies designed to test the efficacy of particular programs or instructional methods in *educational* settings. Educational researchers who are interested in applying theories and procedures developed at the pure or basic level generally conduct such studies. For example, an educational researcher might attempt to set up controlled conditions in several classrooms for the purpose of comparing, say, cooperative learning in social studies with independent student learning. The experimental conditions might call for randomly assigning students and teachers to different treatment modes or conditions where the same material is studied. Pre- and posttests may be administered to all participants and comparisons made to determine whether a statistically significant difference occurred between or among treatments. Typcially, an *independent variable*, the treatment(s) is tested to see what effects it has on a *dependent variable*, the outcome (for example, achievement). In addition, other variables may be taken into account by the researcher, including gender, age, socioeconomic status, and so forth.

Level II research is applied research because (a) it is conducted in the same or similar settings that are actually found in schools, and (b) it makes no attempt to develop a theory, but rather attempts to make instructional or curricular applications of a given theory. At its best, Level II research provides practical insights that cannot be derived directly from pure research. Thus, even though we all can agree that reinforcement has been shown to be a powerful psychological concept by pure researchers, it remains for the Level II researcher to demonstrate how it might be advantageous to systematically apply reinforcement in teaching in classroom settings.

Level II research is crucial to the process of validation of programs or methods of instruction. But time and time again, this step is simply ignored or poorly crafted as program developers or purveyors urge teachers and administrators to adopt a particular product. To return to the ITIP or PET "theory into practice" model for a moment, in retrospect we can see that it claimed its validity on the basis of such pure or basic research constructs as reinforcement, transfer, retention, and so forth, which are in fact well established. But it was almost totally lacking in any proof of improved learning when one takes those constructs and "packages" them as a template for use by teachers in classroom settings. The same thing can be said for a number of other programs that have swept the country such as "Assertive Discipline," "Outcome-Based Education," and "Higher Order Thinking Strategies," to name a few.

One of the best sources for school personnel to search at Level II is the journal *Review of Educational Research,* which is published by the American Educational Research Association (AERA). This journal carries reviews, syntheses, and meta-analyses of various programs, projects, and packages. Doing so will give you insight into the quantity and nature of applied research that has been conducted in a given area. Other useful journals include the *Educational Researcher, The Journal of Educational Research,* and the research journals of the various professional organizations such as the National Council of Teachers of Mathematics and the International Reading Association.

A final point about Level II research is that each study, even if it represents good research, is severely limited in its generalizability. If, for example, a study were conducted of teaching methods of reading and literature with fourth grade inner-city children, then whatever the results, it would be unwise to generalize them to, for example, rural eighth grade students. This is why large numbers of good investigations about a given program should be carried out before school districts jump on this or that bandwagon. Cooperative learning, to cite an example where this has been done, has been and continues to be investigated in such a wide variety of school-based settings that its Level II foundation is quite secure, especially compared to most other innovations. Level II research in education is invariably improved by carefully crafted replication studies, something that is all too rare in our field.

LEVEL III RESEARCH

Level III research is evaluation research designed to determine the efficacy of programs at the level of school or district implementation. It is by far the least likely of the three types to be carried out in any systematic way, and because of this, programs (good, bad, or indifferent) usually go through phases from initial enthusiasm to gradual abandonment, replaced by the next fad.

Examples of Level III research include evaluation studies that examine the overall effects on teachers and students of a particular district- or schoolwide innovation. If a district changes, for example, from basal reading instruction to whole language learning, it is the job of evaluation researchers to determine exactly what changes were brought about and what the results of those changes were. This might involve interviews with teachers, students, and parents, the application of classroom environmental scales and observations to determine student perceptions of whole language learning, assessments of the amount and nature of support for the innovation, and analyses of achievement data over time.

It is important to note that an educational theory may have sound research support at Levels I and II, and yet still may not be successful when implemented on a larger scale. This could happen for a number of reasons. For example, Level II research may have been conducted with highly trained teachers or with teachers who were quite supportive of the new program and who volunteered for the Level II research. When the program is implemented on a districtwide scale, however, there may well be many teachers who are skeptical of it, who are reluctant to participate, who are poorly trained, or who have decided on their own to make certain adaptations to the program. The availability of strategic and tactical support in the form of administrative and inservice leadership, as well as parental reaction, also represent factors which become known only over time. These and other variables make it crucial that Level III research or program evaluation be conducted.

A generation ago when the New Math swept the country, it had a pretty firm foundation at Levels I and II, but what little evidence we did gain at Level III showed us that many teachers were actually subverting the New Math, preferring to teach traditional arithmetic in its place whenever they could. Mixed to negative parental reaction was seriously underestimated to say the least. And even the more farsighted of developers probably underestimated the drumbeat of criticism that arose in the popular press. So, even if you are convinced that the theory behind some new program is sound, and even if you have seen published evidence of controlled studies in classroom settings that are supportive of the theory's application, you're still not home-free until you have seen the results of evaluation studies that indicate that this program really works in large numbers of regular classrooms.

Now you may be thinking that this represents quite a few gates for a new program to have to open before it proves its worth. And that is exactly the point! If we are to become less susceptible to fads, then it will be because we have become more deliberate and cautious along the way to adopting new programs.

Figure 3.1 (p. 21) illustrates the process that ideally unfolds in the cycle of educational innovation. We begin with theories derived from pure or basic research. We then test the theory under experimental or quasi-experimental conditions in school settings. And we move from there to the program evaluation stage where assessment is made based on data from real classrooms which operate under typical day-to-day conditions.

It is well to note that these levels are somewhat arbitrary, and there is not necessarily always a linear flow from pure to applied to evaluation research. Sometimes there is, but more often the situation is more chaotic than that. In some cases, the theoretical construct is less the source of energy than is the simple fact that something is available for educational use that was not available previously. Computers and calculators are obvious examples of this. But even in the case of these technological innovations, research to determine academic outcomes is necessary. Here is a simple example of this point. In the United States, it is common for teachers of mathematics to use the overhead projector to illustrate problem solutions. In Japan, mathematics teachers typically use the chalkboard (Stigler & Hiebart, 1999). It turns out that by using the chalkboard the entire sequence remains in public view while when using the overhead projector it is necessary to scroll forward because the screen cannot accommodated the entire sequence. This represents a researchable issue and brings into question the ready acceptance of every innovation.

SUMMARY

In the world of prescription medications, the Food and Drug Administration (FDA) subjects new medicines to a long and exhaustive review prior to allowing them to be prescribed by doctors and dispensed by pharmacists. And even this process is a far cry from releasing a product to over-the-counter sales. Some critics of this system have pointed out that it often takes years from the time we read about an experimental drug in the newspapers until that drug is available to the public. The role of the FDA is to play gatekeeper as tests are conducted, effects examined, potential drug interactions investigated, and so on. As a result, some drugs never make it to the marketplace, while others do after a period of time.

With respect to educational innovations, however, we have no counterpart to the FDA. Therefore, programs can be rushed into the schools with little or no testing at any stage of the game. This may please those who are in a hurry to jump on the latest bandwagon, but it disadvantages those who would prefer to be consumers of thoughtfully tested and refined programs. In so many instances, whole districts have adopted particular curriculums and teaching procedures that had basically no research foundation. This renders our profession vulnerable to criticisms that are difficult to refute.

In this chapter, it is suggested that research be conducted at three distinctly different levels along the way to validating or invalidating educational innovations. Those three levels are (a) basic or pure research, (b) applied research in school settings, and (c) evaluation research where the effects of the large-scale implementation of an innovation are studied. All of this takes time, and rightly so. This is serious business. The only way to improve educational practice is to approach educational innovation with such a deliberate, measured sense of its worth.

Of course, schools adopt new ideas on the basis of something more than educational research. Economic, political, and cultural considerations will always play a role in this process. That is a simple matter of reality. But where we can be more thoughtful about change on the basis of a thorough examination of the merits of any given change, we ought to proceed cautiously.

Years ago there was a radio show called "It Pays to Be Ignorant." The theory behind the show was that people could win cash prizes and major household appliances by proving to the world, or at least to the huge nationwide radio audience, that they really were ignorant when it came to answering questions put to them by the genial host of the show. It was a great concept and a successful program. But it doesn't pay to be ignorant when it comes to spending the public's tax dollars on educational innovations that really haven't proven themselves.

THE FOLLOWING CHAPTERS

This book is an attempt to provide teachers, administrators, district inservice personnel, preservice and graduate students, and other interested persons with a brief overview and analysis of current innovations in education. The process of selecting these topics involved a careful examination of a wide variety of state and school district inservice offerings, trends noted in educational journals, agendas from national and regional conferences, college and university courses, and staff development institutes. During this process it became clear that many of the offerings were simply variations of a more limited number of basic ideas or concepts. It is these basic concepts, or golden threads, that are the focus of the following chapters. Of course, the manifestation of the concepts may differ somewhat from one region of the country to another, or from one packager to another. The focus, however, remains on programs that have truly nationwide impact, whatever their regional calling cards happen to be.

Each of the following chapters contains a common format for the presentation of the topic under review. Thus each chapter begins with an overview of the concept in an attempt to clarify exactly what is being talked about. This involves such basic issues as definitions of terms, not always an easy task as we shall see. Generally, this has required synthesizing the writing and ideas of numerous authors because for many of these topics there is no single developer who speaks for or represents the entire area. For example, the *brain-based teaching* movement in education is not dependent on the work of one person; rather, it represents a compilation of ideas from numerous investigators and promoters. Even in the instances in which one individual is clearly identified with the topic, for example, Madeline Hunter for the Hunter Model, the discussion is expanded past that individual to include descriptions of the programs as they are being implemented and expanded by others. The "main players" are identified in each particular field of endeavor, that is, those most closely associated with the topic and related programs. While reference is made to various individuals and their programs as examples, the responsibility for interpretations and descriptions of the concepts and programs rendered in this book rests here.

You will also be provided where possible with specific examples of the structural effects these programs have, or would have, if implemented, in the schools. For example, a teacher who adopts a whole language approach will organize (a) the classroom, (b) the curriculum, and (c) instruction differently from the way a teacher following, say, a basal-reader approach would. Similarly, a school following a standards-based education model will have a different focus and decision-making process from that found in a goal-free approach to schooling. Each of these chapters, will show in specific terms what changes might occur if you implement a given program. In other words, ideas have consequences when they become reality, and it is necessary to be clear about that with you.

Included in each chapter is a critique of the given topic. It is fair to say that the work of the proponents of these ideas and programs is not above criticism, and we ought not to be reluctant to do just that. Some programs have been carefully developed and come complete with a sound research foundation. Others are "faddish" and are lacking both a theoretical and research base. In some cases, certain programs are antithetical to one another and the attempt to adopt both or to blend them will lead only to a confusion of purpose. Clear cautionary notes regarding implications for wholesale changes in an educational system will be sounded. Who knows, maybe what you are presently doing is better than what will happen if you implement a certain highly touted program.

Proponents' claims about the degree to which the programs are "research based" will be thoroughly examined. The term *research-based* can be a little like the term *low fat* found on product labels. It can be rather misleading. At the very least, one must know how to interpret it.

Finally, each chapter contains bibliographic references for those who wish to pursue the issues further.

REFERENCES

Bruner, J. (1966/1996). *Toward a theory of instruction.* Cambridge, MA: Harvard University Press.

Gardner, H. (1986). *Frames of mind.* New York: Basic Books.

Piaget, J. (1960). *The child's conceptions of the world.* Atlantic Highlands, NJ: Humanities Press.

Stigler, J., and Hiebart, J. (1999). *The teaching gap: Best ideas from the world's teachers for improving education in the classroom.* New York: The Free Press.

4

SETTING STANDARDS

*A critical mass of schools is establishing, with more
assurance than ever, that children can achieve at high
standards regardless of race or economic disadvantage.*

Michael Schmoker

*This standards-based movement seems to be hanging
around a bit longer than we imagined it would.*

Kenneth Sirotnik and Kathy Kimball

*The standards movement holds the promise of
revolutionizing teaching and learning in our schools.*

Mary Diez

*I'm a little bit tired of people getting credit for improving
education by doing the cheapest thing they can do, which
is to call for the manipulation of test scores or to
create new standards.*

Asa Hilliard

The current standards movement was officially inaugurated with the
publishing of *Curriculum and Evaluation Standards for School Mathematics*
(1989) by the National Council of Teachers of Mathematics. Prior to that,
several influential publications in the mid-1980s were instrumental in setting the process in motion. Among those were *A Nation at Risk* (1983),
Diane Ravitch's *The Schools We Deserve* (1985), E. D. Hirsch Jr.'s *Cultural
Literacy* (1987), and Allan Bloom's *The Closing of the American Mind* (1987).
Each in its own way made the same case: that American schools were failing to make the grade academically, largely because we have no
agreed-on rigorous core curriculum.

By 1989, President George Bush had convened the National Gover-
nors' Association at an Education Summit in Virginia to set national educational goals to be achieved by the year 2000. Bush's successor, President

Bill Clinton, continued the effort that included six goals, among them the curious goal: "By the year 2000, U.S. students will be first in the world in science and mathematics achievement." The year 2000 has been claimed by history, and the results are somewhat less than that. One can only imagine that perhaps our elected leaders had themselves attended too many high school basketball games where the cheer "We're number one" has become so common over the years. This goal was set without any apparent reference to historical evidence that we never have been "number one" in these areas of the school curriculum.

More recently, the Department of Education has issued its *2001–2005 Strategic Plan*. It is structured around four major goals:

1. Build a solid foundation for learning for all children.
2. Reform the U.S. education system to make it the best in the world.
3. Ensure access for all to postsecondary education and lifelong learning.
4. Make the Department of Education a high-performance organization.

These goals seem at once less expansive (except for goal number two), and yet more purposefully vague than those set by Goals 2000. But what do these goals really mean? What do they signify? In the old days of the Soviet Union, five-year plans were pretty much par for the course. They typically looked good on paper.

IT WAS BETTER IN THE OLD DAYS, OR WAS IT?

It is always tempting to disparage the present state of things, and to look simultaneously backward and forward in time, in much the way the Roman god Janus was typically portrayed, to better times. In fact, Columbia University professor William Bagley (1938) in a journal article written more than six decades ago and in his address to the National Education Association Annual Convention of 1938 emphasized these points:

♦ American elementary and secondary students fail to meet standards of achievement by students in other countries.

♦ An increasing number of high school students are basically illiterate.

♦ Notable deficiencies exist in mathematics and grammar throughout the grade levels.

♦ More money is being spent on education than ever before, but such problems as the crime rate continue to increase.

Bagley, in case you haven't guessed, was an essentialist whose brief was that progressive influences had brought American education to the depths of despair.

PLUS ÇA CHANGE, PLUS C'EST LA MEME CHOSE

"The more things change the more they remain the same." Needless to say, the goal of being first in the world in mathematics and science achievement was certainly not in evidence in 1938, nor was it in 2000; and it has yet to be achieved. The other goals, there are six altogether, can be argued for, at least on the grounds that they do not represent measurable outcomes. Therefore, whether "all children will start school ready to learn," to note another goal, has been achieved as a goal is dubious but debatable.

THE MOVEMENT GATHERS STEAM

During the decade of the 1990s other major professional education organizations followed the NCTM lead of setting standards, each in its own respective subject matter area. At this point, standards have been published by the professional organizations representing the five core areas of the school curriculum—mathematics, reading, writing, science, and social studies—as well as in such areas as health, the arts, and life skills. The idea in each case is to identify the salient characteristics of school subjects in order to give teachers and students a clear sense of what those subjects are actually about. Why is this necessary? The answers to that question appear to range from concerns over lagging achievement, especially as noted in international comparisons, to a felt need for order, common content coverage, and overwhelming pressure from business and universities. Business and universities are key players simply because these are mainly the two places where students go after high school.

THE ROLE OF THE STATES

The American school curriculum is in many ways a curious artifact of our educational history. Not only is there no national curriculum, but the fact of the matter is that beyond the state, district, and building levels, classroom teachers are basically given free rein to emphasize whatever they want in the subjects they teach. There is no controlling legal authority that has the power to say to a classroom teacher, "this is what and how you must teach." Thus two teachers teaching U.S. History in adjoining rooms of the same school may cover widely divergent topics. This is less so in areas such as algebra or biology, but even a cursory examination of textbooks makes the point that the curriculum is not completely agreed on in any subject. There is no common core. In the same building, one

FIGURE 4.1. STANDARDS DEFINED

The term standards has come to refer to two different but related ideas: content and performance. Content standards identify *what* students should know and be able to do, and performance standards identify *how* students will demonstrate their proficiency.

Academic Content Standards describe what every student should know and be able to do in the core academic areas (e.g., reading, mathematics, science, history, etc.). Content standards should apply equally to students of all races and ethnicities, from all linguistic and cultural backgrounds, both with and without special learning needs.

Performance Standards answer the question "How good is good enough?" They define how student demonstrate their proficiency in the skills and knowledge framed by states' content standards.

An example from the Washington State Commission on Student Learning, Essential Academic Learning Requirements in Mathematics:

The **content** standard in mathematics requires students to: *understand and apply concepts and procedures from probability and statistics.*

The corresponding **performance standard** (4th grade level, probability benchmark) requires students to demonstrate their mastery of the standard by showing that they:

- Understand the difference between certain and uncertain events.
- Know how to list all possible outcomes of simple experiments.
- Understand and use experiments to investigate uncertain events.

SOURCES: Adapted from *Standards: What Are They? Improving America's Schools,* Spring, 1996. U.S. Department of Education, and from the *Essential Academic Learning Requirements Tech Manual,* 1998, Olympia, WA: Washington State Department of Education.

primary teacher may take a whole-language approach to the teaching of reading while that teacher's next door neighbor takes a phonics-based approach. Of course, state and district guides do prescribe certain coverage, but just as in the case of the doctor's prescription, the patient does not have to swallow it.

Further evidence of the unique (when compared to most other countries) nature of our curriculum is found in the obvious discontinuities among textbooks, standardized tests of achievement, and content emphasis by classroom teachers. It is not at all unusual for teachers to note that skills and knowledge sought on standardized achievement tests were not even taught by them. The linkage between standardized tests and textbooks is tenuous at best, given the fact that any two textbooks that "cover" the same subject will actually cover some topics in common as well as other topics not held in common. In other words, the curriculum is not standardized.

The standards movement is just that, an attempt to standardize the curriculum through the publishing of content standards by the influential professional associations representing the various subject matter disciplines. The thinking is that a standardized curriculum is a more tightly coupled curriculum. For the first time textbook publishers and test authors have a clear frame of reference for what material should be taken into account. So, too, do classroom teachers. Of course, we have no national curriculum so the standards suggested by the professional organizations are exemplary at best. At present, 49 states have or are in the process of adopting standards for the various subjects of the school curriculum. Thus, it appears more possible now than ever before to get everyone on the same page, so to speak.

As each state sets about the business of articulating standards, we might ask why. Why not one national set of standards? The answer is found in the Ninth Amendment to the U.S. Constitution, which makes it clear that all matters not specifically delegated to the federal government fall within the jurisdiction of the individual states. Education is not mentioned in the Constitution, therefore, by inference it is a state matter. However, the professional organizations such as the National Council of Teachers of Mathematics, The International Reading Association, the National Council of Teachers of English, the National Science Teachers Association, the National Council for the Social Studies, and others do have national prominence to say the least, and their setting of standards for the various disciplines of the core curriculum has indeed proven to be highly influential at the state level. Still, one of the pressing problems that has emerged is that there is not complete agreement on what standards are. Recently, I was at a meeting of middle school experts, one of whom, having examined the mathematics standards proposed by one particular state, said, "these aren't standards, they're activities." So problems of definition and articulation will no doubt continue to plague the process. Figure 4.x describes and illustrates several key terms in this regard.

Another curiosity is that although we have witnessed the development of discipline-based standards in nearly every state, we have yet to see much evidence of standards held in common across the curriculum, except by inference. This is so in spite of the fact that all the national (professional organization documents) and state standards reports stress the need for subject matter integration, project-based learning, and so on. In Canada, for example, the Ontario Ministry of Education and Training has published *The Common Curriculum: Policies and Outcomes Grades 1-9*. This thoughtful document sets forth a curriculum framework on the basis of four program areas as opposed to the traditional discipline-based approach. Each of the program areas addresses various elements of content integration and application. (Hargreaves and Earl, 2000).

ACCOUNTABILITY AND STANDARDS

It is one thing to publish standards in order to better inform all those involved in the education of our children. It is yet another thing to expect that teachers, once informed, will follow suit. State and district guides, for example, have been around for years as a means of informing educators of the essential knowledge and skills they should teach. However, as often as not, such guides are paid little notice. It is not at all uncommon for teachers, having been given the district guide at the beginning of the school year, to say that they are unable even to find it when asked, something that they would have little trouble doing if they took the district guide as seriously as, say, their car keys.

Given such a history, one could reason that some teachers will take the standards seriously and many will not, relegating them to the same dust-gathering status as other documents. But this time around, in addition to seeking greater standardization of curriculum content and offering the hope of linking curriculum content with textbook coverage and achievement test coverage, the standards movement is also accompanied by articles of assessment. Several states, most notably Washington, Vermont, and Maryland, have focused on the development of "high-quality" performance assessments designed to measure the extent to which standards-based curriculum and teaching result in improved student abilities to solve complex problems. An example of such a performance assessment problem is found in Figure 4.2.

FIGURE 4.2. EXAMPLE OF PERFORMANCE ASSESSMENT

**Mathematics Sample Short-Answer
Mathematical Concepts and Procedures Item**

Component: The student understands and applies the concepts and procedures of mathematics: algebraic sense.

Benchmark: The students recognizes, creates, and extends patterns and
sequence.

The ancient Greeks discovered that certain numbers, when arranged in dot patters, form definite shapes. **Triangular numbers,** for example, have dot patterns that can be arranged into
triangles. A sequence of triangular numbers is shown below.

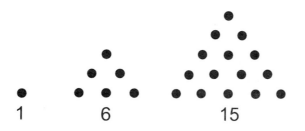

What is the next triangular number in this sequence? Clearly
explain or show the reason for your answer.

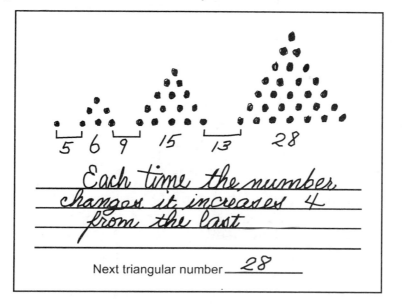

SOURCE: Washington State Commission on Student Learning.

The development of assessment instruments tied to the standards may or may not have been the original intent of the professional associations. The fact is, however, that this is what has happened and is continuing to happen. Standards-referenced test instruments, typically in the form of "performance assessment" tests, are cropping up in nearly every state. Thus what began as a curriculum movement in which *content* standards were articulated, has become as well an outcomes or assessment movement in which *performance* standards are increasingly prescribed.

Another way to think of the evolution of the standards movement is offered in an insightful article by Marzano and Kendall (2000). They suggest that it is crucial to consider the difference between content standards, which describe what students should know and be able to do, and curriculum standards, which describe what should take place in the classroom or, in other words, the desired methods of instruction. They give as an example of a content standard from NCTM: "Use estimation to check the reasonableness of results." Note how generally applicable such a skill would be. On the other hand, they give as an example of a curriculum standard, also from NCTM: "Describe, model, draw and classify shapes." Marzano and Kendall's clear preference is for the setting of clear content standards because content standards represent achievement goals without being prescriptive as to how teachers might go about teaching. Thus, if a state or district wished to suggest methods of instruction designed to reach the goals, that is another matter.

POINTS OF ORIGIN: LEVEL I

The origins of the standards movement can be traced in part to its essentialist philosophical roots. In fact, standards are often known as *essential* learnings. Essentialist philosophy, which generally disdains, but sometimes cooperates with progressive educational philosophy as we shall see, can be described as follows:

> Essentialism is rooted in the belief that there is a core of essential knowledge and skills that must be transmitted to students. This essential core is represented by the various subject matter disciplines that represent the essence of school learning. Essentialism represents a search for objective truth that can be known, and this results in emphasis on discipline-based science, mathematics, language, arts, history, physical education, and other essential school subjects.

Of course, things are never that simple. The standards movement also has roots in the social efficiency tradition, a phenomenon that has been with us since the early days of the twentieth century. Social efficiency asks the question: "How can we make teaching and learning more efficient and productive in order to best serve society?" The efficiency movement, which began in industry and which was clearly articulated in Frederick Winslow Taylor's *The Principles of Scientific Management* (1911), soon jumped the rails from industry to education, and the search was on for ways to make schools more effective, which meant then and means now, more efficient.

Efficiency as an educational concept represents what is known as the technical interest. The technical interest, as described by the philosopher Jurgen Habermas (1971), is a means-end approach. That is, the technical interest seeks means to control situations toward certain predetermined ends. In other words, "if we do this, we will get that." Put another way, prediction equals control. This should be familiar territory to those acquainted with such standards-movement precursors as behavioral objectives, time-on-task analysis, competency-based education, and outcomes-based education.

According to Habermas, the more the technical interest encroaches into the life-world of such interests as the practical and the reflective, the more our lives become diminished. One can be assured that teachers and students, who live in the practical world of classroom life, have not been in the forefront of the standards movement. Speaking from an anecdotal perspective, I can say that more and more teachers are telling me that they no longer involve their students in project learning and other related activity-centered experiences. They are simply "too busy" getting their students ready to do well on the standardized tests and performance assessments.

ESSENTIALIST GOALS, PROGRESSIVE MEANS

Although the standards movement clearly represents an essentialist goal structure, the means suggested for achieving the goals are just as clearly progressive. For example, a recommendation that comes from nearly all the major professional groups is that there be *less* whole-class, teacher-led direct instruction, and that there be *more* experiential, hands-on learning. This seems at first glance to give rise to some measure of discontinuity. Consider, for example, Stevenson and Stigler's (1991, 1994) observation of Japanese mathematics teachers, whom they note are more academically successful than their U.S. counterparts, and who do use a whole-class, teacher-directed approach.

This point takes us back to Marzano and Kendall's cogent observation that content standards and curriculum standards are basically two different things. Thus a content standard may demand a certain skill, knowledge, or ability, while a curriculum standard may suggest "best" means for instructing students toward such achievement. However, this matter does raise serious concern over the wisdom of linking the achievement of certain content goals with certain methods of instruction in the absence of clear and convincing evidence that those methods are the best route to those goals.

In *Best Practice: New Standards for Teaching and Learning in America's Schools* (1998), Zemelman, Daniels, and Hyde write:

> A more general, progressive paradigm is emerging across content boundaries and grade levels. This coherent philosophy and spirit is reaching across the curriculum and up through the grades. Whether it is called Best Practice, or Whole Language, or integrated learning, or interdisciplinary studies, by some other name, or by no name at all, this movement is broad and deep and enduring. It is strongly backed by educational research, draws on sound learning theory, and, under other names, has been tested and refined over the years. (p. 7)

The authors identify "thirteen interlocking principles, assumptions, or theories that characterize this model of education." (p. 7) Figure 4.3 lists these thirteen principles. Whether everyone would agree with the extent to which these clearly progressive principles of teaching and learning, if used by teachers and students, will bring about higher levels of achievement remains another matter. What we can see, however, is that the standards movement is an amalgam. The legendary frontiersman Davy Crockett, at least in his Disney incarnation, used to describe himself as half alligator, half bear, with a touch of snapping turtle. Bad mathematics, perhaps, but a colorful description. Perhaps the theoretical construct of the standards movement is somewhat Crockettesque in that it seems to be half essentialist, half progressive, with a touch of social efficiency.

RESEARCH AT LEVELS II AND III

Given that the standards movement is reasonably recent, one might expect not to find much research connected with it. This is increasingly less the case as investigators make their inquiries. The research that looks at the effects of setting standards on achievement is not easily classified. Typically, it looks more like Level III research than it does Level II because what could be called *program effects* are at stake.

Mayer (1998) investigated the extent to which the NCTM teaching standards in mathematics were a factor in raising achievement among eighth and ninth grade algebra students. Specifically, he asked: "Do students taught in NCTM-like classrooms perform differently on standardized assessments than students taught in traditional classrooms?" (p. 54). Mayer identified classrooms in 41 schools in a large school district in which algebra was taught using either a primarily "traditional" emphasis or using primarily NCTM-prescribed instructional procedures such as

FIGURE 4.3. PRINCIPLES OF BEST LEARNING PRACTICES

- **Student-centered.** The best starting point for schooling is young people's real interests; all across the curriculum, investigating students' own questions should always take precedence over studying arbitrarily and distantly selected "content.

- **Experiential.** Active, hands-on, concrete experience is the most powerful and natural form of learning. Students should be immersed in the most direct possible experience of the content of every subject.

- **Holistic.** Children learn best when they encounter whole ideas, events, and materials in purposeful contexts, not by studying subparts isolated from actual use.

- **Authentic.** Real, rich, complex ideas and materials are at the heart of the curriculum. Lessons or textbooks that water-down, control, or oversimplify content ultimately disempower students.

- **Expressive.** To fully engage ideas, construct meaning, and remember information, students must regularly employ the whole range of communicative media—speech, writing, drawing, poetry, dance, drama, music, movement, and visual arts.

- **Reflective.** Balancing the immersion in experience and expression must be opportunities for learners to reflect, debrief, abstract from their experiences what they have felt and thought and learned.

- **Social.** Learning is always socially constructed and often interactional; teachers need to create classroom interactions that "scaffold" learning.

- **Collaborative.** Cooperative learning activities tap the social power of learning better than competitive and individualistic approaches.

- **Democratic.** The classroom is a model community; students learn what they live as citizens of the school.

- **Cognitive.** The most powerful learning comes when children develop true understanding of concepts through higher-order thinking associated with various fields of inquiry and through self-monitoring of their thinking.

- **Developmental.** Children grow through a series of definable but not rigid stages, and schooling should fit its activities to the developmental level of students.

♦ **Constructivist.** Children do not just receive content; in a very real sense, they re-create and reinvent every cognitive system they encounter, including language, literacy, and mathematics.

♦ **Challenging.** Students learn best when faced with genuine challenges, choices, and responsibility in their own learning.

SOURCE: S. Zemelman, H. Daniels, and A. Hyde. (1998). *Best Practice: New Standards for Teaching and Learning in American Schools, 2nd ed.* Portsmouth, NH: Heinnenman.

---

student-led discussion, group investigation, writing about problems, different means of solving problems, and multiple solutions. He found that the measured knowledge of algebra of both lower and higher GPA students "grows faster" in the NCTM-like classrooms among students at the eighth grade level. At the ninth grade level, which was dominated by students who were not selected to take algebra in their eighth-grade year, and who were therefore typically "lower skilled" students, there seemed to be little achievement difference between students in traditional classrooms and those in NCTM-like classrooms.

Mayer's findings should be considered highly tentative because his study did not attempt to control a range of factors affecting external and internal validity. Nonetheless, his work does represent real-world-of-school research and a set of findings that offer qualified endorsement to the use of the NCTM principles for students who qualify for and take eighth-grade algebra.

Certainly there is no shortage of reporting from states and school districts about how the implementation of standards-based reforms have resulted in increased student achievement. Whether the standards movement is to be given all or part of the credit, the fact is that National Assessment of Educational Progress (NAEP) mathematics and reading scores have risen in recent years in a number of states that have taken reform seriously. The problem with attempting to unravel cause and effect relationships or even more realistically trying to figure out meaningful associations is that any findings, positive or less so, are fraught with uncontrolled variables such as changed or differentially defined dropout rates, greater or lesser retention of students, inclusion or exclusion of special-needs students, inclusion or exclusion of limited-proficiency English students, and other factors that could severely restrict meaningful comparisons.

In spite of these issues, we find the Seattle Public Schools, where emphasis on high academic standards has been coupled with site-based management, reporting 1999 reading and mathematics test scores at both third and eighth grade levels well above statewide averages, a rare outcome for this large urban district. In Milwaukee and Philadelphia, similar success stories have been reported in the wake of adopting higher academic standards. Again, problems surface when one considers the confounding effects arising in each of these situations because a number of reforms have been implemented simultaneously of which a focus on higher academic standards is only one.

On the seven National Assessment of Educational Progress (NAEP) tests given to fourth and eighth graders during the years 1990 to 1996, Texas and North Carolina, two states that have placed great emphasis on the standards-based reform and accountability, made the greatest average gains in the nation (National Alliance of Business, 1998). While these outcomes initially appear to be a positive thing, on further examination one encounters so many rival hypotheses for why this might be so as to make it difficult to attribute these gains to the implementation of standards. In other words, broad policy decisions typically contain so many uncontrolled educational variables as to make cause and effect conclusions nearly impossible.

The Council for Basic Education (CBE) assessed the "rigor" of mathematics and language arts standards on the basis of a review of standards documents from 43 states (Joftus and Berman, 1998). The Council's review yielded a number of significant findings, among them that state mathematics standards tend to be more rigorous than language arts standards. Most states' mathematics standards "contain few major gaps in the concepts and skills included," and even states with less rigorous standards tend to address the most essential skills and concepts. On the other hand, CBE investigators noted that while most states' standards do address basic skills they often do not address "literature study, research, or even language study such as word origins and differences between standard usage and slang" (p. 1).

So the evidence is clear that standards, while subscribed to by nearly every state, mean different things to different people. CBE's conclusion is that there is considerable range to be found with some states setting "very rigorous" standards, others setting "rigorous" standards, and still others setting standards with low levels of rigor. The CBE findings comport with assessments by a number of other researchers who noted similar discrepancies in the quality of standards set by various states

The eminent researcher Robert Linn (2000) notes four reasons why, in spite of quality issues, the standards movement has sustained itself. He notes that testing and test results are and probably will remain an integral part of the movement. Those reasons include the fact that tests are relatively (compared to other curricular/instructional changes) inexpensive, that testing changes can be implemented rather quickly, that test results are highly visible and draw media attention, and that testing can bring about other changes that would be difficult to legislate. He writes that in spite of the problems posed by standards-based assessment, there are some cues that policy makers and other educators should take to heart. Lin has developed these as a checklist which is presented in Figure 4.4.

FIGURE 4.4. TEN SUGGESTIONS FOR POLICYMAKERS

1. Set standards that are high, but attainable.
2. Develop standards, *then* assessments.
3. Include all students in testing programs but provide accommodations for
   - Those with the most severe disabilities.
   - Students who have not yet transitioned into English language programs.
4. Develop new high-quality assessments each year that are comparable to those of previous years or results will be distorted.
5. Important decisions about students and schools must not be based on one single test.
6. Compare change from year to year rather than from school to school.
7. Set both long- and short-term school goals for all schools.
8. Uncertainty should be reported in all test results.
9. Unintended negative effects must be considered as well as intended positive effects when evaluating testing systems.
10. Testing alone will not improve the educational system as a whole; the way to narrow the achievement gap is to provide all children with the teachers and resources needed to reach our high expectations.

SOURCE: Linn, R. (2000). Standards-based accountability: Ten suggestions. *CRESST Policy Brief.* [Online. Available August 1, 2000 at http://www.cs .ucla.edu.]

THE CRITICS' CORNER

Obviously not everyone is enamored of the standards movement. Alfie Kohn has called the standards movement a "horrible idea." Kohn notes that the standards movement is "fatally flawed" in five separate ways. Kohn argues that the standards movement gets the following things wrong: motivation, pedagogy, evaluation, school reform, and improvement. He discusses these issues at length in *The Schools Our Children Deserve* (2000). Kohn points out that the movement oversimplifies why children might want to learn, how they are best taught, and how improvement might best be brought to a complex system. The idea of demanding higher test scores, Kohn notes, will accomplish little more than studying for tests, emphasis on rote learning, and tighter control over classrooms by people who don not spend their time in classrooms.

Marzano, Kendall, and Cicchinelli (2000), who are not particularly critical of the movement, note an apparently overlooked problem with addressing the standards. Their calculations show that, given the demands of the standards and accompanying benchmarks from the various subject matter areas, it would take in excess of 15,000 hours to adequately address the necessary content. This would mean some drastic alteration of the amount of time spent in school because K-12 education has only a little more than 9000 hours at present. Those readers of this book who possess some mastery of fractions will note that this would call for 15/9 of the time we presently spend. Put another way, Marzano, Kendall, and Cicchinelli say the implication for coverage would be to extend school from K-12 to K-21. They conclude that one possible solution is to extend the amount of time given to instruction, and another possible solution is to decrease the number of standards.

Maehr and Maehr (1996) offer rather pointed criticisms of the standards movement when they write:

> The recommendation to establish and apply "standards" emerges as a prime example of looking to past evidence of known flaws, and being unmindful of a changed and changing world into which these standards are now supposed to work....It sounds good on its face perhaps, but it is a simplistic solution at best and a demonic one at worst. Implied is a school that doesn't exist, a commitment that cannot work, a course of action that will prove debilitating to many students and the schools they attend. (p. 21)

Maehr and Maehr go on to list four "major concerns" that they have about the call for standards. They point out that while it is easy to point to failing schools, in fact it is society that has failed. They note that schools already have standards and that adding on new ones in the absence of clear mission is folly. They question the extent to which standards and their accompanying assessment protocols are in fact motivators toward excellence. And they predict an erosion of school culture in which true learning and growth and development are sacrificed in the attempt to meet external standards.

Asa Hilliard (1998) takes the standards movement to task in no uncertain terms. He notes that many of the people advocating tougher standards "have no idea of the importance of quality teaching and leadership." Hilliard argues that without a national curriculum, the result of allowing each state to set its own standards will inevitably lead to validity problems in any meaningful kind of national assessment.

In an article not meant to be directly critical of standards, James Popham (1998) makes a useful distinction between types of standardized tests and their accompanying results, which of course, are pointed to by standards advocates as proof of declining achievement as well as the ultimate measures of how well standards might it. Popham distinguishes between *aptitude* tests, which predict how well students are likely to perform in some subsequent educational setting and *achievement* tests, which measure what students know. The most familiar aptitude tests are the SAT (*Scholastic Assessment Test*) and the ACT *Assessment*. Both of them are used as predictors of college or university academic performance.

Achievement tests, he notes, typically cover four subject areas (mathematics, language arts, social studies, and science), and are designed to provide information to be used for comparisons between and among groups regarding student knowledge and skills. Popham lists the five most used achievement tests as the *California Achievement Test, Comprehensive Test of Basic Skills, Iowa Test of Basic Skills, Metropolitan Achievement Test,* and *Standard Achievement Test.*

Popham cites three reasons why schools should not be judged on the basis of standardized test scores. The first reason he notes is that of the mismatch between what is taught and what is tested. Of course, the response of standards advocates is that by setting clear standards, it becomes far more possible to close the gap between curriculum and assessment. This is so because textbook companies will have a clearer idea of what to include, and teachers will have a clearer idea of what is essential.

Popham's second reason is that standardized tests do not measure the most important things that teachers teach. And by definition, they cannot do so. Here is his reasoning. Standardized tests need to produce a large spread of scores. This means that the most effective test items are those that are answered correctly by only about 50% of the test takers. He writes that test items that are answered correctly "by large proportions of students, for instance, 80 percent or more, are usually not put in standardized tests in the first place..." (p. 2). The problem is that these are the very significant items that teachers typically teach. So, a kind of reverse Darwinian procedure emerges in which success is weeded out.

The third problem noted by Popham is that over time teachers become familiar with the content of standardized tests, and that leads to an inflation of test results because teachers knowingly or not end up teaching to the test. Does this really mean higher achievement? Probably not. It means that teachers are taking their cues about what to teach from the tests.

WHERE DOES THIS LEAVE US?

The standards movement would appear to be one that will not go quietly into that dark night. It may well have a certain staying power, a certain elemental appeal. Who could really argue that the setting of standards in the subject matter disciplines is a wrong-headed idea? As we have seen, the movement does have its detractors, but their objections seem to be mainly over the assessment issues. To convene a body of experts in the field, subject matter and pedagogical authorities, and to ask them to decide on the salient characteristics of, say, geometry, is hardly an affront to a geometry teacher's dignity or professional academic freedom. Even the most "creative" teacher, one who has developed his/her own course of study, would surely want to know what the experts say is significant, if for no other reason than that this could be a point of departure, a model from which to deviate.

Further, while the content standards themselves do represent a disciplinary approach to curriculum, there is no reason to think that a team of teachers from different disciplines would be restricted in their attempts to integrate studies. In fact, one could argue that standards are helpful in such a situation because they define the essence of the various aspects of content to be merged by a team. One of the arguments against interdisciplinary teaching has always been that subjects such as mathematics tend to get short shrift. A team that starts with a set of standards representing each subject is armed with a means of preventing that from happening.

It should also be noted that the professional organizations that have taken the lead in the development of standards have in every case encouraged team teaching, higher order thinking, interdisciplinary learning, inquiry, constructivist approaches, experiential learning, even less use of and reliance on standardized tests. Therefore, it is incumbent on educators to think through the difference between advocating standards and simply assuming that standardized tests are the main or only way we can know whether standards are meaningful guides to teaching and learning. There may be all the difference in the world in these two points of view.

REFERENCES

Bagley, W. (1938, April). An essentialist's platform for the advancement of American education. *Educational Administration and Supervision.*

Beane, J. (1996). On the shoulders of giants! A case for curriculum integration. *Middle School Journal, 28,* 6–11.

Bloom, A. (1987). *The closing of the American mind.* New York: Simon and Schuster.

Cohen, D., & Hill, H. (1998). *Instructional policy and classroom performance: The mathematics reform in California.* ED417942. SE061214.

Deci, E., Spiegel, N., Ryan, R., Koestner, R., & Kauffman, M. (1982). Effects of performance standards on teaching styles: Behavior of controlling teachers. *Journal of Educational Psychology, 74*(6), 852–859.

Diez, M. (2000, May 8). Teachers, assessment, and the standards movement. *Education Week, May 3, 2000.* [Online] Available at: http://www.edweek.org.

Education Commission of the States (1997, December). *Standards: When students get behind.* [Online] Available at: http://www.ecs.org/ecs/ecsqweb.nsf/ [July 31, 2000].

Feinberg, W. (1999, Spring). The influential E. D. Hirsch. *Rethinking Schools Online, 13,* 3. [Online] Available at: http://www.rethinking schools.org/ [May 8, 2000].

Flink, C., Boggiano, A., & Barrett, M. (1990). Controlling teaching strategies: Undermining children's self-determination and performance. *Journal of Personality and Social Psychology, 59*(5), 916–924.

Habermas, J. (1971). *Toward a rational society* (Jeremy J. Shapiro, Trans.). London: Heinemann.

Hargreaves, A., & Earl, L. (2000). *Learning to change.* San Francisco: Jossey-Bass.

Hill, C. (2000, June 12). Developing educational standards. *Putnam Valley Central Schools Web site.* [Online] Available at: http://putwest.boces.org/Standards.html.

Hilliard, A. (1998). The standards movement: Quality control or decoy? *Rethinking Schools, 12,* 4. [Online] Available at: http://www.rethinking schools.org [May 8, 2000].

Hirsch, E. D. (1987). *Cultural Literacy: What Every American Needs to Know.* New York: Vintage Books.

Joftus, S., & Berman, I. (1998). *Great expectations? Defining and assessing rigor in state standards for mathematics and English language arts.* Washington, DC: Council for Basic Education. (ERIC Accession No. ED416080 SE0611160.)

King, D., & Taylor-King, S. (1998). *The policy-making influence of teacher educators on professional teaching standards boards.* Paper presented at the 50th Annual Meeting of the American Association of Colleges for Teacher Education (New Orleans, LA, February 27, 1998). (ERIC Accession No. ED417169. Clearinghouse SP037815.

Kohn, A. (2000, April 13). *The Case against "tougher standards."* [Online] Available at: http://www.alfiekohn.org.

Kohn, A. (2000). *The schools our children deserve: Moving beyond traditional classrooms and tougher standards.* Somerset, NJ: Mariner Books.

Linn, R. (2000, August 1). Standards-based accountability: Ten suggestions. *CRESST Policy Brief.* [Online] Available at: http://www.cse.ucla.edu.

Lederman, N., & Niess, M. (1997). Integrated, interdisciplinary, or thematic instruction? Is this a question or is it questionable semantics? *School Science and Mathematics, 97* (2), 57–58.

Lonning, R., & DeFranco, T. (1997). Integration of science and mathematics: A theoretical model. *School Science and Mathematics, 97*(4), 212–215.

Lonning, R., DeFranco, T., & Weinland, T. (1998). Development of theme-based, interdisciplinary, integrated curriculum: A theoretical model. *School Science and Mathematics, 98* (6), 312–316.

Marzano, R., & Kendall, J. (1997). The fall and rise of standards-based education. *A National Association of State Boards of Education (NASBE) Issues in Brief.* [Online] Available at: http://www.mcrel.com/standards/articles/ [February 29, 2000].

Marzano, R., & Kendall, J. (1998, December 8). *What Americans believe students should know: A Survey of U. S. adults.* [Online]. Available at: http://www.mcrel.org.

Marzano, R., & Kendall, J. (1998). The status of state standards. [Excerpt from *A comprehensive guide to designing standards-based districts, schools, and classrooms.* [Online] Available at: http://www.mcrel.org/standards/ [May 8, 2000].

Marzano, R., & Kendall, J. (1999). Awash in a sea of standards. *Standards at McREL.* [Online] Available at: http://www.mcrel.org/standards/articles/aways.asp [May 8, 2000].

Marzano, R., Kendall, J., & Gaddy, B. (1999). Essential knowledge: The debate over what American students should know. *Standards at McREL advance briefing.* [Online] Available at: http://www.mcrel.org [May 8, 2000].

Mason, T. (1996). Integrated curricula: Potential and problems. *Journal of Teacher Education, 47*(4), 263–270.

Mayer, D. (1998). Do new teaching standards undermine performance on old tests? *Educational Evaluation and Policy Analysis, 20*(2), 53–73.

Meier, D. (2000). *Will standards save public education?* Boston: Beacon Press.

National Alliance of Business (2000, February). The real message of tests: Stay the course with standards. *Work America: The Business Voice on Workforce Development, 17*(2), 1, 4–5.

National Council of Teachers of Mathematics (1995). *Assessment standards for school mathematics.* Reston, VA: author.

Popham, J. (1999, January 7). Your school should not be evaluated by standardized test scores! [Online] Available at: http://www.aasa.org/issues /assessment8-26-98.htm.

Raber, S., Roach, V., & Fraser, K. (Eds.). *The push and pull of standards-based reform: How does it affect local school districts and students with disabilities?* Alexandria, VA: Center for Policy Research. ED417531 EC306273.

Ravitch, D. (1985). *The schools we deserve: Reflections on the educational crises of our time.* New York: Basic Books.

Rust, E. (2000, January 19). Higher standards, stronger tests: There's no turning back. *Education Week.* [Online] Available at: http://www.edweek. org/ew/ew_printstory.cfm?slug=19rust.h1.

Shaughnessy, C., Nelson, J., & Norris, N. (1998). *NAEP 1996 mathematics cross-state data compendium for the grade 4 and grade 8 assessment.* Washington, DC: U.S. Government Printing Office. (ERIC Accession No. ED417083 SE0612070.)

Stevenson, H., & Stigler, J. (1991). How Asian teachers polish each lesson to perfection. *American Educator, 15*(1), 12–20, 43–47.

Stevenson, H., & Stigler, J. (1994). *The learning gap: Why our schools are failing and what we can learn from Japanese and Chinese education.* New York: Touchstone Books.

Taylor, F. W. (1911). *The principles of scientific management.* New York: Harper & Row.

Vars, G. (1991). Integrated curriculum in historical perspective. *Educational Leadership, 49,* 14–15.

Wheelehan, D. (1997). *National standards bibliography.* [Online] Available at: http://www.sccoe.k-12.ca.us/natstandards.htm [July 28, 2000].

Zach, T., Zon, C., Ackley, D., Olds, S., & Wainio, M. (1998). Standards for improvement. *Thrust for Educational Leadership, 27,* 4. [Online] Available at: http://www.acsa.org/publications/Leadersship_Jan_98/leadership_ jan_98_.html [January 29, 2000].

Zemelman, S., Daniels, H., & Hyde, A. (1998). *Best practice: New standards for teaching and learning in America's schools.* Portsmouth, NH: Heinemann.

5

SELF-ESTEEM AND SELF-EFFICACY

The literature suggests that associations between self-esteem and expected consequences are ambiguous and vague.

Beverly Cross

There is no getting around the fact that most educators who speak earnestly about the need to boost students' self-esteem are unfamiliar with the research that has been conducted on this question....Very few people in the field seem to have any feel for the empirical literature as a whole—what the evidence really says and how meaningful it is.

Alfie Kohn

Surely, one cannot argue for a single, one-size fits all definition of self-esteem.

Jerome Dusek

...There is little evidence that self-esteem programs bring about the desired outcomes.

Joseph Kahne

If you search for a more strongly held belief within the American school system than the belief in the importance of self-esteem to school success—and indeed to success in general—you won't find one. It is a deeply embedded cultural belief that permeates nearly every facet of teaching and curriculum.

A recent search turned up literally hundreds of recently published book titles on the topic, including *My Self, My Family, My Friends: 26 Experts Explore Young Children's Self-Esteem* (Farber and Schwartzberg,

2000) and *Building Self-Esteem in Children* (Berne and Savary, 1999, Cross-road Books). Indeed, the notion that positive self-esteem promotes achievement is widely accepted as fact. Trying to convince certain teachers that it might not be so is like trying to convince them the sun rises in the west. This cause-effect relationship idea is so prevalent and strong that Barbara Lerner (1996) has suggested that, "Many teachers will be hard pressed to think of a contrasting theory. The self-esteem theory of educational development has been the reigning orthodoxy for so long that they were never taught anything else" (p. 10). There are rival theories, as we shall see, but they are given little credence in education circles.

What Is Self-Esteem?

Well, for starters, Lewis and Knight (2000) write, "No clear consensus exists regarding the definitions of self-concept and self-esteem, so discussion of these constructs can be confusing" (p. 52). And Maureen Stout (2000) adds, "Despite the enormous amount of writing on the subject of self-esteem, both in the popular press and in academia, few self-esteem advocates appear to feel the need to establish a generally acceptable working definition of it" (p. 11). In recent years, the term "self" seems to have taken on a life of its own. There is even a trendy magazine called *Self*. One book on learning theories (Schunk, 2000), indexes the following terms: self-actualization; self-concept; self-efficacy; self-evaluation; self-fulfilling prophecy; self-instruction; self-instructional training; self-judgment; self-monitoring; self-reaction; self-regulation; self-reinforcement; self-reports; self-schemas; and self-worth. Psychologists, counselors, and educators use a range of terms to capture the elusive concept of self-esteem. Generally, however, "self-concept," "self-esteem," "self-regard," and "self-image" are used interchangeably by educators, and all refer to how we view ourselves, our abilities, our appearance, our self-worth, and so on; in other words, one's perception of oneself. The idea is that, for each of us, our self-measure can vary considerably, both quantitatively and qualitatively. On a continuum, we see ourselves as valued, or not valued, capable or less so, worthwhile or not. The idea that self-esteem is a viable construct and one worth considering from an educational point of view is a fairly recent one, and one for which the case to be made is problematic at best.

It is instructive to consider some of the instruments that purport to measure self-esteem, because instruments provide us, for better or for worse, with operational definitions. For example, the *Coopersmith Self-Esteem Inventory* (Coopersmith, 1987) defines self-esteem as "the evaluation a person makes and customarily maintains of him- or herself; that is an expression of approval or disapproval, indicating the extent to which a person believes him- or herself competent, successful, and significant and worthy." The *Culture-Free Self-Esteem Inventories* (Battle, 1992) define self-esteem as "a composite of an individual's feelings, hopes, fears, thoughts, and views of who he is, what she is, what he has been, and what she might become." And the *Piers-Harris Children's Self-Concept Scale* (Piers and Harris, 1984) defines self-concept as a "relatively stable set of self-attitudes reflecting both a description and an evaluation of one's own behavior and attitudes." Although the word choice varies somewhat, you will note that the definitions are more similar than different. This, then, is at least a place to start.

In pursuit of further clarification, three ideas should be noted. First, psychologists have differentiated between *global* and *narrow* constructs of self-esteem. For example, one might have an overall high opinion of oneself but could hold oneself in very low esteem as an athlete. One might score very high on an academic self-esteem inventory, but low on a musical one. This suggests that self-esteem is not a broad construct at all, but that each of us has multiple constructs of self-esteem. Thus, one's self-esteem may be dependent on the area of life in question. A term often associated with more narrowly-defined self abilities is *self-efficacy,* a term described by the psychologist Albert Bandura (1997) as personal beliefs about one's capabilities to learn or perform actions at designated levels.

Such distinctions are at odds with the view held by those educators who consider self-esteem as a unified, global construct. However, more and more evidence seems to be emerging to support a multidimensional and differentiated rather than a global view of self-esteem (DuBois and Hirsch, 2000).

Second, the construct is also convoluted by the tendency to equate self-esteem with human dignity, thereby rendering it an entitlement of personhood in a civil society. Keep in mind that just because all people are of equal worth, it does not follow that they can perform all tasks with equal skill. The doctrine of equal value as human beings is certainly a broad construct of self-esteem. But it confuses attempts to get at the more narrow constructs of self-esteem or self-efficacy in specific areas of endeavor. Perhaps it is useful in this regard to separate the idea of "being" from that of "doing." That, however, is much easier to propose than to carry out.

Third, there is the issue of perceptions of reality. The broad construct of self-esteem (equal value as human beings) should not necessarily cause a problem here, but the narrow constructs can because some people's views of themselves are so far removed from reality that it does them a disservice. In fact, they may be better or worse at certain things than they think they are. Here is an example. In a five-nation comparison of mathematical abilities of 10-year-olds made in 1989 (Stigler and Hiebert, 1999), American children finished last in mathematics achievement and South Korean children finished first. However, the American children had the highest self-estimate of their mathematical abilities, and the South Korean children had the lowest.

A review of the literature indicates a broad and sustained interest in the topic. Dubois and Hirsch note that they were able to identify 1463 articles pertaining to self-esteem at the early adolescent level alone (2000). Whether the construct is real or imagined, it is, nonetheless, a part of American culture, and it continues to be a major focus of attention among educators and educational researchers.

THE CLAIMS AND THE PROGRAMS

At the heart of the matter are the claims made by educators and psychologists, basically humanistic psychologists, that feeling good about oneself is important for constructive life choices, that it helps prevent destructive behaviors, and even that it leads to higher achievement. Basically, the idea is that people who view themselves favorably are able to work and learn more effectively. It is claimed that self-esteem and academic achievement are positively associated, that there is a causal relationship between the two (in the esteem-achievement direction), and, therefore, to increase achievement, we should try to raise students' self-esteem. Consider the following comment in Carl Rogers' classic book, *Freedom to Learn* (1969, 1994). Rogers quotes a teacher with whom he was working at the time as saying, "I cannot explain exactly what happened, but it seems to me, that when their [the students] self-concept changed, when they discovered they *can*, they did! These 'slow learners' became 'fast learners'; success built upon success" (p. 22).

Consider as well this comment by Madeline Hunter (1994) in an attempt to justify the wide ranging benefits of her teaching model: "Outside evaluation demonstrated substantial increases in student learning and self-esteem..." (p. 34). Yet nowhere does there seem to be published empirical evidence that self-esteem was carefully measured in connection with the use of Hunter's model under anything approaching controlled conditions. And it is well to keep in mind that even those instrument developers who believe in the global self-esteem construct would say that self-esteem is a deeply imbedded phenomenon not subject to rapid change.

The strength of these beliefs runs deep, and as Lerner pointed out, it is so ingrained that teachers cannot even come up with a rival theory. The cause-and-effect theory, however, goes well beyond achievement. In the late 1980s, legislation was passed which created the California Task Force on Self-Esteem. With a $700,000 budget the task force was to place self-esteem at the center of a social science research agenda, with the intent of ameliorating the pressing social issues of welfare dependency, drug and alcohol abuse, school failure, child abuse, and teenage pregnancy. John Vasconcellos, who created the legislation, stated:

> As we approach the twenty-first century, we human beings now—for the first time ever—have it within our power to truly improve our human condition. We can proceed to develop a social vaccine. We can outgrow our past failures—our lives of crime and violence, alcohol and drug abuse, premature pregnancy, child abuse, chronic dependence on welfare, and educational failure. (California Task Force, 1990, p. ix)

What Jonas Salk had achieved in the crusade against polio, the California Task Force would achieve in the crusade against low self-esteem.

The California Task Force proposed to vaccinate children against a disease that had plagued students for years. After all, nothing is as powerful as an idea whose time has come. As the belief that self-esteem, and therefore achievement and other things, could be boosted by informed teachers became more widespread, two concurrent developments emerged. First, educational practices in general began to change in an attempt to alleviate any "damage" being done to students by traditional practices and to promote more self-esteem that is positive by the use of different strategies and curriculum. Practices dropped, or at least attacked, included various grading procedures in which students failed, tracking of students by ability, negative reinforcement, the monocultural curriculum, competition, and autocratic procedures in general. These were replaced by positive reinforcement from teachers, grade inflation, self-talk, identifying personal strengths, opportunities to study one's own culture, counseling, creative spelling, ebonics, and so on. Obviously, this coincided with many other developments that led to more "progressive" educational practices, but the self-esteem movement was evident in virtually all of them.

The second development was the use of prepackaged self-esteem curriculum programs which germinated, quickly sprouted, and which continue to flower to this day. It is a big business. Examples include *Esteem Builders, Power of Positive Students* (POPS), *Phoenix Curriculum,* and even the *DARE* program for drug prevention. These are merely a few of the better-known programs. All focus, variably, on the activities mentioned in the preceding paragraph. The philosophies behind two of these programs are presented in Figure 5.1.

FIGURE 5.1. DESCRIPTIONS OF TWO SOCIAL VACCINE–
SELF-ESTEEM PROGRAMS USED NATIONWIDE

The Phoenix Curriculum*

The goal of the Phoenix Curriculum is to help teenagers gain an understanding of their potential and an appreciation of themselves. The curriculum consists of a 10-module program for grades 6, 7, and 8, divided into three units focusing on self-esteem, getting along with others, and goal setting and achievement; and a 20-module program for high school divided into 5 units focusing on self-esteem, personal relationships, responsibility, happiness and success, and goal setting and achievement.

The Phoenix Curriculum provides an organized, well-focused approach to overcome boredom, negativity and defeatism. The real strength of the program is that, as students learn about goal setting and personal choice, it allows them to take more and more responsibility for themselves and for learning. Students learn to trust themselves and to take pride in who they are. Once they have that self-confidence—the belief that they can achieve whatever they set their minds to—teachers can proceed with the traditional part of their job: providing opportunities for learning.

The Power of Positive Students**

We accept, and research supports, the relationship between self-concept and achievement in school. Because the school experience is a primary influence on how students perceive themselves, and because students with a positive self-concept are more effective learners, self-esteem must be a major concern of those who plan and implement the school curriculum. The psychological, social, emotional and moral development of a child is not incidental to education but the foundation on which it is built. Building self-esteem as part of the curriculum is a worthy end in itself.

Our plan, however, goes beyond pedagogic reform. The purpose is to modify the total instructional environment to sustain the positive feelings that most children have about themselves when they enter school….Any effective plan requires the cooperation of all persons who compose a child's human environment.

Sample techniques and strategies employed:

♦ To achieve a positive climate, and a positive self-concept, we repeated in endless variations, morning, noon, and night, the message, "You can succeed if you want to," and "Everybody is somebody."

♦ We held districtwide programs...to see and hear nationally known personalities who credit their success to positive thinking.

♦ We thoroughly briefed members of the community, and enlisted their support for the program.

♦ We informed our central administrative staff of the theoretical base, aims, and methodology of the plan, and kept them current through weekly meetings.

♦ We deliberately surrounded children with assurances of their self-worth.

♦ We held slogan contests.

♦ We looked for ways to introduce positive thinking into our topics.

SOURCE: * Youngs, B. B. (1989). The Phoenix curriculum. *Educational Leadership, 46*(5), 24. ** Mitchell, W. H., and McCollum, M. G. (1983). The power of positive students. *Educational Leadership, 40*(5), 48–51.

Consider for a moment the following excerpt from *Bridges: A Self-Esteem Activity Book for Students in Grades 4–6* (McGuire and Heuss, 1994). The activity in question is titled "How to Develop a High Self-Esteem."

How does a person who has low self-esteem go about raising it? Well, the best way is to change his thought patterns. It's true— we feel the way we THINK we feel! The more positive you are, the better you'll feel. And the better you feel, the higher your self-esteem will be. GO FOR IT! (p. 59)

This use of teacher and student time away from such real issues as character formation, academic achievement, and hard work, with its focus on feeling good, is presented by the authors as though "raising" one's self-esteem were a simple matter of doing this and the many other activities found in the program. In economic theory, the concept of "opportunity cost" suggests that choosing to do one thing also means giving up certain others. What is the opportunity cost of spending time in these activities? The school day contains only so many hours. The reader is informed on the book's back cover that the authors' "mission" is to promote positive self-esteem, but nowhere in the activity book is there a shred of theory, research, documented findings, or linkages between self-esteem and anything else beyond feeling good about oneself.

It is also worth mentioning that some advocates have adopted the causation theory as a useful explanation of why certain minority groups continue to lag academically. Indeed, many multicultural curricula are designed to promote students' self-esteem based on their ethnic identity and on the idea that all cultures are worthwhile and have made valuable contributions (e.g., Vann and Kunjufu, 1993). The research, however, doesn't necessarily take us there. Frase and Streshly (2000), citing research done by Rothman (1989), write, "African-American self-esteem is as high and sometimes higher than that of whites," but it is in the public mindset that this is not so.

THE CRITICS

In recent years, the critics of these strategies and programs have become more and more vociferous. The attacks have come from a wide range of sources on either side of the political spectrum. They have come largely from the popular press, but also from some conservative essentialist writers in education. Cartoons regularly lampoon the efforts and programs by educators in this area. There have been editorials by nationally syndicated columnists, such as Charles Krauthammer, George Will, and John Leo, blasting the ludicrousness of it all, and generously citing the more bizarre examples to be found. Some see it as simply the latest incarnation of the long-standing emphasis on positive thinking and self-help.

Most of the critics are in basic philosophical disagreement with the causation theory, and they point to the almost total lack of empirical data to support that theory. For example, Thomas Sowell (1993, p. 97), a senior fellow at the Hoover Institution stated that, "The very idea that self-esteem is something *earned*, rather than being a prepackaged handout from the school system, seems not to occur to many educators." Alfie Kohn (1994, 277) stated that, "the whole enterprise could be said to encourage a self-absorption bordering on narcissism," and that the programs are superficial, consisting of such drivel as, "I am special because ...," essays "all about me," and chanting hollow phrases such as "I think" and "I feel."

It is more difficult to find critics within the educational establishment, but there are a few. For example, Elizabeth McPike (1996), the editor of *American Educator,* the journal of the American Federation of Teachers (AFT), wrote: "...[W]ell-intentioned but misguided notions about self-esteem have become, if anything, even more deeply embedded in the culture of many, many schools. These notions get played out in various ways and constitute one of the most serious threats to the movement to raise

academic and disciplinary standards and improve the learning opportunities and life chances of our nation's children" (p. 9). Roy Baumeister
(1996) goes even further, advising educators to "beware the dark side" of
teaching self-esteem and advises schools to "forget about self-esteem, and
concentrate on self-control." And, as we shall see, a number of researchers
are also quite troubled by the claims of causation, and even relationship,
between self-esteem and achievement and prosocial behaviors. But these
critics within the profession are rare. Even more rare are those who challenge the multicultural claims about self-esteem and students' success as
have O'Donnell and O'Donnell (1995).

LEVEL I RESEARCH

It is best to think of the Level I research in two separate ways: First, let
us consider theoretical models, followed by a look at empirical studies
examining the relationship between self-esteem and achievement and
pro-social behaviors.

Chapter 3 described how educational theories often derive from a
variety of sources: philosophy, experience, observations, and basic
research (often done in other fields, such as psychology). Consider two
scenarios. First, someone may conduct exploratory research—collecting
data on a variety of people, analyzing them statistically looking for relationships between variables. Then, on the basis of those relationships,
either a theory of causation—that is, that one variable has a directing
influence on the other variable—or a theory of relationship—that is, that
where one variable is found, the other(s) probably will be also—is developed. For example, an economist may find a positive correlation or relationship between a person's amount of education and income. The data
show that as the amount of a person's education increases, his or her
income also increases. One might theorize a cause-and-effect relationship
between the two variables: education determines income. This makes a
certain amount of sense. Educated people in our society can usually
demand a higher salary than those less educated.

However, the nature of correlation is sometimes confusing. In this
case, one could just as easily have theorized that income drives education,
because people with money are more likely to be able to afford to go to
college. This theory also seems plausible. But, it is just as plausible that
both variables are driven by something else. The German social scientist,
Max Weber, advanced a theory in the late nineteenth century of the relationship between Protestantism and success in capitalist ventures. Weber
had noted a significant statistical correlation between the two variables.
His critics, however, have pointed out that highly developed capitalist
enterprises existed prior to the advent of Protestantism and can also be
found in Asian cultures where Protestantism is hardly present. Weber

was well aware that other preconditions, material and psychological, are often present for the development of successful capitalism, and even he admitted that a cause-and-effect relationship is tentative at best.

The second scenario develops somewhat differently. Based on a philosophical or worldview of human nature, one might develop a theory independent of much empirical data. At this point, it is a theory with little or no evidence. It becomes the work of empirical researchers to see if the theory fits "reality," that is, whether there is reason to think it is true or workable in certain circumstances. Sometimes evidence is gathered to a degree that the theory is accepted as "true" or valid. And sometimes the evidence is lacking and the theory is rejected as insufficient to explain reality. A celebrated example of this is the phenomenon known as "phrenology." The theory of phrenology, conceptualized by the Austrian doctor Franz-Joseph Gall around the turn of the eighteenth century, posited that the conformation of the skull is indicative of mental faculties and character traits. Phrenology enjoyed popular appeal until well into the twentieth century when it became discredited for lack of scientific evidence. As a field, education is replete with such examples, the most recent of which is the Instructional Theory into Practice (ITIP) model that was referred to earlier.

Self-esteem theory appears to have developed in this second way. Scheirer and Kraut (1979) concluded that many of the self-esteem ideas can be traced back to early humanist psychologists. They state:

> Professional psychologists as early as William James emphasized that a person's beliefs about himself will influence his decisions and actions. The forefathers of American social psychology, C. H. Cooley and George Herbert Mead, described the self as a social entity formed by appraisal reflected from other persons. Following Mead and Cooley, symbolic interactionists hypothesized that a positive self-concept will lead to constructive, socially desirable behavior, and conversely that a distorted self-concept will lead to deviant, socially inadequate behaviors. (p. 131)

Thus a correlation between self-esteem and prized behaviors, not to mention a cause-and-effect relationship, was hypothesized early on. What is noteworthy here is that these things were *theorized* as ways to explain human failure and "deviant, socially inadequate behaviors." One might just as easily have theorized the opposite, that people's socially inadequate behavior leads them to feeling bad about themselves. Or, a third hypothesis is that the causative agents sit somewhere outside the correlation.

Earlier mention was made of Lerner (1996) who noted that self-esteem theory has been the reigning orthodoxy for so long that, "Many teachers will be hard pressed to think of a contrasting theory." What many educators have never even thought of is that there are rival theories to this orthodoxy. For example, Lerner contrasts the orthodoxy with the ideas of Alfred Binet (of Stanford-Binet fame), who theorized that:

> ...[A] self-critical stance was at the very core of intelligence, its sine qua non and seminal essence....[H]e saw self-criticism as the essence of intelligence, the master key that unlocked the doors to competence and excellence alike....[H]is view on the natural inclinations [one of egotism] of children [was] not novel at all,...that egotism was the natural state of childhood. Teachers who took this view saw it as their job to help children overcome their egotism...and [learn] to see themselves and their accomplishments in a realistic perspective in order to take realistic steps toward excellence. (p. 10)

Lerner calls this "earned self-esteem" as opposed to "feel-good–now self-esteem." In this contrasting theory, self-esteem is earned. "It is not a precondition for learning but a product of it" (p. 10). This point of view, one echoed by John Hewitt (1998), as well as the point of view of other rival theories, seems hardly to have been given serious consideration if one were to judge by the curricular artifacts available.

What empirical evidence exists to support the reigning self-esteem *theory*? Not much that anyone has apparently been able to find. In fact, the thousands of studies done on self-esteem in the past four decades have been reviewed numerous times (e.g., Scheirer and Kraut, 1979; Hansford and Hattie, 1982; Byrne, 1984; California Task Force on Self-Esteem, 1990; Skaalvic and Hagtvet, 1990; Kohn, 1994; Baumeister, Smart, and Boden, 1996) and the conclusions are always the same: The *relationship* between self-esteem and achievement and other related behaviors is minimal at best, and more likely nonexistent. And most of the researchers consistently point out that even with those factors for which a small relationship is found, it is usually so small as to have no practical significance. Additionally, these small correlations are in no way supportive of any type of cause-and-effect relationship.

Scheirer and Kraut (1979) examined the wealth of research and concluded that, "...little direct evidence exists in either psychological or sociological literature that self-concept has an independent influence on behavior" (p. 132). Regarding academic achievement in particular, they stated, "...the overwhelmingly negative evidence reviewed here for a causal connection between self-concept and academic achievement should create caution among both educators and theorists who have heretofore assumed that enhancing a person's feelings about himself would lead to academic achievement" (p. 145), and that, "...neither the internal needs model nor the identification with one's ethnic group model has stimulated an educational program with positive results linking self-concept with academic achievement" (p. 144).

Things had not changed much 25 years later when Alfie Kohn concluded:

- ♦ "...[T]he findings that emerge from this [self-esteem] literature are not especially encouraging for those who would like to believe that feeling good about oneself brings about a variety of benefits" (p. 273).

- ♦ "In sum, high self-esteem appears to offer no guarantee of inclining people toward pro-social behavior—or even of steering them away from antisocial behavior" (p. 275).

- ♦ "The implication is that the better the research, the less significant the connection it will find between self-esteem and achievement" (p. 275).

Among the more interesting developments in this intriguing realm are the actions of the California Task Force on Self-Esteem (1990). The Task Force was composed almost wholly of strong proponents of the self-esteem theory. The report of the Task Force stated, however, that, "We who served on the task force were determined that our findings would be grounded in the most current and valid research available" (p. 43). And what did they conclude?

> The associations between self-esteem and its expected consequences are mixed, insignificant, or absent. The nonrelationship holds between self-esteem and teenage pregnancy, self-esteem and child abuse, self-esteem and most cases of alcohol and drug abuse....If the association between self-esteem and behavior is so often reported to be weak, even less can be said for the causal relationship between the two. (Smelser, 1989, 15, 17)

This did not stop advocates of the causal theory, however, who forged ahead with a wealth of new programs. How could this have happened, given the evidence? Joseph Kahne (1996), who studied this outcome from the California Task Force for Self-Esteem, noted that, "Findings that questioned the likelihood of ameliorating social problems by promoting self-esteem were ignored. More precisely,...they were overruled" (p. 12). Such is the strength of cultural beliefs, so much so that evidence itself seems not to matter and can simply be overruled by those who do not believe it. The task force itself offered this explanation: "...Many of us on the task force are convinced that a sizable number of practitioners in functioning [self-esteem] programs are well ahead of academic researchers in their appreciation of self-esteem's central role in the social problems that plague our society" (p. 43). So much for humility.

One other matter of note: From the decades of research on self-esteem, an interesting counter-theory has emerged, which suggests that self-esteem strategies may have detrimental effects. Wesley Burr (1992) suggested that out of this emphasis on self-esteem have emerged greater selfishness, excessive individualism, and processes that are undermining the health of families. Baumeister, Smart, and Boden (1996) have taken this charge a step further. Their examination of the research concluded that there is a lack of empirical evidence to support the idea that low self-esteem leads to antisocial behavior. They write, "The traditional view that low self-esteem is a cause of violence and aggression is not tenable in light of the present evidence" (p. 26). From the research, however, they have theorized, "that one major cause of violent response is threatened egotism, that is, a favorable self-appraisal that encounters an external and unfavorable evaluation....In particular, unrealistically positive or inflated view of self, and favorable self-appraisals that are uncertain, unstable, or heavily dependent on external validation, will be especially vulnerable to encountering such threats" (p. 12). Finally, they theorize that, "An uncritical endorsement of the cultural value of high self-esteem may therefore be counterproductive and even dangerous" (p. 29).

New research even draws into question the cherished notion that higher self-esteem leads to more socially-acceptable behaviors. Whether linkages can be established between self-esteem and adjustment by children and adolescents remains problematic in the sense that any such linkages that might exist appear to be highly differentiated and complex. Dubois and Tevendale (1999) note that even directional patterns of influence, that is to say, between cause and effect, are probably recursive. They go on to write:

> ...[T]here appears to be a potential for high levels of self-esteem to have *negative* (italics added) or unfavorable consequences for the adjustment and well-being of young adolescents, rather than only the health-promoting benefits that have been assumed previously (p. 8).

Dubois and Hirsch's conceptual model of self-esteem in early adolescence is presented in Figure 5.2. It illustrates the many factors imbedded in the construct, including context, developmental status, and types of adjustment. The model emphasizes the bidirectional nature of self-esteem.

FIGURE 5.2. GENERAL CONCEPTUAL MODEL OF SELF-ESTEEM IN EARLY ADOLESCENCE

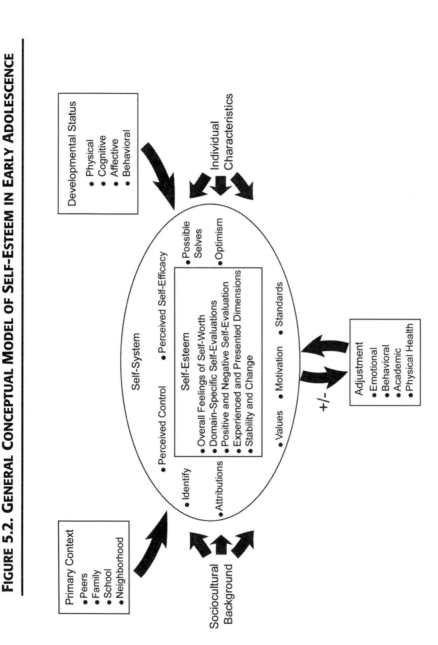

In summary, what does the Level I research say? Basically, it says that the construct of self-esteem as a global, unified entity is probably not established and most probably does not exist as such, that self-esteem is more likely differentially held by individuals depending on context, and that it represents a complex, interrelated set of factors. As to its cause and effect properties, the latest theoretical thought is that it is bidirectional, serving as both cause and effect in such matters of adjustment and achievement. While research findings do support that higher self-esteem is in some sense desirable, it does not account for more than approximately 5% of the variance in criterion measures of achievement, a moderate contribution to say the least. (Dusek, 2000) Given the latest theory building and research findings, self-efficacy seems a more reasonable school-based pursuit than does self-esteem.

LEVELS II AND III RESEARCH

Not surprisingly, the popular educational literature is replete with anecdotal stories that inform the reader of schools and students "turned around" by "innovative" school programs and practices designed to promote self-esteem. But it is difficult to disagree with Alfie Kohn (1994), who concluded that, "Hard data to support the efficacy of such interventions [self-esteem programs] are...virtually nil." Even the sympathetic California Task Force on Self-Esteem reached similar conclusions. They concluded that, "There is no solid evidence that counseling and psychotherapy can increase self-esteem." If that type of intense treatment cannot change self-concepts, it seems improbable that slogans and other such efforts will have little effect on achievement and other pro-social behaviors.

It is one thing to ponder whether teachers can play a significant role in raising the self-esteem of their students, a prospect that seems complex and problematic, in spite of claims made by program developers. However, there is a certain amount of research to indicate that certain elements of self-esteem, especially self-efficacy, do play a role, however limited and however directional, in certain valued school outcomes.

Sterbin and Rakow (1996) investigated the linkages between academic achievement on standardized tests and locus of control and self-esteem. Reviewing some 12,260 student test scores from the National Education Longitudinal Study 1994 database, they did find moderate but positive correlations between locus of control and achievement ($r = .29$) and self-esteem and achievement ($r = .16$). They concluded that the findings suggest that the constructs of locus of control and self-esteem need improved, more situation-specific operational definitions. Finally, they stated that "self-esteem is significantly related to socioeconomic status, gender, and locus of control, variables that must be taken into account before the effects of self-esteem on achievement can be assessed" (p. 1).

Pajares and Viliante (1997) studied the influence of writing self-efficacy, writing apprehension, perceived usefulness of writing, and writing aptitude on 218 fifth-graders' essay-writing performance. They noted that "students' beliefs about their abilities directly influenced apprehension, perceived usefulness, and performance, and partially mediated the effects of gender and writing aptitude on apprehension, perceived utility, and performance" (p. 1). Writing aptitude emerged as a clear predictor of writing performance. The significance of this thoughtful study is that the investigators recognized the emergent knowledge of self-efficacy as differentiated, situation specific, and certainly related to perceived importance of task.

A study by Roeser and Eccles (1998) examined the relationships between adolescents' perceptions of their middle school and achievement among other variables. They found that student perceptions of their school's climate, including such matters as school goal structure, provision for autonomy, and positive teacher regard of students were associated with increased academic success. Of course, this is correlational rather than cause and effect research, but it is supportive of clear school goals, student autonomy and choice making, and a positive attitude on the part of teachers toward their students.

A meta-analysis conducted by Multon et al. (1991) tested the hypotheses that self-efficacy beliefs related positively to academic performance and persistence outcomes. The investigators reported a positive and statistically significant relationship between self-efficacy beliefs and academic performance and persistence outcomes across a wide variety of school subjects. It is important to note here that we are talking about self-efficacy and not about global self-esteem.

A thoughtful qualitative study conducted by Cross (1997) involved the attitudes and beliefs about self-esteem held by 68 urban teachers. Using primarily interview techniques, she found the teachers in her sample overwhelmingly considered low self-esteem endemic with urban students. Further, she concluded that these teachers believed that through instructional and curricular interventions they could affect self-esteem leading to improved behavior and academic achievement. Among other things, she concluded that the teachers in her sample tended to oversimplify the complexities inherent in such matters as directionality as well as cause and effect, and that the teachers held largely unexamined ideological and political assumptions based on little empirical evidence and only tangentially connected to theory and practice.

There is one major Level III research study worth noting. The U.S. Office of Education initiated Project Follow Through, a comprehensive program in the primary grades of 170-plus communities (see Chapter 14).

The largest and most expensive educational study ever conducted by the Office of Education, it involved research on a wide range of instructional approaches from open classrooms to very highly structured, teacher-controlled methodologies. Researchers (Stebbins et al., 1977) concluded that the models of instruction that produced the largest gains in self-esteem were those that assumed that *competence* enhanced self-esteem (Lerner's "earned self-esteem") and not the other way around. Those instructional programs concerned with affective outcomes and their causal influence on learning (Lerner's "feel-good-now self-esteem") produced minimal or even negative affective outcomes, as well as the lowest academic achievement. The sad note, however, is that given their popularity and the time and money spent on self-esteem programs, there is so little school-based evidence to support them.

CONCLUSION

Finally, it is up to you to decide whether self-esteem programs in school settings are a worthwhile endeavor. There is limited evidence at Levels I, II, and III to support their pursuit. Caution, therefore, is the watchword if you decide to go ahead. Some time ago I had a conversation with a professor of education who works at another university. She is a staunch advocate of raising self-esteem in the classroom through specific strategies that lead, in her opinion, to higher achievement. To the remark that the evidence is lacking, she simply replied that the work is too important for us to be sitting around waiting for research results that may not be useful anyway. So, as Abraham Lincoln once observed, "People who like that kind of thing find that's just the kind of thing they like." And, apparently, many are sold on the idea. The question ultimately is not whether we all want young people to have a positive opinion of themselves. Of course, we do. Rather, the question is how does that come about? Perhaps the answer is found in the pursuit of old-fashioned virtues such as disciplined effort, helping others, showing courtesy and kindness, and applying ourselves diligently when it comes to hard work on serious matters. But that, too, is just a theory waiting to be tested.

A final note is in order here. It is probably time for teachers to stop thinking of self-esteem as a global construct. Too much evidence exists to indicate that it is situation specific, that it is multidimensional, that it varies tremendously for a given individual based on perceptions of importance and self-efficacy, and that it is bidirectional and recursive in relation to significant school and life outcomes. We end up where we started this chapter, to paraphrase the poet T. S. Eliot. Cross (1997, p. 90) writes: "The challenge is for teachers to disengage themselves from the popular and to some degree academic fixation on self-esteem."

REFERENCES

Bandura, A. (1997). *Self-efficacy: The exercise of control.* New York: W. H. Freeman.

Battle, J. (1992). *Culture-free self-esteem inventories* (2nd ed.). Austin, TX: PRO-ED.

Baumeister, R. F. (1996, Summer). Should schools try to boost self-esteem. *American Educator, 14–19.*

Baumeister, R. F., Smart, L., and Boden, J. M. (1996). Relation of threatened egotism to violence and aggression: The dark side of high self-esteem. *Psychological Review, 103*(1), 5–33.

Burr, W. (1992). Undesirable side effects of enhancing self-esteem. *Family Relations, 41,* 460–464.

Byrne, B. M. (1984). The general/academic self-concept nomological network: A review of construct validation research. *Review of Educational Research, 54*(3), 427–456.

California Task Force to Promote Self-esteem and Personal and Social Responsibility (1990). *Toward a state of esteem: The final report of the California Task Force to Promote Self-esteem and Personal and Social Responsibility.* Sacramento: California State Department of Education.

Coopersmith, S. (1987). *Coopersmith self-esteem inventory.* Palo Alto, CA: Consulting Psychologists Press.

Cross, B. (1997). Self-esteem and curriculum: Perspectives from urban teachers. *Journal of Curriculum and Supervision, 13,* 70–91.

Dubois, L., & Hirsch, B. (2000). Self-esteem in early adolescence: From stock character to marquee attraction. *Journal of Early Adolescence, 20,* 5–11.

Dubois, L., & Tevendale, H. (1999). Self-esteem in childhood and adolescence: Vaccine or epiphenomenona? *Applied and Preventive Psychology, 8,* 103–117.

Dusek, J. (2000). Commentary on the special issue: The maturing of self-esteem research with early adolescents. *Journal of Early Adolescence, 20,* 231–241.

Falk, R., & Miller, N. (1998). The reflexive self: A sociological perspective. *Roeper Review, 20,* 150–153.

Frase, L., & Streshly, W. (2000). *Top 10 myths in education: Fantasies that Americans love to believe.* Lanham, MD: Scarecrow Press.

Hansford, B. C., & Hattie, J. A. (1982). The relationship between self and achievement/performance measures. *Review of Educational Research, 52*(1), 123–142.

Hewitt, J. (1998). *The myth of self-esteem: Finding happiness and solving problems in America.* New York: St. Martins.

Kahne, J. (1996). The politics of self-esteem. *American Educational Research Journal, 33*(1), 3–22.

Kaisa, A., Stattin, H., & Nurmi, J. (2000). Adolescents' achievement strategies, school adjustment, and externalizing and internalizing problem behaviors. *Journal of Youth and Adolescence, 29*(3), 289–306.

Kohn, A. (1994). The truth about self-esteem. *Phi Delta Kappan, 76*(4), 272–283.

Lewis, J., & Knight, H. (2000). Self-concept in gifted youth: An investigation employing the piers-harris subscales. *Gifted Child Quarterly, 44*(1), 45–53.

Lerner, B. (1996, Summer). Self-esteem and excellence: The choice and the paradox. *American Educator,* 9–13, 41–42.

McGuire, J., & Heuss, B. (1994). *Bridges: A self-esteem activity book for students in grades 4–6.* Boston: Allyn and Bacon.

McPike, E. (1996, Summer). Editor's introduction. In B. Lerner (Ed.). Self-esteem and excellence: The choice and the paradox. *American Educator,* 9–13, 41–42.

Mecca, A. M., Smelser, N. J., & Vasconcellos, J. (Eds.) (1989). *The social importance of self-esteem.* Berkley: University of California Press.

Mitchell, W. H., & McCollum, M. G. (1983). The power of positive students. *Educational Leadership, 40*(5), 48–51.

Multon, K. et al. (1991). Relation of self-efficacy beliefs to academic outcomes: A meta-analytic investigation. *Journal of Counseling Psychology, 38,* 30–38.

O'Donnell, T. F., & O'Donnell, W. J. (1995). Multicultural myths. *American School Board Journal, 182*(7), 23–25.

Pajares, F., & Viliante, G. (1997). Influence of self-efficacy on elementary students' writing. *Journal of Educational Research, 90,* 353–360.

Piers, E. V., & Harris, D. B. (1984). *Piers-Harris children's self-concept scale (the way I feel about myself).* Los Angeles: Western Psychological Services.

Roeser, R., & Eccles, J. (1998). Adolescents' perceptions of middle school: Relation to longitudinal changes in academic and psychological adjustment. *Journal of Research on Adolescence, 8,* 123–158.

Rogers, C. (1969/1994). *Freedom to learn.* Columbus, OH: Charles E. Merrill.

Rothman, S. *The myth of black low self-esteem.* Northampton, MA: Smith College Center for the Study of Social and Political Change.

Scheirer, M. A., & Kraut, R. E. (1979). Increasing educational achievement via self-concept. *Review of Educational Research, 49*(1), 131–150.

Schunk, D. (2000). *Learning theories: An educational perspective.* Upper Saddle River, NJ: Prentice-Hall.

Skaalvic, E., & Hagtve, K. (1990). Academic achievement and self-concept. *Journal of Personality and Social Psychology, 58*(2), 292–307.

Smelser, N. J. (1989). *Self-esteem and social problems: An introduction.* In A. M. Mecca, N. J. Smelser, and J. Vasconcellos (Eds.). *The social importance of self-esteem* (pp. 1–25). Berkeley: University of California Press.

Sowell, T. (1993). *Inside American education: The decline, the deception, the dogmas.* New York: Free Press.

Stebbins, L., St. Pierre, R., Proper, E., Anderson, R., & Cerva, T. (1977). *Education as experimentation: A planned variation model (Vol. IVA–D).* Cambridge, MA: Abt Associates.

Sterbin, A., & Rakow, E. (1996). Self-esteem, locus of control, and student achievement. (ERIC document 406429.)

Stigler, J., & Hiebert, J. (1999). *The teaching gap.* New York: Touchstone Books.

Stout, M. (2000). *The feel-good curriculum.* New York: Perseus Books Group.

Vann, K. R., & Kunjufu, J. (1993). The importance of an Afrocentric, multicultural curriculum. *Phi Delta Kappan, 74*(6), 490–491.

Walz, G. R., & Bleur, J. C. (1992). *Student self-esteem: a vital element of school success.* Alexandria, VA: American School Counselor Association.

Youngs, B. B. (1989). The Phoenix curriculum. *Educational Leadership, 46*(5), 24.

6

INNOVATIONS FROM BRAIN RESEARCH

Can a profession whose charge is defined by the development
of an effective and efficient human brain continue to remain
uninformed about that brain? If we do remain uninformed
about the brain, we will become vulnerable to the
pseudoscientific fads, generalizations, and programs that will
surely arise from the pool of brain research.

Robert Sylwester

Over the past 20 years or more, neuroscientists have amassed
a wealth of knowledge on the brain and its development from
birth to adulthood. And they are beginning to draw some
solid conclusions about how the human brain grows and how
babies acquire language, sight and musical talents, and other
abilities. The question now is: How much of these data can
educators use? The answer is uncertain.

Debra Viadero

Many well-meaning educators have gone way beyond the
research.

Eric Jensen

In 1998, Vilayanur Ramachandran, a senior scientist from the University of California at San Diego, announced that there are more possible brain states than there are particles in the universe. (Howard, 2000). His comment serves as one more reminder of the tremendous and not fully realized potential of human learning.

Take a moment to consider the following: synapse formation; dendritic field; computerized axial tomography; positron-emission tomography; magnetic resonance imaging; glial cells; neurons; dendrites;

neurotransmitters; peptides; corpus callosum; and anterior commissure. These terms, which are a focus of brain research, have little meaning to most teachers and administrators. Yet, the research in this area may well have implications for how we should teach and how schools should be organized. Robert Sylwester (1995, 1998), a leading figure in the field of brain research and school learning, points out that educators have stressed the environmental aspects of learning potential, largely without an understanding of how the brain actually works. However, advances in medical research have made possible the startling recognition that the human brain is on the verge of understanding itself! In light of this development, Sylwester concluded that, "Our profession has tended to think of the nurture side as dominant, but these new theories argue that nature plays a far more important role than previously believed—or that the dichotomy itself is not an irrelevant issue. They also suggest that many current beliefs about instruction, learning, and memory are wrong" (1995, pp. 14–15).

The current fascination with brain research flows from the belief that if we can figure out how the brain functions, that is, how information is received, stored, retrieved, and otherwise processed, we can then design educational programs based on that knowledge. Brain research represents for many the ultimate pedagogical frontier. Once this new territory is explored and mapped, the promise of maximizing the learning potential of each student will be realized. Sylwester's bold statement in the previous paragraph gives notice: We may need to make fundamental changes in the ways we go about the business of learning and teaching.

The basic research in this area began with Paul Broca's celebrated nineteenth-century theory of hemispheric dominance (Sternberg, 2000). Research into this and other areas of brain function continued apace throughout the twentieth century, and in 1981, Roger Sperry received the Nobel Prize for his cerebral specialization research. In more recent years, medical research into brain function has expanded into a variety of areas to include brain development in childhood, short- and long-term memory, attention, emotions, gender differences, effects of aging, consciousness, creativity, sensory input, intelligence, sexuality, and others. It is all very technical and overwhelming for those outside the world of scientific investigation even to consider.

THE PENDULUM IS WELL INTO ITS SWING

It was not long after certain findings from brain research became publicized that educators jumped into the breach with ideas about how the findings should alter educational practices (Reiff, 1992; Carnine, 1990; Caine & Caine, 1990, 1997; Howard 2000; Springer & Deutsch, 1989; Sternberg, 2000; Wittrock, 1981). A wide range of educational "theories" has emerged on the heels of medical investigations. Two decades ago Robert Sylwester (1981) wrote, "The brain is the most magnificent three pounds of matter in the universe. What we now know about the human brain and what we'll discover in the years ahead may well transform formal education." Whether what we think we know about the brain will prove useful or not, educators have jumped on the bandwagon with article after article about the educational implications of medical research. Sylwester (1981, p. 8) went on to say, "…but can we afford to wait until all problems are solved before we begin to study the education issues implicit in this research? When mass media begin to report discoveries, parents will expect us to respond."

In at least a comparative sense, Sylwester was cautious, believing that it was too early to implement curricular and instructional changes based on the medical research. He was no doubt well aware of the tendency of some educators to make wild claims and advocate unproven methodologies based on theories alone, and he remains cautious to this day. As he has more recently written, "We've already demonstrated our vulnerability with the educational spillover of the split-brain research: the right brain/left brain books, workshops, and curricular programs whose recommendations often went far beyond the research findings" (1995, p. 6).

Certain other educators are less restrained in their enthusiasm. It is charitable to say that they at least think they have responded to the medical findings by developing activities and strategies designed to influence life in classrooms. The topic has become common fare at conventions, workshops, and inservice meetings. Those who wish confirmation of this claim need only review the list of presentations found in the catalogues of major education conferences or peruse journals in education.

An article by Guild and Chock-Eng (1998), titled *Multiple Intelligences. Learning Styles, Brain-Based Education: Where Do the Messgages Overlap?*, points to the enthusiastic and wide ranging implications claimed on behalf of brain-based teaching. The authors conclude that the overlap yields "theories" that are learning and learner-centered, aimed at the whole person, supportive of diversity, and supportive of teachers and students as reflective practitioners. Elsewhere we see classroom teachers giving kids peppermints, playing classical music, plugging in various scent-producing gadgets, handing out raisins before tests, and repainting their rooms in calming colors, all in the name of brain-based teaching findings. Neuroscientist Craig Kinsley of the University of Richmond says some of the claims "border on pseudoscience." Citing soft lighting as an example, Kinsley says a likely consequence will be "more kids needing glasses." (Hendrick, 2000).

An example of teaching/learning claims derived from medical research is reflected in the work of Caine and Caine (1990, 1997). They write that they have developed "brain principles as a general theoretical foundation for brain-based learning. These principles are simple and neurologically sound. Applied to education, however, they help us to reconceptualize teaching by taking us out of traditional frames of reference and guiding us in defining and selecting appropriate programs and methodologies" (1990, p. 66).

A summary of Caine and Caine's brain-based learning theory is presented in Figure 6.1. Each of the 12 learning principles has direct implications for teaching and learning. For example, Principle Two states that "brain-based teaching must fully incorporate stress management, nutrition, exercise, drug education, and other facets of health into the learning process" (p. 66). Principle Six states that "vocabulary and grammar are best understood and mastered when they are incorporated in genuine, whole-language experiences. Similarly, equations and scientific principles are best dealt with in the context of living science" (p. 67). These are interesting conclusions in any educational context, but to state that they are based on brain research gives them, one supposes, heightened credibility. At any rate, these assertions sailed past the editorial gatekeepers of *Educational Leadership*, a policy journal in the field of education, which in the year 1998 alone carried 16 separate articles on brain-based education.

FIGURE 6.1. CAINE AND CAINE'S BRAIN-BASED LEARNING PRINCIPLES AND TEACHING MODEL

Principles:

- Principle One: The Brain Is a Parallel Processor.
- Principle Two: Learning Engages the Entire Physiology.
- Principle Three: The Search for Meaning Is Innate.
- Principle Four: The Search for Meaning Occurs Through "Patterning."
- Principle Five: Emotions Are Critical to Patterning.
- Principle Six: Every Brain Simultaneously Perceives and Creates Parts and Wholes.
- Principle Seven: Learning Involves Both Focused Attention and Peripheral Perception.
- Principle Eight: Learning Always Involves Conscious and Unconscious Processes.
- Principle Nine: We Have Two Types of Memory: A Spatial Memory System and a Set of Systems for Rote Learning.
- Principle Ten: The Brain Understands and Remembers Best When Facts and Skills Are Embedded in Natural Spatial Memory.

♦ Principle Eleven: Learning is Enhanced by Challenge and Inhibited by Threat.

♦ Principle Twelve: Each Brain Is Unique.

Teaching Models:

	Traditional	*Brain-Based*
Source of Information	Simple. Two-way, from teacher to book, worksheet, or film to student	Complex. Social interactions, group discovery, individual search and reflection, role-playing integrated subject matter.
Classroom Organization	Linear. Individual work or teacher-directed.	Complex. Thematic, integrative, cooperative, workstations, individualized projects.
Classroom Management	Hierarchical. Teacher-controlled.	Complex. Designated status and responsibilities delegated to students and monitored by teacher.
Outcomes	Specified and convergent. Emphasis on memorized concepts, vocabulary, and skills.	Complex. Emphasis on reorganization of information in unique ways, with both predictable outcomes, divergent and convergent, increase in natural knowledge demonstrated through ability to use learned skills in variable contexts.

SOURCE: Adapted from Caine, R. N., & Caine, G. (1994). *Making connections: Teaching and the human brain.* Menlo Park, CA: Addison-Wesley.

The application of basic brain research to education has also resulted in an emphasis on learning styles, particularly among proponents of hemisphericity (right and left brain preference) in learning. It is worth noting that both learning styles advocates and brain research educators support a whole-brain approach to teaching. That is, they both claim that it is necessary to teach to both sides of the brain, thereby providing a wide and complementary range of strategies and activities to stimulate learners.

Harvard psychologist Ellen Langer (1997) proposes a "flexible thinking" model based on emergent findings in brain-mind research. Langer attempts to dispel a number of myths about thinking and learning that seem to have permeated educational settings. These myths, she claims, are barriers to creative, productive thinking. Among those myths are the idea that basic facts should be thoroughly memorized, that focusing on one thing at a time is productive, that rote memory work ought to be a staple in learning, that intelligence is knowing a lot of information, and that most questions have right and wrong answers. Langer counters these "myths" with her findings that overlearning stifles insight and individuality, that learning ought to be fun and therefore more likely meaningful, that life-long learning is a key to success, and that memorization is a barrier to creativity.

Pierce Howard (2000), the author of a massive synthesis of research and development in brain-based learning, writes, "the advances in brain research are breathtakingly rapid....Who knows where the next major advance will be and what difference it will make in our lives?...As research expands our sense of what is true and what is real, paradigms begin to shift, sometimes imperceptibly, sometimes earth-shakingly. In looking over the way cognitive science affects our lives I see ten paradigms that seem to me to be in the middle of the major shifts" (p. 745).

Among those ten major shifts noted by Howard, all of which have basic implications for teaching and learning, are the following five:

1. A shift in emphasis from external to internal motivation in learning.
2. A shift in emphasis on aging as detrimental to learning to a "use it or lose it" approach to life-long learning.
3. A shift from thinking of intelligence as a single-faceted concept to a multifaceted concept.
4. A shift from thinking of nurture as the main factor in learning to nature as the main factor.
5. A shift from thinking of the brain as a computer to thinking of the brain as a pharmacy.

Bernice McCarthy's 4MAT System is an example of a hybrid program that incorporates brain research and learning styles. McCarthy (1987, 1996) has developed a comprehensive instructional approach to meeting individual needs by combining research on brain hemispheres with David Kolb's Learning Cycle (1985). The 4MAT System identifies the learning needs of four types of learners and accompanying strategies for the integration of both right and left brain processing skills.

Other educational implications cited by brain-based teaching advocates include:

◆ Balanced teaching in order to engage both hemispheres;

◆ Growth spurts and their implications for individualization, pacing, year-round schooling, acceleration, and failure policies;

◆ Matching structure and content of curricula, environments, activities, and interactions to cognitive abilities;

◆ Curriculum integration to provide meaningful contexts and connections among and between subjects;

◆ Schema theory, to furnish a learning environment that provides stability and familiarity as well as challenge and discovery;

◆ Wider ranges of contextual and sensory cues in learning in order to increase the number of links made with each new concept, thus leading to improved long-term memory and transfer.

Much of what Langer, Howard, and others cite as points of teaching/learning emphases based on brain research represents pretty much the progressive educational agenda, one which has been around for more than a century. Progressives were arguing in behalf of many of these same issues before there was much brain research in the modern sense. However, the fact that much of the progressive agenda is in basic agreement with emergent findings only ought to cause us to reconsider it in a time of emphasis on standardized testing and uniform curricula.

RESEARCH ON EDUCATION AND THE BRAIN

The research at Level I is classic basic research into brain function. The researchers themselves admit that the research base is just developing and that it has barely scratched the surface. Sylwester identifies two approaches taken by scientists who study the brain: from the bottom up and from the top down. The bottom-up approach characterizes the work of neuroscientists who focus on the working of small units—individual cells or small systems of cells. The top-down approach focuses on complex cognitive mechanisms or functions, such as movement, language, and abstract analysis. These studies include the normal and abnormal functioning of single neurons, networks of neurons, and the factors that affect neuron activity. All of this (and much more) is accomplished through the use of CAT scans, EEGs, PETs, MRIs, and other tests. Some of this research is conducted on animals, as well as on people with brain damage or mental illness. Other studies are done in laboratory experiments with normal primates and humans, using brain imaging technology to determine chemical composition, electrical transmission, and blood flow patterns which occur normally and during the conduct of certain tasks. All of this sounds very technical, and it is.

A variety of theories and ideas have emerged from the basic research into brain function. Two of the earliest theories still prevalent in education circles coalesce around two major concepts: hemisphericity and growth spurts.

Sperry's research supports the idea that the two hemispheres of the brain serve differing but complementary functions. A person uses both hemispheres when learning or functioning, but one may dominate the other and determine a person's style or preferred way of learning. Each hemisphere is thought to contribute specialized functions to tasks. The left hemisphere of the brain is associated with verbal, sequential, analytical abilities. The right hemisphere is associated with global, holistic, visual-spatial abilities. Two related ideas are full *lateralization* and *parallel processing.* In lateralization, the left hemisphere dominates in language expression while the right hemisphere dominates in nonverbal processing. In parallel processing, research indicates that the brain hemispheres perform many tasks simultaneously.

The concept of different functions for the two hemispheres of the brain seems now to be widely accepted, with the left brain controlling linear activity and the right brain controlling global activity. Programs have emerged to teach to both sides of the brain or to compensate for a weaker hemisphere. However, this conclusion is questioned by a number of researchers and psychologists. For example, Zalewski, Sink, and Yachimowicz (1992) concluded that "there is little empirical support for educational programs that supposedly train students to compensate for hemisphericity through teaching integrative process techniques," and that "the notion of cerebral dominance has limited theoretical or practical value for educators..." (pp. 55–56). Howard (2000) notes that while there are volumes of research that document the specialized hemispheric functions, a topic which has captured the imagination of many, "the practical, day-to-day implications are few. In addition many of the findings are exaggerated with fantastic conclusions drawn from scant data....However, to make a big deal, for example, out of 'teaching to the right brain' makes appealing to one's creativity sound like something new. Hemisphere research has only confirmed that we have a more creative side and a more linear side." (pp. 48–49)

Herman Epstein's medical research, done in the 1970s, seems to indicate that the brain grows in spurts rather than in a continual, uninterrupted process. This finding is often used to support the Piagetian model of cognitive development. Growth spurts in school age children often occur between the ages of 6 and 8, 10 and 12, and 14 and 16. And they often occur in summer when school is not in session. Myelination has to do with the process of nerve fiber maturation, which occurs in stages that seem to parallel Piagetian stages of cognitive growth and development. Connecting nerve systems are the last to myelinate in childhood, indicating that a child could be said to have a "functionally split brain."

A number of other topics are currently the focus of investigation. Nobel Prize winner Gerard Edelman (1992) proposed a biological brain theory model based on evolutionary theory emergent from a type of jungle environment. He stresses the biological nature of learning and consciousness, which may have implications for the classroom, but it is not certain at this point what they might be. Another Nobel Prize winner, Francis Crick, has undertaken a biological search for the soul (or consciousness) within neural networks. His book, *The Astonishing Hypothesis: The Scientific Search for the Soul* (1994) has generated considerable interest. The implications of Crick's book for education are also unclear, but its nearly total focus on materialism certainly puts it at odds with many religious beliefs, a sure-fire prescription for controversy.

Exploration in the area of gender differences and brain function continues apace. For example, it has been well-documented that males and females differ in the way they solve intellectual problems and experience emotions. Males generally perform better on certain spatial tasks and mathematical reasoning, while females typically outperform males on tasks of perceptual speed and verbal fluency. The extent to which these differences exist due to environmental factors or combinations of factors is problematic, but it is also theorized that they are due to different hormonal influences during brain development (Kimura, 1992). Howard (2000) insightfully reminds us "that the final word has not been written on the causes and changeability of sex and gender differences. Keep in mind that all of this research deals with averages, and that individuals do not obey the law of averages" (p. 243).

Noteworthy are two other avenues of thought emerging from recent findings in brain research. Daniel Goleman (1995, 1998) has become famous with his construct of emotional intelligence, about which he cites research on the brain and emotion. His thesis is that individual success can be predicted better by emotional health than by standardized IQ tests. He says: "In a very real sense we have two minds, one that thinks and one that feels." And Peterson (1994) presents an interesting look at brain research and the idea of critical periods, that is, that certain periods of development are crucial if not vital to the development of specific cognitive and neurological functions. Each of these has potential implication for how schools go about the business of teaching and learning.

There are a number of other areas of brain research that may well have educational implications, but they remain elusive simply because the medical knowledge itself is still quite limited. These include endorphin molecules, memory, hyperactivity, attention span, and creativity. Just to cite an example, researchers at the UCLA Medical Center have discovered that children below the age of 10 have brain activity that is unusually rich in the secretion of theta waves, thought to be associated with creativity. Whether in the future this knowledge will stop teachers from handing out worksheet after worksheet to these naturally creative little characters remains a matter for speculation. The general opinion of experts is that we have barely scratched the surface in our knowledge of the human brain.

A review of materials for this chapter yielded scores of "research findings" and "implications" for education from brain research. Please recognize that the following list is only a sample of what educators and researchers are saying based on brain research. The intent is not to endorse these recommendations or even to suggest that ample evidence exist in their support.

- ◆ Critical periods exist for learning some skills.
- ◆ Early experience, education, and environment play a primary role in determining who we are.
- ◆ Research on hemisphericity is inconclusive.
- ◆ Emotion drives attention, and attention drives learning and memory.
- ◆ Music trains the brain for higher forms of thinking.
- ◆ Knowledge is retained longer if children connect not only aurally but also emotionally and physically to the material.
- ◆ Complex subjects such as trigonometry or foreign language should not wait for puberty to be introduced.
- ◆ Teens' biological clocks are set later than those of their fellow human beings and therefore high school should start later in the morning.
- ◆ Children need to be more physically active in the classroom.
- ◆ If sensory neural connections are not repeatedly stimulated in the first few months of life when the brain is still in its formative period, they atrophy and die.
- ◆ Females seem to have stronger connections between the two halves of their brain than do males.

♦ Diet, exercise, and sleep patterns play important roles in learning.

This is quite a list, but it represents only a fraction of the ideas emerging from the pedagogical claims made in the name of brain research. Some of the claims are far more wide-ranging than the few that appear above.

Howard Gardner (2000), whose research and development has led to his celebrated multiple intelligences theory, noting the rapid advances in brain-function research writes that, "Only when it comes to the highest cognitive functions, like metamemory or creativity, has brain science yet to make its contributions." He lists seven findings from brain research that he says "ought to be kept in mind by anyone concerned with education." (p. 81). They are:

1. The tremendous importance of early experience.
2. The imperative "use it or lose it" and of stimulation through sensory activity.
3. The flexibility (plasticity) of the early nervous system, which underscores the importance of learning in the early years.
4. The importance of action and activity in learning.
5. The specificity of human abilities and talents and the wide range of differences in individuals.
6. The possible organizing role played in early childhood by music.
7. The crucial formative role of emotions in learning.

Complicating any attempts at an analysis of the research at Levels II and III is the variety of claims being made in the name of brain research. On many of the very specific claims, research at Level II has not been able to catch up with all the various findings and possible implications for education. At this point, however, there are too few objective, well-designed studies identifying specific educational purposes and methodologies based on brain research to provide an acceptable and reliable base in support of such claims. Moreover, the topic becomes confusing because so many innovators are now claiming brain research as a reason to do this or that. For example, learning styles advocates often point to brain research in support of their claims, but the applied research that does exist is often of poor quality. Similarly, brain-based teaching advocates such as Caine and Caine (1997) call for brain-based educational methodologies that include the integrated curriculum, thematic teaching, and cooperative learning. So the Level II research in these areas may well point to the efficacy of specific methodologies, but to do so may or may not necessarily be an accurate inference flowing from the brain research findings to date.

Medical and psychological research will continue and, of course, educators will undoubtedly continue to draw inferences for teaching and learning from it. But we are too close to the frontiers of knowledge in this area to legitimately cite research that promises improved test scores, or very much of anything else for that matter. This is not to say, however, that no evidence exists.

Gordon Shaw (1993, 2000) reports his findings related to the so-called "Mozart Effect." In the Mozart Effect experiment, college students in an experimental group listened to the first ten minutes of Mozart's *Sonata for Two Pianos in D Major*. Students in the control group did not. Shaw and his colleagues found a statistically significant difference in spatial-temporal reasoning in favor of the experimental group, an effect which lasted for generally 10 to 15 minutes. Needless to say, these findings have created considerable controversy. Certainly Howard Gardner, without commenting directly on this particular research in *The Disciplined Mind* (2000), is thoroughly supportive of the importance of classical music in learning and goes to some length to make the point.

Shaw and his colleagues did a pilot study in 1997 with a group of three-year-old preschool children. The experimental condition consisted of six months of piano keyboard training. The result was a statistically significant difference in favor of the experimental group in spatial-temporal reasoning over control groups including one group that received language training on computers.

These findings, as you might expect, offer both promise of real advancements in teaching and learning as well as an invitation to the unwary to implement musical programs in ways that probably go beyond any reasonable evidence.

Shaw and his colleagues also cite the success stories of work in inner city Los Angeles at the elementary level, reporting advances in spatial-temporal reasoning skills on the basis of an animated computer-based curriculum called Spatial-Temporal Animation Reasoning (STAR). The program emphasizes experiences in symmetry, finding patterns, spatial logic, rotating objects, and so on.

Many of the school restructuring efforts seem to coincide with what certain educators are saying the brain research points to; that is, problem-focused learning, cooperative learning, smaller groups, project learning, search for deeper meaning, and so on, but those ideas have been touted on grounds independent of brain research as well. Possibly, however, future research in brain function will lend support to these efforts.

CONCLUSION

It is no doubt advisable for educators to attempt to stay informed of the research in brain function. The problem is, however, that it tends to be highly technical research from another field, that of medical research. The extent to which this basic research will trickle down to the point that it yields real educational implications remains to be seen. Much of what is touted by brain-based teaching advocates resembles good sense teaching, so in that sense it may be harmless at worst and useful at best. Still, one thing we do not need is to be accused of implementing programs, however well intentioned, based on quackery, something that has happened from time to time in the history of education. We may be a number of years away from any major revelations that are directly applicable to life in classrooms or that provide a coherent set of principles for teaching and learning.

This is a tremendously exciting field of endeavor, with frontiers as challenging as those found in outer space. The research base at Level I will continue to grow exponentially. Our education-based application knowledge right now is quite primitive, but it won't stay that way. Look for a host of new insights down the road. But do proceed with caution in investing your time in inservice activities in which methodologies are founded primarily on "brain research" because they will often tend to be faddish and probably not securely linked to actual research. The fact that the direct classroom applications are not presently there should not blind us from the realities that will emerge in the future. This area will in time come to have more to offer to teaching and learning than we can presently imagine.

REFERENCES

Caine, R. N., & Caine, G. (1990). Understanding a brain-based approach to learning and teaching. *Educational Leadership, 48*(2), 66–70.

Caine, R. N., & Caine, G. (1994). *Making connections: teaching and the human brain.* Menlo Park, CA: Addison-Wesley.

Caine, R. N., & Caine, G. (1997). *Education on the edge of possibility.* Alexandria, VA: Association for Supervision and Curriculum Development.

Carnine, D. (1990). New research on the brain: Implications for instruction. *Phi Delta Kappan, 71*(5), 372–277.

Crick, F. (1994). *The astonishing hypothesis: The scientific search for the soul.* New York: Scribner.

Edelman, G. M. (1992). *Bright air, brilliant fire: On the matter of the mind.* New York: Basic Books.

Garger, S. (1990). Is there a link between learning style and neurophysiology? *Educational Leadership, 48*(2), 63–65.

Goleman, D. (1995). *Emotional intelligence.* New York: Bantam.

Goleman, D. (1998). *Working with emotional intelligence.* London: Bloomsbury.

Guild, P., & Chock-Eng, S. (1998). Multiple intelligences, learning styles, brain-based learning: Where do the messages overlap? *Schools in the Middle, 7*(4), 38–40.

Hand, J. (1989). Split-brain theory and recent results in brain research: Implications for the design of instruction. In R. K. Bass & C. R. Dills (Eds.). *Instructional development: The state of the art, II.* Dubuque, IA: Kendall/Hunt.

Hendrick, B. (2000, August 24). Brain-based learning relies on scents, sweets, sounds. *Pioneer Planet.* St. Paul, MN: Cox News Service.

Howard, P. (2000). *The owner's manual for the brain: Everyday applications from mind-brain research.* Austin, TX: Bard Press.

Jensen, E. (1998). *Teaching with the brain in mind.* Alexandria, VA: Association for Supervision and Curriculum Development.

Kimura, D. (1992, September). Sex differences in the brain. *Scientific American, 267*(3), 118–125.

Kolb, D. A. (1985). *The learning style inventory.* Boston, MA: McBer & Co.

Langer, E. (1997). *The power of mindful learning.* Reading, MA: Addison-Wesley.

Levy, J. (1983). Research synthesis on the right and left hemisphere: We think with both sides of the brain. *Educational Leadership, 40*(2), 4, 66–71.

McCarthy, B. (1987). *The 4MAT system: teaching to learning styles with right/left mode techniques.* Barrington, IL: Excel.

McCarthy, B. (1996). *About Learning.* Barrington, IL: Excel.

Peterson, R. W. (1994). School readiness considered from a neurocognitive perspective. *Early Education and Development, 5*(2), 120–140.

Reiff, J. C. (1992). *What research says to the teacher: Learning styles.* Washington, DC: National Education Association Professional Library.

Restak, R. M. (1984). *The brain.* Toronto: Bantam.

Shaw, G. (2000). *Keeping Mozart in mind.* San Diego: Academic Press.

Shaw, G., Kruger, J., Silverman, D., Aertsen, A., Aiple, F., & Liu, H. (1993). Rhythmic and patterned firing in visual cortex. *Neurological Research, 15,* 46–50.

Sprenger, M. (1999). *Learning and memory: The brain in action.* Alexandria, VA: Association for Supervision and Curriculum Development.

Springer, S., & Deutsch, G. (1989). *Left brain right brain* (3rd ed.). New York: W. H. Freeman.

Sylwester, R. (1990). An educator's guide to books on the brain. *Educational Leadership, 48*(2), 79–80.

Sylwester, R. (1994). What the biology of the brain tells us about learning. *Educational Leadership, 51*(4), 46–51.

Sylwester, R. (1995). *A celebration of neurons: An educators guide to the human brain*. Alexandria, VA: Association for Supervision and Curriculum Development.

Wittrock, M. C. (1981). Educational implications of recent brain research. *Educational Leadership, 37*(1), 12–15.

Zalewski, L.J., Sink, C., & Yachimowicz, D.J. (1992). Using cerebral dominance for education programs. *The Journal of General Psychology, 119*(1), 45–57.

7

TEACHING FOR INTELLIGENCE

Intelligence, in a word, reflects a micro-culture of praxis: the reference books one uses, the notes one habitually takes, the computer programs and databases one relies upon, and perhaps most important of all, the network of friends, colleagues, or mentors on whom one leans for feedback, help, advice, even just for company.

Jerome Bruner

Although we cannot turn mentally retarded individuals into intellectual geniuses, we can achieve meaningful increases in intellectual abilities. Any conclusions to the contrary can result only from failing to cite or take seriously the full range of the relevant data.

Robert Sternberg

The day that the IBM computer Deep Blue defeated world chess champion Garry Kasparov was the day that the average person began to think in new ways about the nature of intelligence. If a machine could beat the world's best player at a game of such demanding skill, then what does it mean to be intelligent? Presently one other such challenge remains for the computer, the ancient Chinese game of Go, the only game left that it has not solved.

This chapter and the one that follows examine the research base for two closely related topics, teaching for intelligence and thinking skills. The decision to separate them into two parts is based on the observation that teaching thinking skills seems to have manifested itself in the tactical form of specific concrete programs, often commercial ones, while teaching for intelligence represents a more strategic, generic set of ideas about teaching and learning. In this chapter, we examine several views of the broad construct of intelligence and how educators are bringing some of these ideas to the classroom. In the next chapter, we look at the more specific efforts that are being made to teach those very elusive mental processes called thinking skills.

WHAT IS INTELLIGENCE?

The debate over what constitutes intelligence is quite involved, and of long duration. At the heart of the matter is the perception that some people seem to be more mentally astute than others do, seem to learn more readily and thoroughly than others do, and seem to be able to solve certain problems more effectively than others do. But the "smart/dumb" dichotomy is much too simplistic to describe what is meant by intelligence, at least as psychologists and researchers in the field use it.

A number of unresolved issues complicate the discussion. Is intelligence a unified construct, or are there multiple types of intelligence? What roles do environment and heredity play in determining an individual's intelligence? Is intelligence specific to the culture in which one lives? Can intelligence be taught? And how can intelligence or the forms of intelligence, best be measured? Perhaps in the coming years answers to these questions will become more definitive as research on brain function moves forward.

Different individuals have answered each of these questions in a variety of ways over the years. Charles Spearman (1927) maintained that there is something called *general intelligence,* which is a basic capacity affecting all mental tasks. Proponents of this view note that those who do well on one type of mental task tend to do well on most others. Evidence of this is the fact that math and reading scores correlate quite highly, suggesting that there must be a general factor present to explain this. Spearman was able to document statistically that it is possible to derive a single quotient from the results of various tests of mental ability. He called this quotient g for general intelligence.

L. L. Thurstone (1938), however, maintained that there are several—more than 200—distinct mental abilities, including numerical ability, spatial ability, and verbal ability. He reached this conclusion in spite of the fact that tests of these presumably separate entities showed high intercorrelations. Thurstone's point was that a distribution of scores from different tests of mental ability could also be analyzed in ways that showed that they gathered around a number of distinct centers with each center measuring a particular cognitive ability (Singham, 1995). Thurstone's view is probably closer than Spearman's to that subscribed to by most professionals today.

Hernstein and Murray's (1995) controversial book *The Bell Curve: Intelligence and Class Structure in American Life* caused considerable debate, when, in the minds of many people, they attributed intelligence mainly to heredity. Their interpretation of already existing data seemed to shift the center of gravity toward nature in the long-standing nature/nurture debate. In essence, Hernstein and Murray appeared to conclude that there is a unitary construct called intelligence that can be measured by IQ tests, and that Spearman's thesis was essentially correct. Critics have attacked everything from the implied social and political agenda they attribute to Hernstein and Murray to their "overly simplistic" analysis of the data. Those interested in pursuing the issues outlined here would do well to read Mano Singham's (1995) thoughtful analysis of the problems associated with this type of research on intelligence.

While the layperson may continue to think of and talk about intelligence as if it were a single entity, certain professionals have been moving in another direction. Howard Gardner (1993, 2000) has proposed what has become a very popular model that he calls "multiple intelligences" and, as we shall see, school districts from around the country have jumped at the chance to put his ideas into action. Gardner's work has been especially attractive to those educators who have become discouraged with the traditional idea that intelligence is based nearly exclusively on genetically endowed abstract reasoning abilities. They see students who show great "aptitude" or "talent" for this or that and wonder why, as Gardner has, the concept should not be expanded. We will return to Gardner's work later in this chapter.

A more recent development in the field is the work of Daniel Goleman (1995, 1998) who maintains that there is an entity that he calls *emotional intelligence*. Citing research on the brain and emotion, Goleman's thesis is that individual success can be better predicted by emotional health than by standardized IQ tests. He writes, "In a very real sense we have two minds, one that thinks and one that feels." Whether or not attention to this concept of intelligence will prove useful for educators and beneficial for children remains unknown. However, offered here for your consideration is this prediction: within the next few years this new theoretical model will be used to develop innovative educational programs much as Howard Gardner's theory has been used. The idea will simply prove too attractive to some program developers for this not to happen.

From the potentially wide range of issues and topics one could reasonably connect to the idea of teaching for intelligence, four stand out as the most significant innovations. Each is drawn from theoretical study and research in the general area of intelligence. While there is some overlap among the four, they represent distinctly different approaches both to the study of intelligence and to the educational implications that might be drawn from such study. The common thread found among them is the long gestation period of theorizing and problem solving out of which they each emerge.

Let us look first at the theory of Reuven Feuerstein and his educational program *Instrumental Enrichment*. It relates intelligence to the teaching of thinking and problem-solving skills in much the same way as do certain of the thinking skills programs examined in the Chapter 8. In this sense, Feuerstein's work emerges from the classic definitions of intelligence as the construct has been measured by IQ tests. The notable idea is that intelligence, according to Feuerstein, can be enhanced through appropriate teaching strategies.

Next, we examine Howard Gardner's theory of Multiple Intelligences and its rapidly expanding use in the schools. Gardner is concerned with the *content* of intelligence; that is, the different abilities behind intelligent behavior. Gardner points to recent advances in cognitive studies that he is convinced show best how to conceptualize intelligence. In brief, he thinks of intelligence basically as a person's biopsychological potential.

Third, we turn our attention to the theory building of Robert Sternberg and the resulting programs based on his Triarchic Theory of Intelligence. Sternberg's work is an example of the focus on cognitive *processes* used by people in thinking operations His research is based primarily in a field of psychology known as information processing.

Fourth, we will look at the work of Daniel Goleman and others in the emergent area known as emotional intelligence. Emotional intelligence is defined as "the ability to perceive and express emotion, assimilate emotion in thought, understand and reason with emotion, and regulate emotion in the self and others." (Mayer, Salovey, and Caruso, 2000).

REUVEN FEUERSTEIN'S INSTRUMENTAL ENRICHMENT

The work of Israeli clinical psychologist Reuven Feuerstein, is based on a theory that intelligence is dynamic and not static, meaning that it can be altered with appropriate interventions. One of Feuerstein's more notable contributions to the field was his development of the *Learning Potential Assessment Device* (Feuerstein, 1979), an instrument that measures the product of someone's thinking as well as the process itself. The student is presented with different problem-solving tasks, and, when needed, the test examiner *teaches* the student how to solve such problems in order to assess the extent to which the student has learned from the teaching. Thus, what emerges from the test-taking situation is a more dynamic assessment, one that predicts the student's potential. According to Feuerstein, cognitive development is dependent on direct intervention over time that teaches the mental processes necessary for learning how to learn. These interventions are sometimes called mediated learning experiences. In this sense, Feuerstein's work builds on Lev Vygotsky's idea of the Zone of Proximal Development, which is the range between which a learner can solve problems independently and the learner's ability to benefit from expert guidance.

Feuerstein's theorizing has led to the development of an elaborate curriculum called *Instrumental Enrichment,* which provides the kinds of needed mediated learning experiences (Feuerstein & Jensen, 1980, May; Feuerstein, Rand, Hoffman, & Miller, 1980). Frances Link (1991) describes the program as:

> ...[A] direct and focused attack on those mental processes, which, through absence, fragility, or inefficiency, are to blame for poor intellectual or academic performance....In terms of behavior, *Instrumental Enrichment*'s ultimate aim is to transform retarded performers, to alter their characteristically passive and dependent cognitive style to that of active, self-motivated, independent thinkers. (p. 9)

The program consists of a 3-year series of content-free lessons, called "instruments," which are grouped in 14 areas of cognitive abilities (see Figure 7.1). It is intended for upper elementary, middle, and secondary level students. Students do "instruments" with paper and pencil for about two to three hours a week. The teacher serves as the mediating agent and the instruments are supposed to parallel the subject matter being taught by the teacher. In this sense, the program integrates with the existing course of study while "enriching" it with intelligence-enhancing exercises. The program is sufficiently sophisticated to make it crucial that teachers have a considerable amount of training in its use.

FIGURE 7.1. FEUERSTEIN'S 14 INSTRUMENTS

Organization of Dots
Orientation in Space I
Comparison
Analytic Perception
Categorization
Instructions
Temporal Relations
Numerical Progressions
Family Relations
Illustrations
Transitive Relations
Syllogisms
Representational Stencil Design
Orientation in Space II

DOES IT WORK? THE RESEARCH

Advocates of the program say it does. Frances Link (1991) states: "Empirical data exist to document improvement in cognitive functions; improvement in self-concept; improvement in reading, writing, and mathematics subjects after two years of implementation" (p. 11). The claims imbedded in this statement are wide ranging, and perhaps not all are capable of being substantiated to the extent that one might hope.

A point of fundamental distinction between Feuerstein's program and many of the thinking skills programs detailed in Chapter 8, is that there is a Level II research base for *Instrumental Enrichment*. Within a few years of its development, a number of studies had been conducted on its effects. Savell, Twohig, and Rachford (1986) reviewed the initial body of research conducted in Israel, Venezuela, Canada, and the United States. They concluded that the evidence to that point showed positive effects for nonverbal measures of intelligence in all four countries, "in middle and low social class groups, in groups considered normal, as well as groups considered culturally or educationally disadvantaged," as well as in the hearing impaired. The effects, however, on other outcomes such as self-esteem, impulsivity, classroom behavior, and achievement were either "absent, inconsistent, or difficult to interpret." The positive results, however, were tied to those studies in which teachers had at least 1 week of training and students were involved with *Instrumental Enrichment* for at least 80 hours over a 2-year period.

Sternberg and Bhana (1986) conducted a second review of the research. They expressed concern about "teaching to the test," particularly the IQ-type tests, on which Savell et al. found positive gains. Nevertheless, Sternberg and Bhana were mildly supportive of the program. They stated, "we believe that when the full program is administered by carefully trained, intelligent, motivated, and conscientious instructors, gains can be attained on standard kinds of IQ and aptitude measures" (p. 63). If they are right, the results seem promising. Whether this will translate into higher achievement remains to be determined.

Since that time there have been a few studies in the literature of Level II and Level III research on *Instrumental Enrichment*. For example, studies by Hoon (1990), Offenberg (1992), Kaniel and Reichenberg (1992), and Mulcahy (1993) generally report positive results, suggesting that *Instrumental Enrichment* can improve children's thinking (and therefore intelligence) when implemented over a long period of time and with well-trained teachers. The quality of these studies could be questioned with regard to elements of design and control of variables, but, as reviewers have noted, this is a very difficult area in which to conduct research. The indications from the research to date are that there may well be something here worth pursuing. Mayer (2000), in summing up Feuerstein's work, writes, "There is evidence that instrumental enrichment can be successful in improving students' performance on tests of intellectual ability." (p. 529)

HOWARD GARDNER AND THE
THEORY OF MULTIPLE INTELLIGENCES

Howard Gardner's *Frames of Mind* was published in 1983 and was intended primarily for a limited audience of psychologists and other workers in the field of intelligence. Gardner was critical of the then prevailing views of intelligence, especially the idea of intelligence as a single construct. His work as an investigator in Harvard's Project Zero had convinced him, much as Thurstone had been convinced before him, that intelligence is composed of a number of factors distinctly different from one another. Where Thurstone had thought that the number of different kinds of intelligence might be in the range of 200, Gardner more modestly settled on 7, since expanded to 8. He does speculate that there may be more, but he has been able to document eight. Gardner noted that brain research had shown that stroke victims, for example, who might show considerable language loss, still maintained other capabilities. This was proof to him that certain functions are separate enough to make the case for different intelligences. Studying individuals of great ability in one area but who might not excel at all in other areas also shaped Gardner's thinking about separate intelligences.

Gardner questioned the value of the *general intelligence* construct, along with the more traditional views of intelligence that defined it operationally by tests focused primarily on logic, verbal, and quantitative abilities. Instead, he states that his interest is on those intellectual processes that are not covered by the *general intelligence* concept. Gardner rejects "the distinction between talent and intelligence; in my view, what we call 'intelligence' in the vernacular is simply a certain set of 'talents' in the linguistic and/or logical-mathematical spheres." Gardner has now identified eight intelligences and is looking for more (see Figure 7.2). He writes that,

> Although all humans exhibit the range of intelligences, individuals differ—presumably for both hereditary and environmental reasons—in their current profile of intelligences. Moreover, there is no necessary correla tion between any two intelligences, and they may in deed entail quite distinct forms of perception, memory, and other psychological processes. (Gardner & Hatch, 1989, p. 5)

FIGURE 7.2. HOWARD GARDNER'S MULTIPLE INTELLIGENCES

1. **Linguistic intelligence,** which involves sensitivity to the meaning of words, their order and syntax, the sounds, rhythms, and inflections of language, and the uses of languages.

2. **Musical intelligence,** which consists of sensitivities to rhythm, pitch, and timbre. It also has an emotional component. Gardner relates musicians' descriptions of their abilities that emphasize an individual's natural feel for music and not the reasoning or linguistic components of musical ability.

3. **Logical-mathematical intelligence** that emerges from interaction with objects. By a sequence of stages the person is more able to perform actions on objects, understand the relations among actions, make statements about actions, and eventually see the relations among those statements.

4. **Spatial intelligence,** which is the capacity to perceive the physical world, accurately, to perform transformations and modifications on these perceptions, and to produce or recreate forms.

5. **Bodily-kinesthetic intelligence,** which involves a person's ability to use the body in highly specific and skilled ways, both for expressive (the dancer) and goal-directed (the athlete) purposes.

Personal intelligence which takes two forms:

6. **Intrapersonal intelligence** is the ability to access one's own feelings and to label, discriminate, and symbolically represent one's range of emotions in order to understand behavior.

7. **Interpersonal intelligence** involves the ability to notice and make distinctions about others' moods, temperaments, motivations, and intentions.

8. **Naturalist intelligence** is the ability to draw on features of the natural world to solve problems (the chef, gardner, florist).

Gardner has cautioned that "MI theory is in no way an educational prescription," and that "the theory does not incorporate a 'position' on tracking, gifted education, interdisciplinary curricula, the layout of the school day, the length of the school year, or many other 'hot button' educational issues" (1995, p. 206). Gardner (2000) believes that many of the current uses of the theory are misdirected, and states simply that the theory implies that we need to broaden our definition of intelligence to include those other areas of mental abilities, to cultivate them in children, to approach learning in a variety of ways, and to personalize education. One change flowing at least in part from Gardner's work is the broadening of means of assessing learning. He thinks this trend will continue and that it will bring about corresponding changes in the creation of environments more conducive to alternative and fair assessment practices. Gardner (1993) further mused that, "I hope that in the next twenty years, a number of efforts will be made to craft an education that takes multiple intelligences seriously....Perhaps, if careful studies are done, we will even know *why* some educational approaches work and why some do not" (p. 250).

Gardner (2000) does provide certain classroom-focused insights to the use of multiple intelligences. Beginning with his assertion that "deep understanding should be our central goal (p. 186)," he goes on to cite three ways that a "multiple-intelligences perspective" can enhance understanding by learners. The first he calls *powerful points of entry*. Noting that students can be quickly engaged or not, depending on how compelling an introduction to a topic is, cites narrative, numerical, logical, and aesthetic entry points among others.

Gardner's second idea for enhancing understanding is through *offering apt analogies*. Metaphors, similies, and useful examples give students opportunities to think about content and ideas from varying perspectives and in ways that peak their imagination. And Gardner's third way of enhancing understanding through multiple intelligences is *by providing multiple representations of the central or core ideas of a topic*. Deviating from conventional wisdom, he says, he does not believe there is one best way to represent a set of ideas or a central theme. He uses the term *model languages* to describe the many ways and forms that ideas can be represented, including musically, graphically, spatially, and artistically.

RESEARCH ON MULTIPLE INTELLIGENCES: A BRIDGE TOO FAR?

At Level I Gardner claims that "MI theory is based wholly on empirical evidence and can be revised on the basis of new empirical findings" (1995, p. 203). *Frames of Mind* includes a survey of a wide range of literature and psychological research on intelligence that serves as the basis for MI theory. It is actually quite extensive, and work has been done to develop assessment instruments in an attempt to measure the intelligences (see Gardner & Hatch, 1989). A considerable amount of effort has been carried out through Harvard Project Zero to measure the intelligences and to implement some ideas in school settings. But to this stage, from a technical measurement viewpoint, the results have been mixed at best.

As Gardner himself has said, educators have interpreted this theory in literally hundreds of ways. For example, at one school it was concluded that

> We have found that multiple intelligences is more than a theory of intelligence; it is, for us, a philosophy about education with implications for how kids learn, how teachers should teach, and how schools should operate....For example, teachers can help a child whose strength is bodily-kinesthetic use that talent to learn multiplication facts or spelling words; capitalize on children's interpersonal intelligences by using the study of personalities as a pathway to the study of history; or use graphs and tables to record the similarities and differences among Native American tribes to help students with strong logical-mathematical intelligence. (Hoerr, 1994, p. 30)

Other far reaches include having kids singing (musical intelligence) the multiplication facts or dancing to the four basic food groups. Unquestionably, there is little hard evidence that these uses of the theory actually lead students to learn more. Whether Gardner has liberated or highjacked a term that has been used with consistent meaning for 100 years is, one supposes, a matter of perspective.

The questions for researchers are whether school-based implementations of this theory lead to higher academic achievement (dependent variable) or to increases in the eight intelligences (independent variable). The jury is still out on academic achievement, but the possibilities for enhancing forms of intelligence seem promising.

At the empirical and programmatic Levels II and III, findings from school-based applications of Gardner's theory are reported by Campbell and Campbell (1998), who describe the implementation of multiple intelligences in the curriculums of six schools, ranging from elementary to high school. In each case, they report broad achievement gains as a result of implementation, which in each case began in 1993 and continues through the present. Anyone seriously interested in pursuing multiple intelligences infusion in the school curriculum would be well advised to read Campbell and Campbell's book.

ROBERT STERNBERG AND THE TRIARCHIC THEORY OF INTELLIGENCE

While Gardner is representative of psychologists who have focused on the *content* of human intelligence, Robert Sternberg of Yale University has emerged as a leader among those interested in intelligence as a *process*.

Sternberg is widely known as a leading *information processing* (IP) theorist. He has synthesized his research-based construct into a theory of intelligence that quantifies IP abilities. By Sternberg's definition, to think productively is to be able to process information effectively. His theory identifies a three-part (triarchic) description of mental abilities: contextual intelligence, experiential intelligence, and componential intelligence (2000). He has also identified six factors basic to successful information processing (see Figure 7.3).

Sternberg's pioneering efforts in information processing and a resultant theory of intelligence (1990a, 2000) emphasize thinking processes common to everyone. New perceptions of what intelligence, and therefore thinking skills, means have begun to emerge from his work. Sternberg has developed what he calls a "triarchic theory of intelligence," one that breaks down cognitive behavior into thinking, adapting, and problem solving. Thinking, which he calls "componential intelligence," includes planning, performance, and knowledge acquisition. Adapting, which he calls "contextual intelligence," is composed of selecting, reshaping, and maximizing ideas. And problem solving, which he calls, "experiential intelligence," involves insight, automaticity, creativity, and efficiency.

FIGURE 7.3. ROBERT STERNBERG'S SIX FACTORS

---

1. **Spatial ability,** or the ability to visualize a problem spatially, skills one would associate with geometry, geography, architecture, mechanical drawing, art, map making and interpreting, and so on.

2. **Perceptual speed,** or the ability to grasp a new visual field quickly, something that brings to mind the playing of Nintendo video games, and so on.

3. **Inductive reasoning,** or the ability to reach conclusions and generalize from evidence or other information.

4. **Verbal comprehension ability,** or the ability to comprehend text either quickly or at deeper levels.

5. **Memory,** or the ability to store and retrieve information, ideas, and so on.

6. **Number ability,** or the ability to manipulate numerical ideas and to learn algorithms.

Lohman (2000) describes three kinds of reasoning processes found in Sternberg's theory based on complex information processing and intelligence. Those processes are: selective encoding (distinguishing relevant from irrelevant information in problem solving); selective comparison (deciding what information is needed to solve a problem); and selective combination (combining encoded and compared information in order to solve a problem). Here is an example you can try for yourself: If a drawer contains 10 brown socks and 8 blue socks, what is the least number of socks you would have to take out of the drawer (assuming you were not looking) in order to ensure having a matched pair? The answer is three. The numbers 10 and 8 represent basically irrelevant information.

It should be noted that Sternberg is uncertain that cognitive theories such as his own can necessarily improve teaching. A theory of intelligence is one thing; implementing such a theory in a classroom is quite another. He also addresses the idea of whether thinking skills can be applied generically or whether they are domain-specific, a matter of great importance to those who teach subjects in school settings. He suggests that people, rather than the skills themselves, are the issue. He suggests that some pupils (as well as teachers) are domain specific while others are domain general. Yet, he does maintain that we can "achieve meaningful increases in intellectual abilities" (1996, p. 51).

In seeming contradiction to his statement of skepticism about school-based applications, Sternberg, focusing specifically on the aspects of intelligence related to creativity, has identified a number of strategies "that teachers and administrators may use to make students, staff—and themselves—more creative" (1995/1996, p. 81). Among those "strategies" are encouraging the questioning of assumptions, modeling creativity, allowing mistakes, encouraging risk taking, and letting students define problems.

RESEARCH ON THE TRIARCHIC MODEL

The Level I research base carried out by Sternberg and his colleagues in the development of the triarchic theory is substantial. He built his work on the already extensive development of theories of information processing. The logical next step appears to be the development of instruments or measuring devices of some kind designed specifically to test intelligence as a process, as he suggests it is. His work has been put into practice on a limited scale through the Yale Practical Intelligence for School Curriculum, and an evaluation study that shows these skills can be taught (Sternberg, Okagaki, & Jackson, 1990). The relative newness of Sternberg's theory means that it has not been put into practice to the extent that either Feuerstein's or Gardner's models have been. Time will tell whether the theory remains credible, and, in the likely event that it will, to what extent it can be used successfully in school settings.

DANIEL GOLEMAN AND THE
THEORY OF EMOTIONAL INTELLIGENCE

The idea of emotional intelligence surfaced a little more than a decade ago. Not everyone was enamored with the thought. Stanley Greenspan (1997, p. 185) wrote, "Recently the notion of 'emotional intelligence' has been put forward to describe, for example, the kind of perceptiveness involved in the ability to read other people's emotional cues. How this capacity is used, however—whether to empathize with a distraught friend, motivate a research group, or sell someone the Brooklyn Bridge— is not taken into account."

Nevertheless, the idea has captured the imagination of the public, and emotional intelligence appears to be here to stay. This is in large measure do to the popularizing of the concept by Daniel Goleman (1995, 1998) whose books on the topic have become best sellers. Extravagant claims were made in the name of emotional intelligence, and the popular press quickly joined in, as an October 2, 1995, *Time* magazine cover story, "What's Your EQ?" would attest.

Some differences of opinion regarding the exact definition or nature of emotional intelligence exists. Leading analysts and researchers of emotional intelligence appear to have split into at least three camps.

Mayer and Salovey (2000) write, "...we recognized that our own theoretical work would be more useful if we constrained emotional intelligence to a mental ability concept and separated it from the very important traits of warmth, outgoingness, and similarly desirable virtues" (p. 402). They define emotional intelligence as a construct consisting of four broad areas of specific tasks: emotional perception; assimilation; understanding; and management.

Bar-on's theoretical work on emotional intelligence, by way of contrast, combines what Mayer and Salovey qualify as mental abilities, including emotional self-awareness with other traits such as "personal independence, self-regard, and mood; this makes it a mixed model" (Mayer et al., p. 402).

A third, and certainly the most widely-known, view is held by Goleman (1995, 1998). Goleman's model, which he calls The Emotional Competence Framework, encompasses five broad areas (see Figure 7.4). Those areas are (a) self-awareness; (b) self-regulation; (c) motivation; (d) empathy; and (e) social skills. Certainly, by Mayer's definition, this qualifies as a mixed model. In fact, Goleman states that his model can be summed up in one word, "character."

FIGURE 7.4. THE EMOTIONAL COMPETENCE FRAMEWORK

Personal Competence

These competencies determine how we manage ourselves.

Self-Awareness
Knowing one's internal states, preferences, resources, and intuitions

◆ *Emotional awareness:* Recognizing one's emotions and their effects

◆ *Accurate self-assessment:* Knowing one's strengths and limits

◆ *Self-confidence:* A strong sense of one's self-worth and capabilities

Self-Regulation
Managing one's internal state, impulses, and resources

◆ *Self-Control:* Keeping disruptive emotions and impulses in check

◆ *Trustworthiness:* Maintaining standards of honesty and integrity

◆ *Conscientiousness:* Taking responsibility for personal performance

◆ *Adaptability:* Flexibility in handling change

◆ *Innovation:* Being comfortable with novel ideas, approaches, and new information

Motivation
Emotional tendencies that guide or facilitate reaching goals

◆ *Achievement drive:* Striving to improve or meet a standard of excellence

◆ *Commitment:* Aligning with the goals of the group or organization

◆ *Initiative:* Readiness to act on opportunities

◆ *Optimism:* Persistence in pursuing goals despite obstacles and setbacks

Social Competence
These competencies determine how we handle relationships.

Empathy
Awareness of others' feelings, needs, and concerns

♦ *Understanding others:* Sensing others' feelings and perspectives, and taking an active interest in their concerns

♦ *Developing others:* Sensing others' development needs and bolstering their abilities

♦ *Service orientation:* Anticipating, recognizing, and meeting customers' needs

♦ *Leveraging diversity:* Cultivating opportunities through different kinds of people

♦ *Political awareness:* Reading a group's emotional currents and power relationships

Social Skills
Adeptness at inducing desirable responses in others

♦ *Influence:* Wielding effective tactics for persuasion

♦ *Communication:* Listening openly and sending convincing messages

♦ *Conflict Management:* Negotiating and resolving disagreements

♦ *Leadership:* Inspiring and guiding individuals and groups

♦ *Change catalyst:* Initiating or managing change

♦ *Building bonds:* Nurturing instrumental relationships

♦ *Collaboration and cooperation:* Working with others toward shared goals

♦ *Team capabilities:* Creating group synergy in pursuing collective goals

SOURCE: D. Goleman (1998). *Working with Emotional Intelligence.* London: Bloomsbury Publishing.

At the level of operational definition, that is, measuring emotional intelligence, instruments fall into two categories: measures of ability and self-report measures. Mayer et al. (2000, p. 405) write, "Ability measures have the advantage of representing an individual's performance level on a task. By contrast, self-report measures are filtered through a person's self-concept and impression management motives." Brief mention follows of three measurement instruments. Those interested in a more in-depth analysis, one which is beyond the scope of this book, are encouraged to peruse the listed references.

The Multifactor Emotional Intelligence Scale (MEIS), developed by Mayer, Caruso, and Salovey, is a test consisting of 12 ability measures divided into four branches: perceiving; facilitating; understanding; and managing emotion. The test has shown high reliability outcomes (alpha reliability of $r = .96$). They write, "Findings from the MEIS indicate that emotional intelligence may qualify as a conventional intelligence operationalized as a mental ability" (p. 408).

Bar-on's *Emotional Quotient Inventory* (1997) is a self-report instrument that has shown some promise in spite of few reported predictions of actual behavioral outcomes (Mayer et al., 2000). A factor analysis of the *EQ* instrument yielded factors more or less consistent with specific skills found in his four broad areas of intrapersonal skills, interpersonal skills, adaptability, stress management, and general mood.

Goleman's self-report scale consisting of 10 items is probably more useful as a discussion springboard or informal self-assessment than as a research tool. The instrument, which is reported in the *Utne Reader* (1995), contain problematic situations to which the respondent selects a position from several possibilities, and, one imagines, rationalizes it to self and/or others. The scale has shown to have low reliability (Davies, Stankov, & Roberts, 1998).

What are the implications for school settings? They probably fall somewhere in a range between Mayer, Salovey, and Caruso's rather restrained sense of any immediate curricular/instructional applications and Goleman's unbounded enthusiasm.

CONCLUSION

The pioneering works of Feuerstein, Gardner, Mayer et al., Sternberg, and others suggest that intelligence can be taught and enhanced. This idea runs counter to traditional assumptions that intelligence is something you are endowed with only. There is much evidence to suggest that intelligence can be raised, including the well-known illustration of recent generational gains in intelligence test scores by Japanese school children. That they and other Asian countries have witnessed a considerable rise in the average height of the population in the space of a generation is also well documented. The thinking that better diet, health care, and so forth, have brought this about in a relatively short time span encourages those who advocate intervention strategies.

The work cited in this chapter is both more foundational and theoretical than the examples in the closely related chapter which follows. In a sense, this chapter serves as potential Level I research for the teaching of thinking skills, our next topic, in school settings. Whether developers take full and thoughtful advantage of the profound ideas flowing from the exciting developments on the frontiers of research into the nature of intelligence remains to be seen.

REFERENCES

Bar-on, R. (1997). *The Emotional Quotient Inventory Technical Manual.* Toronto: Multi-Health Systems.

Ben-Hur, M. (Ed.) (1994). *On Feuerstein's instrumental enrichment: A collection.* Arlington Heights, IL: Skylight Publications.

Bruner, J. (1996). *The culture of education.* Cambridge, MA: Harvard University Press.

Campbell, L., Campbell, B., & Dickinson, D. (1998). *Teaching and Learning Through Multiple Intelligences.* Boston: Allyn & Bacon.

Davies, M, Stankov, L., & Roberts, R. (1998). Emotional intelligence: In search of an illusive construct. *Journal of Personality and Social Psychology, 75,* 989–1015.

Feuerstein, R. (1979). *The dynamic assessment of retarded performers: The learning potential assessment device, theory, instruments, and techniques.* Baltimore: University Park Press.

Feuerstein, R., & Hoffman, M. B. (1985). The importance of mediated learning for the child. *Human Intelligence International Newsletter, 6*(2), 1–2.

Feuerstein, R., & Jensen, M. R. (1980, May). Instrumental enrichment: Theoretical basis, goals, and instruments. *The Educational Forum,* 401–423.

Feuerstein, R., Rand, Y., Hoffman, M. B., & Miller, R. (1980). *Instrumental enrichment: An intervention program for cognitive modifiability.* Baltimore: University Park Press.

Gardner, H. (1993). *Frames of mind,* 10th ed. New York: Basic Books.

Gardner, H. (1993). *Multiple intelligences: Theory in practice.* New York: Basic Books.

Gardner, H. (1995). Reflections on multiple intelligences: Myths and messages. *Phi Delta Kappan, 77*(3), 206–209.

Gardner, H. (2000). *The disciplined mind: Beyond facts and standardized tests, the K-12 education that every child deserves.* New York: Penguin Books.

Gardner, H., & Hatch, T. (1989). Multiple intelligences go to school: Educational implications of the theory of multiple intelligences. *Educational Researcher, 18*(8), 4–9.

Goleman, D. (1995). *Emotional intelligence.* New York: Bantam.

Goleman, D. (1998). *Working with emotional intelligence.* London: Bloomsbury.

Hernstein, R. J., & Murray, C. (1995). *The bell curve: Intelligence and class structure in American life.* New York: Free Press.

Hoerr, T. R. (1994). How the New City School applies the multiple intelligences. *Educational Leadership, 52*(3), 29–33.

Hoon, S. S. (1990). Feuerstein's instrumental enrichment: An exploratory study for activating intellectual potential in slow learners. (ERIC Document Reproduction Service No. ED329813.)

Kaniel, S., & Reichenberg, R. (1992). Instrumental enrichment—Effects of generalization and durability with talented adolescents. *Gifted Education International, 8*(3), 128–135.

Link, F. (1991). *Instrumental enrichment.* In A. Costa (Ed.) *Developing minds: Programs for teaching thinking,* pp. 9–11. Alexandria, VA: Association for Supervision and Curriculum Development.

Lohman, D. (2000). Complex information processing and intelligence. In R. Sternberg (Ed.). *Handbook of intelligence.* Cambridge: Cambridge University Press.

Mayer, R. (2000). Intelligence and education. In R. Sternberg (Ed.). *Handbook of intelligence,* pp. 519–533. Cambridge: Cambridge University Press.

Mayer, J., Salovey, P., & Caruso, D. (2000). Models of emotional intelligence. In R. Sternberg (Ed.). *Handbook of intelligence,* pp. 396–420. Cambridge: Cambridge University Press.

Mulcahy, R. (1993). *Cognitive education project. Summary project.* (ERIC Document Reproduction Service No. ED367682.)

Offenberg, R. M. (1992). *A study of the effects of instrumental enrichment on middle-grade, minority students.* Report No. 9225. (ERIC Document Reproduction Service No. ED361462.)

Savell, J. M., Twohig, P. T., & Rachford, D. L. (1986). Empirical status of Feuerstein's "Instrumental Enrichment" (FIE) technique as a method of teaching thinking skills. *Review of Educational Research, 56*(4), 381–409.

Singham, M. (1995). Race and intelligence: What are the issues. *Phi Delta Kappan, 77*(4), 271–278.

Spearman, C. (1927). *The abilities of man: Their nature and measurement.* New York: Macmillan.

Sternberg, R. (1990a). Practical intelligence for success in school. *Educational Leadership, 48*(1), 35–39.

Sternberg, R. (1990b). *Metaphors of mind: Conceptions of the nature of intelligence.* New York: Cambridge University Press.

Sternberg, R. (1995/1996) Investing in creativity: Many happy returns. *Educational Leadership 53*(4), 80–84.

Sternberg, R. (1996). The school bell and the bell curve: Why they don't mix. *NASSP Bulletin, 80*(577), 46–56.

Sternberg, R. (1997). *Thinking styles.* Cambridge: Cambridge University Press.

Sternberg, R. (Ed.) (2000). *Handbook of intelligence.* Cambridge: Cambridge University Press.

Sternberg, R. J., & Bhana, K. (1986). Synthesis of research on the effectiveness of intellectual skills programs: Snake-oil remedy or miracle cures? *Educational Leadership, 44*(2), 60–67.

Sternberg, R. J., Okagaki, L., & Jackson, A. S. (1990). Practical intelligence for success in school. *Educational Leadership, 48*(1), 35–39.

Thurstone, L. L. (1938). Primary mental abilities. *Psychometric Monographs, No. 1.*

Yekovich, F. R. (1994). *ERIC/AE Digest. Current issues in research on intelligence.* Washington, DC: Office of Educational Research and Improvement.

8

THINKING SKILLS PROGRAMS

*We have a lot of evidence that teaching content alone, and
hoping it will cause students to learn to think, doesn't work.
The teaching of content alone is not enough.*

Arthur Costa

*There is a danger that the teaching of "thinking skills"—
if it survives to become part of mainstream educational
practice—may one day become to thinking what diagram-
ming sentences and memorizing rules of grammar too often
have become to writing.*

John Baer

*Most teachers do not know what intellectual standards
are nor why they are essential to quality thinking.*

Linda Elder and Richard Paul

Almost all national, state, district, and school lists of goals, and, more recently, standards, include something from the grab bag called thinking skills. Thousands of people have attended the international conferences on critical thinking held annually at Sonoma State University in California and sponsored by the Foundation for Critical Thinking. In addition, the Association for Supervision and Curriculum Development (ASCD) has published a guide describing 27 commercial programs designed for teaching thinking–problem solving–critical thinking skills (Costa, 1991; see also Costa & Kallick, 2000). A number of these programs claim widespread usage and success. The developer of the *MegaSkills Program* claims it is used in nearly 3000 schools in 48 states (Rich, 1998, p. x), and the program has spread to several countries in Asia, including Singapore, Thailand, and China.

Arguing on behalf of an emphasis on higher level thinking in class-rooms, Jeanne Chall (1999, pp. 124–125) writes, "One of the persistent debates...has been whether the major emphasis of instruction should be on knowledge and skills or on the higher mental processes—the ability to think, to solve problems, and create....Although the supporting research on these questions has been available for nearly a century, little attention has been paid to it. Instead the ideal position since the early 1900s has been to develop in students broad meanings and problem-solving ability rather than skills, facts, and knowledge."

Thinking skills is a general term that tends to incorporate problem solving, critical thinking, "higher order" thinking, divergent thinking, and creative thinking. Thinking skills are also tied into various views on intelligence, especially with reference to such terms as gifted and talented. Even for a profession that often seems to have little respect for the mean-ing of words, the terminology is rather loose. The various lists of goals of thinking skills programs one finds in the literature tend to be skills-focused, typically employing such terms as critical thinking skills, higher order thinking skills, problem solving skills, strategic reasoning skills, productive thinking skills, and so on, all used more or less interchange-ably. The common ground seems to encompass the kinds of school experi-ences that purport to transcend memory work, textbook usage, drill and practice, and patterned, repetitive assignments.

Diane Halpern's (1998) definition of critical thinking seems to capture the essence of the thinking skills spectrum of terms. She defines critical thinking as "the use of those cognitive skills or strategies that increase the probability of a desirable outcome—in the long run, critical thinkers will have more desirable outcomes than 'noncritical' thinkers (where desir-able is defined by the individual, such as making good career choices or wise financial investments)" (p. 450).

The implication of all this is that these "skills" are located at a higher place on some taxonomic register and, therefore, ought not to be confused with lower level thinking skills such as using a skill saw, or remembering or explaining—skills for which, if one can believe the rhetoric, there will be less and less demand in this new century. At the risk of getting ahead of the story through the literary device of foreshadowing, let me give you two pieces of advice: (a) be wary of programs that promise to deliver decontextualized "skills" of any kind, and (b) be wary of programs that purport to get students ready for an unknown and infinitely complex future.

THOUGHTS ABOUT THINKING

One would be hard-pressed to find someone who thinks that thinking skills are unimportant. This may well be even more the case nowadays as it becomes increasingly obvious to everyone that the knowledge explosion makes it ever more difficult to "master" content. There are, however, several problems that seem to be endemic to the entire area labeled "thinking skills."

For starters, there is very little agreement about what thinking skills actually are. Notice Halpern's definition tells you what critical thinkers do, but not how they do it. Virtually every curriculum program in existence has a list of skills to be developed, but the concepts are quite abstract in many cases with a range of possible interpretations applied to any given thinking skill. "Classification," for example, is often identified as an important thinking skill because it is so associated with scientific thought and expression. But what is meant by the term "classification?" Putting things in groups? Organizing whole taxonomies? Recognizing that different attributes lead one to assign something to a particular category? And at what point does classifying become stereotyping or eversimplification? This is very vexing because "classification" is a rather concrete skill compared to, say, "evaluation" or "insight."

A related problem is that of measuring thinking skills. It is a rather difficult challenge compared to measuring certain physical skills, such as one's ability to run 100 meters in so many seconds. There are no widely accepted thinking skills tests. Selected portions of standard IQ tests are about as good as anything we have. And the several tests specifically designed to measure thinking skills that are available have little agreed-on validity if for no other reason than they define the various constructs differentially.

With regard to testing, well, one source of invalidity is the failure of most skills tests to actually find out whether a person actually possesses a certain skill. This is most vexing. Nunnes, Schliemann, and Carraher (1993), for example, documented the remarkable skill with which Brazilian street children could perform mathematical operations when it came to vending wares, but who showed literally no skill in their performance of the same operations on paper and pencil tests. Schliemann, Carraher, and Ceci's (1997) review of the literature led them to the conclusion that decontextualized tests of intellectual skills yield invalid estimates of those same skills in real-life contexts. Serpell (2000) notes that "Some researchers have taken this argument a step farther and suggested that cognition itself is socially distributed…and thus that attribution of intellectual power to an individual is somewhat arbitrary" (p. 354). This same argument is made rather convincingly by the psychologist Jerome Bruner (1996).

A third issue is whether thinking skills can be taught successfully to students independent of content. This remains a matter of some debate. Most experts have concluded that they probably cannot, that in fact thinking is contextual, situated, and content-related. So, the issue of transfer is problematic. Can someone who has been taught how to analyze (a typical skill) use "analysis" as a generic skill applicable to chemistry, literature, geography, personal problems, and so forth? It doesn't seem likely, although there may be something to it. And how does one teach others to analyze in a generic sense? Analysis, after all, can be based on evidence, expertise, experience, intuition, or on other factors This would appear to be the essence of the argument: the better one's knowledge is of something, the better one is positioned to do meaningful analysis. Having knowledge, even in considerable store, does not guarantee one's ability to analyze; an absence of knowledge, however, of a given topic or issue precludes any ability to perform meaningful analysis in that field. But here we run into trouble again: what does it really mean to have knowledge of something? I remember rather well having "knowledge" of how an internal combustion engine works on an eighth grade science test: intake, compression, power, and exhaust. But you don't want me working on your car.

Stigler and Hiebert (1999) make the point that content-imbedded instruction, for example, the teaching of mathematics, can incorporate higher level thinking skills, but that much depends on the teacher's expertise. The point is that several teachers can be teaching the same topic, but some may lead students to think more deeply about it than others. Figure 8.1 (pp. 110–111) illustrates the contrasts and comparisons among three styles of teaching mathematics: American, German, and Japanese to school students. Note in particular the points of emphasis on problem solving and challenging students in the German and Japanese lessons.

Apparently not everyone agrees that thinking need be content-imbedded. Edward De Bono (1991, 2000) has maintained that thinking can be directly taught as a skill or set of skills. His thinking skills program, called CoRT, an acronym for Cognitive Research Trust, emphasizes content-free thinking strategies. An example is the "Plus, Minus, Interesting" (PMI) strategy in which students are given an hypothetical situation and are asked to list as many "pluses," "minuses," or "interestings" as they can about the problem. One of the situations is the question, "What if all cars were painted yellow?" The more outcomes a student could list, the more *fluent* he or she is. The more truly different outcomes a student could list, them more *flexible* is her or his thinking. According to de Bono, activities like these enable students to use effective thinking strategies that have transfer value to unknown future situations. This attractive assertion, however, has little empirical support.

Another issue is that of a huge assumption which may, in fact, not be warranted. The assumption is that teachers themselves possess these various thinking skills. If they do not, how could they possibly teach them? In his book, *A Place Called School*, curriculum researcher John Goodlad writes, "The emphasis on facts and recall of facts in quizzes demonstrates not just the difficulty of teaching and testing for more fundamental understanding but the probability, supported by our data, that most teachers simply do not know how to teach for higher levels of thinking..." (Goodlad, 1984, p. 237). The extent to which teachers possess these abilities, or could themselves be taught to model or teach them, is largely unknown. This could well be the germ of a fruitful research agenda.

Lastly, we know very little about *how* people think. We know much more about the products of people's thoughts than we know about how they arrive at those products. Vast philosophical and scientific arguments are waged over the brain versus mind issue, just to name one example. There is some considerable debate about whether thinking is a conscious or an unconscious process (Baer, 1988). So, if we are not sure how people think, how can we proceed with the business of teaching them how to think in such a way that is compatible with given individuals' styles or approaches to situations that demand thinking? Perhaps *apropos* of that, the current model of practice that one can readily deduce from extensive classroom observation is that thinking skills are something students already possess in varying degrees, and like "citizenship," it is something you bring to your work, not something that is directly taught by teachers.

All of this notwithstanding, there seems to be no shortage of would-be innovators willing to jump into the breach. Programs abound, and the thinking skills movement is going full-force across the country.

A useful perspective for considering these matters is offered by Brandt (1984, 1988). He describes teaching *for* thinking as the engagement of content and learning activities and the development of language and conceptual abilities through teacher questioning, student-to-student interaction, group discussions, and so on. Brandt identifies teaching *about* thinking as encouraging students to be aware of their thinking, reflecting on it, and learning to control it, what is often referred to as metacognition. Students are asked to monitor their own thinking and to make deliberate use of various thinking frames, perhaps as found in such programs as Talents Unlimited, CoRT, and Tactics (see "References"). And Brandt suggests that teaching *of* thinking represents the attempt to teach particular mental skills such as summarizing, paraphrasing, and decision making. This last concern is no doubt the weakest area, and the one we know least about.

The thinking skills movement is manifest in two forms: (a) the import and adoption of specifically-designed curricula or programs (see Figure 8.2, page 112, for a sample listing), and/or (b) the development and implementation of a matrix of thinking skills throughout the curriculum by a school district or perhaps by a given school. The former often involves the implementation of one or more of the more popular commercial programs. The latter represents an "infusion" model where teachers agree to introduce and revisit thinking skills across a variety of subject areas. In either case, the efforts are intended to focus on the development in learners of thought processes in which they are perceived to be lacking or in

FIGURE 8.1. HOW DIFFERENT TEACHERS ORGANIZE A MATHEMATICS LESSON

TIME	GERMAN LESSON	JAPANESE LESSON
1 min	Teachers checks homework by calling on students for answers. Students work more difficult homework problems on board. Teacher corrects terminology. Note: Typical for teacher to be careful about notation and language. Unusual to spend this much time checking homework.	Teacher reviews yesterday's lesson and assigns a problem that was not finished.
		Students present solution methods they have founds, and teacher summarizes.
10 min		Teacher presents task for the day and asks students to work on it independently (task is to invent problem for classmates to solve). Note: Typical to present task for the day and allow students to solve it in their own way. Often, task can be solved using method students have learned recently.
20 min	Teacher presents problem for the day—a theorem for students to prove—and leads them through the proof. Teacher emphasizes the procedures that can be used to prove theorems like this. Note: Proving a theorem is unusual, but the teacher leading the students through, a discussion of advanced procedures is common. Often, a student will be at the board for part of the discussion.	
30 min		Teacher suggests they continue their work in small groups. Leaders of groups share problems with teacher, who writes them on board. Students copy problems and begin working on them. Note: Unusual for students to work this long without a class discussion. Typical for students to struggle with task before teacher intervenes.
	Class reviews the theorem by students reading aloud from a handout.	
40 min		
	Teacher assigns homework. Note: Typical to allow no class time for working on homework.	Teacher highlights a good method for solving these problems. Note: No homework is typical.

U.S. LESSON	AUTHORS' NOTES
Teachers asks students short-answer review questions. Note: Typical to begin with "warm-up" activity.	**Opening** Common for lessons in all countries to begin with review. But Germany and the United States begin with relatively long segments of checking homework; Japan begins with a quick review of yesterday's lesson.
Teacher checks homework by calling on students for answers. Note: A common way to check homework.	
Teacher distributes worksheet with similar problems. Students work independently.	**Heart of the Lesson** Germany: Teacher leading students through the development of advanced techniques for solving challenging problems, with students responding to frequent questions.
Teacher monitors students' work, notices some confusion on particular problems, and demonstrates how to solve these. Note: Typical for teacher to intervene at first sign of confusion or struggle.	Japan: Students working on challenging problem and then sharing their results. United States: Teacher engages in quick-paced question/answer with students, demonstrates methods, and asks students to work many similar problems.
Teacher reviews another worksheet and demonstrates a method for solving the most challenging problem.	**Closing** The lessons conclude in different ways: Germany and the United States often with assigning homework; Japan with the teacher summarizing the main point(s) of the lesson.
Teacher conducts a quick oral review of problems like those worked earlier.	
Teacher asks students to finish worksheets. Note: Unusual to not assign homework.	

need of greater proficiency. Invariably, one finds reference to such "skills" as analysis, synthesis, evaluation, decision making, creativity, information processing, problem solving, organization, communication, and reasoning. The current emphasis on standards and the accompanying performance assessment instruments being developed reflect a desire for students to possess such thinking skills as problem solving abilities, insight, and critical thinking. Another difference found among thinking skills programs is whether they are content-free (e.g., CoRT, SOI) or content-imbedded (Philosophy for Children, ThinkerTools).

FIGURE 8.2. SAMPLE THINKING SKILLS PROGRAMS FOR SCHOOLS

Instrumental Enrichment (R. Feuerstein)
Cognitive Research Trust (CoRT) (E. De Bono)
Talents Unlimited (C. Schlichter)
Philosophy for Children (M. Lipman)
Higher Order Thinking Skills (HOTS) (S. Pogrow)
MegaSkills (D. Rich)
Thinker Tools (White & Frederiksen)
Project Impact
Tactics for Thinking
Project Intelligence (R. Herrnstein, et al)
Structure of the Intellect (SOI) (M. Meeker)
Odyssey
Strategic Reasoning
Thinking to Write

Whether these are in fact skills in the same sense as those needed by an expert carpenter or golfer is not always clear. The more tangible an operation (for example, skillfully using bow and arrow, or needle and thread), the more readily we can agree that it is a skill, or set of skills, and something that can be taught as well. But even in such concrete situations, a truly skilled person is someone who can coordinate, articulate, and make seamless or fluid a number of subskills which come together into a whole which, to quote the oft-cited Gestalt expression, is greater than the sum of its parts. Figure 8.3 provides an example of a typical set of thinking skills and accompanying strategies.

Most thinking skills programs are sufficiently complex to require a considerable amount of faculty inservice training if they are to succeed. Teachers are acquainted through training sessions with detailed descriptions of the skills to be taught, sample lesson plans, activities, ways to evaluate, and more. Usually, emphasis is placed upon strategies whereby

FIGURE 8.3. A TAXONOMY OF THINKING SKILLS

◆ I.   **Thinking Strategies**

Problem Solving

1. Recognize a problem
2. Represent the problem
3. Devise/choose solution plan
4. Execute the plan
5. Evaluate the solution

Decision Making

1. Define the goal
2. Identify alternatives
3. Analyze alternatives
4. Rank alternatives
5. Judge highest-ranked alternatives
6. Choose "best" alternative

Conceptualizing

1. Identify examples
2. Identify common attributes
3. Classify attributes
4. Interrelate categories of attributes
5. Identify additional examples/nonexamples
6. Modify concept attributes/structure

◆ II. **Critical Thinking Skills**

1. Distinguishing between verifiable facts and value claims
2. Distinguishing relevant from irrelevant information, claims, or reasons
3. Determining the factual accuracy of a statement
4. Determining the credibility of a source
5. Identifying ambiguous claims or arguments
6. Identifying unstated assumptions
7. Detecting bias
8. Identifying logical fallacies
9. Recognizing logical inconsistencies in a line of reasoning

10. Determining the strength of an argument or a claim

◆ **III. Information-Processing Skills**

1. Recall
2. Translation
3. Interpretation
4. Extrapolation
5. Application
6. Analysis (compare, contrast, classify, seriate, etc.)
7. Synthesis
8. Evaluation
9. Reasoning (inferencing): inductive, deductive, analogical

SOURCE: Adapted from Beyer, B. K. (1988a). Developing a scope and sequence for thinking skills instruction. *Educational Leadership, 45*(7), 27.

teachers can incorporate thinking skills into different subject areas and apply them to various age levels. Some of the programs are designed to stand alone as curriculums in and of themselves. These are often used in so-called gifted and talented pull-out classes.

PROGRAM IMPLEMENTATION

To give you a clearer picture of what these programs are like, let us examine one commercial example and one locally developed example. They are reasonably representative of the range of programs available.

MEGASKILLS

MegaSkills (1998) has developed over a 30-year period, and is presently in use in one form or another in some 3000 schools in 48 states, as well as in a number of other countries. It is without question one of the most widely disseminated thinking skills programs in the United States. Unlike most commercial education programs, MegaSkills is basically the work of one person, founder and author Dorothy Rich. Accolades for the program have poured in from such luminaries as researchers Herbert Walberg of the University of Illinois, Chicago Circle, and Edward Zigler of Yale, former senator Bill Bradley, both the president and the executive director of the NEA, executives of the American Library Association, the National PTA, the National Association of Elementary School Principals, the National Alliance of Busines, and the list goes on.

Here is the essence of the MegaSkills program. Rich (1998) defines megaskills as "the values, the abilities, the inner engines of learning that determine success in school and beyond." She states, "We know they are important. We now know they can be taught and learned..." (from the introduction). Rich has identified 11 megaskills (see Figure 8.4). These so-called megaskills are not a curriculum in themselves; rather they are designed to support endeavor in all areas of the curriculum and in everyday life. Each megaskill has multiple purposes: academic success, character training, work ethic, and so on.

FIGURE 8.4. DOROTHY RICH'S MEGASKILLS

- *Confidence:* Being able to do it.
- *Motivation:* Wanting to do it.
- *Effort:* Being willing to work hard.
- *Responsibility:* Doing what's right.
- *Initiative:* Moving into action
- *Perseverance:* Completing what you start.
- *Caring:* Showing concern for others.
- *Teamwork:* Working with others.
- *Common Sense:* Using good judgement
- *Problem Solving:* Putting what you know and what you can do into action.
- *Focus:* Concentrating with a goal in mind.

One megaskill is problem solving. The program presents a four-step system for solving problems:

1. What is the problem?
2. What solutions can we try?
3. What are the good and bad points of these solutions?
4. What do you think of the solution in this activity?

While there is nothing particularly new about these questions, they are focused on potentially real problem situations, for example, safety in the home. A recurring theme of the program is that of home-school connections. Students are encouraged to make up their own questions as they go about the work of solving particular problems. They are then challenged to do something practical at home such as put up a warning sign where certain medicines are stored. Following the experience of dealing with a concrete, more immediate application, students are asked to explore larger issues such as AIDS prevention, drug use, and crime reduction, using problem-solving methods. Parents are expected to be intimately involved.

What are the academic outcomes of the MegaSkills program? The answer to this question is not easily furnished to the reader. However, Rich does cite a Memphis State University study that followed up workshops conducted at 40 sites around the Memphis area. A pre- and post-assessment based on parent reporting in the wake of program implementation showed that children's homework time dramatically increased, TV watching decreased, parents reported spending more time each day with their children, and parent-child relationships improved. While this is not controlled, cause and effect research, and one could readily speculate on threats to internal and external validity of the study, it does indicate some favorable growth in parent awareness of childhood learning needs. A useful list of research-related publications prepared by the Office of Educational Research and Improvement, U.S. Department of Education, specially prepared for the 1998 edition of MegaSkills is found in an appendix to the book.

WRITING AS A THINKING AND LEARNING TOOL

At a local, noncommercial level, the faculty at Bernards High School, Bernardsville, NJ, initiated a staff development program called Writing as a Thinking and Learning Tool (Figure 8.5). "With no additional expenditure for materials and no burden of added content for teachers, we designed this program to tackle head-on the task of improving students' critical and creative thinking through writing" (Bland & Koppel, 1988, p. 58).

Training for teachers focused on techniques for creating a "thinking environment" in the classroom, the process approach to writing, and strategies for implementing each of the three program components in all subject areas. According to their own evaluation, the project produced these results:

- Improved student problem solving and clarity of thinking.
- Increased and immediate feedback to students about their thinking.
- Increased participation in sharing ideas and opinions by students.
- Growing student ability to transfer thinking skills from one subject to another.

FIGURE 8.5. BERNARDS HIGH SCHOOL'S
DO-IT-YOURSELF CRITICAL THINKING PROGRAM

Purposes:

1. To train any interested teacher of any subject area, grades 7–12, in strategies to improve thinking through the use of writing;

2. To assist the trained teachers in implementing and refining the strategies through peer coaching and inservice workshops;

3. To conduct formal and informal evaluation activities to determine the effect of these strategies on the quality of student thinking, both oral and written.

Program Components:

1. Producing ideas—brainstorming, classifying, prioritizing, inferring, predicting and evaluating. Sample teaching strategies—free association, cubing, mind maps, and clustering.

2. Expressing ideas—prioritize, classify, elaborate, and connect ideas. Sample teaching strategies—think writing, practice essays, serial writing, oral composing, group essays, conferring and questioning.

3. Refining expression—the development of a finished product. Sample teaching strategies—checklists, peer conferences, oral reading.

SOURCE: Bland, C., & Koppel, I. (1988). Writing as a thinking tool. *Educational Leadership*, *45*(7), 58–60.

Most of us would be delighted with such outcomes. It is, however, not clear exactly how the people at Bernards were able to document their findings. Just imagine, for starters, the list of variables at stake. How was thinking ability measured? Were comparison groups used? To what extent was this already happening as a result of traditional teaching or pupil maturation? How was evidence of student ability to transfer thinking skills from subject to subject documented? These nagging questions are seldom addressed with sufficient rigor. They get lost in the enthusiasm that accompanies innovation. Nevertheless, Bernards is to be commended for an attempt at program evaluation, something that rarely happens in any systematic way.

THE RESEARCH BASE FOR
THINKING SKILLS PROGRAMS

Certain problems seem to be inherent in the research on thinking skills. Any evaluation of the research base must be done with the following things in mind:

- It is difficult to conduct research in an area for which there exists no generally agreed-on set of definitions of terms. Mathematics achievement, by way of contrast, can be operationally defined by a set of constructs, although even this isn't easy to reach total agreement on. Mathematics is largely defined by the various textbooks in use, by the goal structure of the National Council of Teachers of Mathematics (NCTM), and by the various standardized tests that are available. One can make no such parallel claims about thinking skills. Remember the Supreme Court justice who said that while he couldn't define pornography, he knew it when he saw it? Let us suppose we could say we know good thinking when we see it. It would be at least a place to start, but even if we could say that, it's a pretty shaky foundation on which to build.

- We are not particularly adept at measuring thinking skills. A few such tests exist, for example, the Cornell Critical Thinking Test. Some IQ and abilities tests contain scales that may be somewhat appropriate to this area, but the "skills" are diverse (see Figure 8.3, p. 113) and difficult to measure and evaluate. We may be years away from valid, reliable, agreed-on instruments of assessment.

- Given the first two problems, it follows that the means to achieve curriculum alignment seem presently insurmountable. What we are left with are measurement instruments specific to a given curriculum or local program. These instruments, while often interesting, are plagued by problems of reliability, validity, and subjectivity.

- Thinking skills no doubt develop over a long period of time, and they routinely defy attempts to trace their realization to a specific unit or curriculum experience. In addition, it has been suggested by more than one observer that school environments in general may not be particularly supportive of the very thinking skills that advocates tend to promote. And as Arthur Costa has noted, "the change in student behavior is bound to be diverse and elusive" (Brandt, 1988, p. 11).

♦ The idea that thinking skills are content-specific and cannot be taught generically must be seriously entertained until such time as it is discredited, and that doesn't seem to have happened. And if this is so, how does one construct content-free tests to measure thinking skills?

Mostly, we are left with observations, impressions, and anecdotal records to document increases in student thinking skills. Any teacher who has ever had to fill out that part of a report card knows what shaky grounds we are on when we give a "+" to Mary for her ability to "solve problems independently." And how many teachers would take either the credit or the blame for the pluses and minuses we marked in the category for the 30 kids in that class?

BASIC RESEARCH ON THINKING

At Level I, one finds a surprisingly small amount of information claimed by thinking skills advocates about basic or pure research in this area. However, it appears that the basic research can be traced mainly to two areas: brain research and cognitive science. It is certainly reasonable to assume that the work of such researchers as Gardner, Feuerstein, and Sternberg, cited in Chapter 7, forms much of the theoretical basis of some, but not all, thinking skills programs.

No doubt we are on the threshold of important knowledge of human brain function. The research referred to in Chapter 6 on brain-based learning will give you some insight into this area. Much is at stake here including heredity, nutrition, and experience.

The work in cognitive science includes such stage theories as those advanced by Piaget (1970) and Kohlberg (1987), research in information processing such as that done by Robert Sternberg (1997, 2000), and research in constructivist thought such as that conducted by Driver (1983), Cobb (1995), and Schwartz and Bransford (1998). The work of Lev Vygotsky (1987) in the area of the codevelopment of language and thought is extremely important. A book well worth reading to acquaint you with these areas is *How People Learn: Brain, Mind, Experience, and School* (Bransford et al., 2000). The authors summarize current findings about how cognitive abilities relate to learning. Among other findings, they cite the following listed in Figure 8.6

Of course, it would be remiss to neglect to mention the work of Benjamin Bloom, whose *Taxonomy of Educational Objectives for the Cognitive Domain* (1956) has influenced the development of more than one lesson plan or district guide over the years. Bloom suggested that a hierarchy of thought exists, and he composed one made up of six levels. At the lower cognitive register are found, in ascending order, knowledge, comprehension, and application; at the higher cognitive register are found, in ascend-

FIGURE 8.6. FINDINGS FROM COGNITIVE SCIENCE

♦ Young children lack knowledge, but they do have abilities to reason with the knowledge they understand.

♦ Children are problem solvers and, through curiosity, generate questions and problems.

♦ Children develop knowledge of their own learning capacities—metacognition—very early. This gives them the ability to plan and monitor their success and to correct errors when necessary.

♦ Adults play a critical role in promoting children's curiosity and persistence by directing their attention, structuring their experiences, supporting their learning strategies, and regulating the complexity and difficulty of levels of information for them.

♦ Spending a lot of time ("time on task") in and of itself is not sufficient to ensure effective learning.

♦ Learning with understanding is more likely to promote transfer than simply memorizing information from a text or lecture.

♦ Knowledge that is taught in a variety of contexts is more likely to support flexible transfer than knowledge that is taught in a single context.

♦ Students develop flexible understanding of when, where, why, and how to use their knowledge to solve new problems if they learn how to extract underlying themes and principles from their learning.

♦ All learning involves transfer from earlier experiences.

♦ Sometimes the knowledge that people bring to a new situation impedes subsequent learning because it guides thinking in wrong directions.

♦ Different domains of knowledge, such as science, mathematics, history, have different organizing properties. It follows that to have an in-depth grasp of an area requires knowledge about both the content of the subject and the broader structural organization of the subject.

♦ Expertise can be promoted in learners. The predominant indicator of expert status is the amount of time spent learning and working in a subject area to gain mastery of content. The more one knows about a subject, the easier it is to learn additional knowledge.

Adapted from J. Bransford, A. Brown, & R. Cocking (Eds.) (2000). *How people learn: Brain, mind, experience, and school.* Washington, DC: National Academy Press, 234–238.

ing order, analysis, synthesis, and evaluation. These six levels of cognition have been accepted by millions as gospel, and have been used as a template for teacher questions, lesson plan objectives, and anything else related to student thinking. Actually, Bloom's *Taxonomy* is an imaginative theoretical construct with little empirical foundation. Is it really true, for example, that synthesis requires greater intellectual endeavor than does comprehension? It is probably the case that to synthesize something, comprehension is required, just as it may well be the case that to comprehend something, synthesis of some kind is required. And is a simple evaluation a "higher" intellectual function than a penetrating analysis? The proof simply isn't there. Bloom's overly simplistic use of the very terms that are the essence of his taxonomy is disquieting. To equate "knowledge," for example, with lower registers of cognition when it ought to be abundantly clear that knowledge of something can be profound as well as trivial is to visit semantic confusion on us.

Is There Any Evidence? Levels II and III Research

Given the ambiguities of research at Level I, it is predictable that the research at Level II is rather tentative. A number of studies investigated the development of higher order thinking skills (a construct which has not really been established) as educational outcomes, but they are scattered throughout the literature on mastery learning, cooperative learning, outcome-based education, and peer coaching, among other topics, and are mainly not research studies on the kinds of programs described in this chapter. However, two exceptions do come to mind.

The *ThinkerTools Curriculum* for teaching physics by using interactive computer software has been subjected to empirical research with rather efficacious results. The curriculum focuses on basic principles of physics, allowing students to use and test their preconceived ideas in model building and experimentation. A recurring theme in the curriculum is an "inquiry cycle" that enables students to monitor and adjust where they are in the inquiry process. Reflective assessment is built into the curriculum both at the individual level and at the level of reviewing the assessments of other students' work. The program's authors, White and Frederiksen report two studies (1997, 1998). In the first study, sixth-grade students who learned physics using *ThinkerTools* outperformed eleventh- and twelfth-grade physics students in the same school system who were taught using traditional methods. Their second study compared urban seventh and ninth graders who learned physics using *TinkerTools* with suburban eleventh and twelfth graders (typically an unfair comparison), with the rsults favoring the younger urban students.

White and Frederickson write, "We found that, regardless of their lower grade levels...and their lower pretest scores, students who had participated in *ThinkerTools* outpeformed high school physics students...on qualitative problems in which they were asked to apply the basic principles of Newtonian mechanics to real-world situations" (1998, pp. 90–91). This would certainly seem to be promising support for the idea that thinking skills can be learned and transferred.

Hembree (1992) examined problem-solving attainment primarily in mathematics instruction and concluded that heuristics training provided the largest gains in problem-solving performance, but with a number of limitations. This tells us, however, little about thinking skills programs per se, either commercially or teacher-developed.

A number of claims can be readily found in popular education journals such as *Educational Leadership,* that describe the benefits of these programs, but there does not appear to be even a modest number of published empirical studies to support most of the supposed benefits. For certain advocates of thinking skills programs (as with many other innovations mentioned in this book) this lack of research poses no obstacle. Stanley Pogrow (1995) seems to have discovered a new type of research, called "pattern sense making," that overrides traditional cause-and-effect studies. For schools using his Higher Order Thinking Skills (HOTS) program he states: "It seemed natural to form a network to exchange information and ideas. The network makes possible a more realistic type of research than is possible in the highly controlled (contrived) settings of limited scope and limited duration in which most educational research takes places." Such an arrangement allows for information flow and spontaneous feedback. This research, Pogrow writes,

> ...has generated fundamental new knowledge about the nature of the learning needs of educationally disadvantaged students. In addition, this approach to research has generated very different conclusions from those of conventional research—conclusions that I believe are more valid and valuable for making national and school policy than those generated from either the prevalent quantitative or qualitative research techniques. (p. 20)

Thus, Pogrow furnishes us with an original theoretical paradigm, he develops a specific program, and he conducts the research himself. Not only are the results efficacious, by his own admission, but his theoretical work has made possible conclusions that are "more valid and valuable" than those derived using other techniques. Hard to know what to say in the wake of that.

The difficulties and ambiguities of thinking skills assessment have not gone unnoticed by those who have reviewed the research. Norris' (1985) review focused more on the general nature of critical thinking than on any cause-and-effect relationships. It is, however, a useful review for anyone contemplating curriculum changes in this area. He concluded that we really don't know much about critical thinking and quite sensibly offered only a few tentative conclusions, among them that critical thinking is not a generic tool and that it is sensitive to context.

Both the Norris review and a review by Sternberg and Bhana (1986) highlighted the problems associated with the research on thinking skills, and those problems remain over a decade later. Sternberg and Bhana's review sought to determine whether thinking skills programs are "snake-oil remedies or miracle cures." They evaluated five programs that had been cited in the annals of program evaluation and found most of the research to be very weak in design and possibly biased. Even setting aside these serious problems, they found the results to be inconclusive and none of the evaluations useful for determining which portions of the programs worked and which did not. They concluded, "Some thinking skills training programs are probably not a whole lot better than snake oil, but the good ones, although not miracle cures, may improve thinking skills" (p. 67).

Cotton (1992) is more sanguine about the research base at Level II and Level III. She examined 33 "key documents, [of which] 22 are research studies or evaluations." The other 11 were reviews or syntheses of research. In these studies, thinking skills were defined in a variety of ways, including analysis, synthesis, evaluation, making predictions, making inferences, and metacognitive activities. She reached these conclusions (pp. 4–6):

+ Thinking skills instruction enhances academic achievement.
+ Research supports instruction in many specific skills and techniques, including study skills, creative and critical thinking skills, metacognition, and inquiry training.
+ Various instructional approaches enhance thinking skills.
+ Computer-assisted instruction helps to develop thinking skills.
+ Research supports the use of several specific thinking skills programs, including a number of those listed in Figure 8.2 (p. 112).
+ Training teachers to teach thinking skills leads to student achievement gains.

In spite of Cotton's optimism, neither the amount nor quality of the research used to support such broad conclusions as these seem justified. Of course, you ought to examine the studies that Cotton reviewed. But short of that, reread any one of the foregoing six conclusions. No doubt you can quickly imagine conditions that would make the claim subject to a number of qualifiers. The claims are somewhat reminiscent of the effective schools claims in that they may confuse cause and effect, are not weighted in helpful proportion, and raise the specter of untoward variables and rival hypotheses. The claims may point in basically the right direction, but the evidence is not sufficient at this point to meet our standards. Perhaps it is better to think of them as promising hypotheses in need of further testing.

In support of the idea that thinking skills can be learned and applied to other contexts, Anderson et al. (2000), citing recent gains in both cognitive and situative research, do note that research "has provided significant information and understanding of conditions in which learning has general effects in human performance" (p. 12). They go on to say that "cognitive research has shown that learning to use specific representational forms can facilitate transfer between specific tasks" (p. 12). This, of course, does not specifically answer the question whether thinking skills can be taught apart from specifc subject matter, but it does support the idea that they can be transferred from one context to another.

The professional literature, especially that chronicled in policy journals such as *Educational Leadership*, not to mention the many teacher magazines, is replete with success stories, but few penetrating analyses. The advocates and enthusiasts are certainly out there in profusion. Thinking skills has become one of the very lucrative inservice and materials areas, and at its worst it preys on the vulnerability of professionals of good will who so much would like to improve the quality of students' thinking. It is pretty safe to say that penetrating questions, problem solving, and perseverance are of considerable help when such strategies are integrated with important content in an atmosphere that is genuinely conducive to the engagement of reflective thought.

CONCLUSION

It would be unreasonable to claim that these programs fail to provide students with thinking skills. On the other hand, there is simply not much convincing evidence that they do. The research in this area is muddled to say the least. We cannot, for example, even define or document the separate existence of thinking skills. Attempts to organize them into hierarchies may bear little resemblance to reality. Most of the evidence in favor of these programs is anecdotal. On the other hand, when one examines the activities and teaching strategies found in most of the programs, they seem to have some potential.

At this time, it would seem a decision to purchase and implement one of these programs and to invest teachers' time in inservice training cannot be reasonably based on the research evidence. Ironically, the pure research base is quite good and is improving almost daily, but the connections between pure research and the work of program builders are primitive. However, if in your professional judgment a particular thinking skills program looks good to you because of the interesting activities and strategies, that may be a logical basis on which to give it a closer look, in which case one hopes you will carefully consider the content and ideas you are trying to teach as well as the environmental conditions in which you want learning to take place.

I can't resist one last comment relative to measuring thinking skills, context, and relevance. Some years ago, I helped to conduct a 3-year study of problem solving by primary-age children. One of the problems they had worked on had to do with growing plants and selling them at a plant sale they held. They even made attractive containers to put their plants in. There were 26 children in this particular first grade classroom, and they took in $96 at their plant sale. Believe me, these young kids who could not have divided 96 by 26 in a paper-and-pencil equation had no trouble at all figuring out how much money each child should receive.

REFERENCES

Anderson, J., Greeno, J., Reder, L., & Simon, H. (2000). Perspectives on learning, thinking, and activity. *Educational Researcher, 29(4)*, 11–13.

Baer, J. (1988). Let's not handicap able thinkers. *Educational Leadership*, 45(7), 66–72.

Beyer, B. K. (1987). *Practical strategies for the teaching of thinking.* Boston: Allyn and Bacon.

Beyer, B. K. (1988a). Developing a scope and sequence for thinking skills instruction. *Educational Leadership, 45(7)*, 26–30.

Beyer, B. K. (1988b). *Developing a thinking skills program.* Boston: Allyn and Bacon.

Bland, C., & Koppel, I. (1988). Writing as thinking tool. *Educational Leadership, 45(7)*, 58–60.

Bloom, B. (Ed.) (1956). *Taxonomy of educational objectives.* New York: Longman.

Brandt, R. (1984). Teaching of thinking, for thinking about thinking. *Educational Leadership, 42*, 3.

Brandt, R. (1988). On teaching thinking: A conversation with Art Costa. *Educational Leadership, 45(7)*, 10–13.

Bransford, J., Brown, A., & Cocking, R. (2000). *How people learn: Brain, mind, experience, and school.* Washington, DC: National Academy Press.

Bruner, J. (1996). *The culture of education.* Cambridge, MA: Harvard University Press.

Costa, A., & Kallick, B. (2000). *Activating and engaging habits of mind.* Washington, DC: Association for Supervision and Curriculum Development.

Costa, A. L. (Ed.) (1985). *Developing minds: A resource book for teaching thinking.* Alexandria, VA: Association for Supervision and Curriculum Development.

Costa, A. L. (Ed.) (1991). *Developing minds: Programs for teaching thinking.* Alexandria, VA: Association for Supervision and Curriculum Development.

Cotton, K. (1992). *Teaching thinking skills.* School Improvement Research Series, Close-up #11. Portland, OR: Northwest Regional Educational Laboratory.

DeBono, E. (2000). *New Thinking for the New Millenium. London:* New Millenium Ent.

DeBono, E. (1983). The direct teaching of thinking as a skill. *Phi Delta Kappan, 64*(10), 703–708.

DeBono, E. (1991). The CoRT Thinking Program. In A. L. Costa (Ed.) (1991). *Developing minds: Programs for teaching thinking,* pp. 27–32. Alexandria, VA: Association for Supervision and Curriculum Development.

Driver, R. (1983). *Pupil as scientist?* London: Open University Press, Milton Keynes.

Elder, L., & Paul, R. (1995). Critical thinking: Why teach students intellectual standards, I & II. *Journal of Developmental Education, 18*(3), 36–37; *19*(1), 34–35.

Gardner, H. (1983). *Frames of mind.* New York: Basic Books.

Goodlad, J. (1984). *A place called school.* New York: McGraw-Hill.

Hembree, R. (1992). Experiments and relational studies in problem-solving: A meta-analysis. *Journal for Research in Mathematics Education, 23*(3), 242–273.

Hobbs, D. E., & Schlichter, C. L. (1991). Talents unlimited. In A. L. Costa (Ed.) (1991). *Developing minds: Programs for teaching thinking,* pp. 73–78. Alexandria, VA: Association for Supervision and Curriculum Development.

Kohlberg, L. (1987). Child psychology and childhood education: A cognitive-developmental point of view. New York: Longman.

Nickerson, R. S., Perkins, D. N., & Smith, E. E. (1985). *The teaching of thinking.* Hillsdale, NJ: Lawrence Erlbaum.

Norris, S. P. (1985). Synthesis of research on critical thinking. *Educational Leadership, 42*(8), 40–45.

Nunes, T., Schliemann, A., & Carraher, D. (1993). Street mathematics and school mathematics. New York: Cambridge University Press.

Paul, R. (1993). *Critical thinking: What every person needs to survive in a rapidly changing world,* 3rd ed. Santa Rosa, CA: Foundation for Critical Thinking.

Phillips, D. (1995). The good, the bad, and the ugly: The many faces of constructivism. *Educational Researcher.*

Piaget, J. (1970). *Science of education and the psychology of the child*. New York: Viking Press.

Pogrow, S. (1995). Making reform work for the educationally disadvantaged. *Educational Leadership, 52*(5), 20–24.

Resnick, L. B. (1987). *Education and learning to think*. Washington, DC: Academy Press.

Schlichter, C. L. (1986). Talents unlimited: An inservice education model for teaching thinking skills. *Gifted Child Quarterly, 30*(3), 119–123.

Schlichter, C. L., Hobbs, D., & Crump, W. D. (1988). Extending talents unlimited to secondary schools. *Educational Leadership, 45*(7), 36–40.

Schliemann, A., Carraher, D., & Ceci, S. (1997). Everyday cognition. In J. Berry, P. Dasen, & T. Saraswathi (Eds.). *Handbook of cross-cultural psychology*, 2nd ed., Vol. 2.

Schwartz, D., & Bransford, J. (1998). T time for telling. *Cognition and Instruction, 16*(4), 475–522.

Serpell, R. (2000). Intelligence and culture. In R. Sternberg (Ed.). *Handbook of intelligence*. Cambridge: Cambridge University Press, 549–577.

Sternberg, R. J., & Bhana, K. (1986). Synthesis of research on the effectiveness of intellectual skills programs: Snake-oil remedy or miracle cures? *Educational Leadership, 44*(2), 60–67.

Sternberg, R. (1997). *Thinking styles*. Cambridge: Cambridge University Press.

Sternberg, R. (2000). *Handbook of intelligence*. Cambridge: Cambridge University Press.

Worsham, A. M., & Stockton, A. J. (1986). A model for teaching thinking skills: The inclusion process (*Phi Delta Kappa Fastback, 236*). Bloomington, IN: Phi Delta Kappa.

Sutherland, P. (1992). *Cognitive development today*. London: Paul Chapman Publishing.

Vygotsky, L. S. (1986). *Thought and language*. Cambridge, MA: MIT Press.

White, B., & Frederickson, J. (1997). *The thinkertools inquiry project: Making scientific inquiry accessible to students*. Princeton: Center for Performance Assessment, Educational Testing Service.

White, B., & Frederickson, J. (1998). Inquiry, modeling, and metacognition: Making science accessible to all students. *Cognition and science, 16*, 90–91.

9

WHOLE-LANGUAGE LEARNING

We believe that discussions about phonics and whole language must move away from an artificial, simplistic dichotomy that does not reflect the reality of practice in whole-language classrooms.

Karen Dahl and Patricia Scharer

A whole-language approach that does not incorporate sufficient attention to decoding skills leaves in its wake countless numbers of youngsters who, in the words of one teacher, are surrounded by "beautiful pieces of literature that [they] can't read."

American Educator

Whole language works. The proof is massive and overwhelming.

Harvey Daniels, Steve Zemelman, and Marilyn Bizar

Whole language is a philosophy of how literacy best develops in learners. It is based in part on first-language acquisition theory (Garcia and Pearson, 1990) which explains how children learn oral language. Advocates argue that oral language develops naturally because there is a need for it, that is, it serves a purpose, and literacy learning is basically analogous in that it works best when it serves a need or purpose (Dole, 2000). Whole language represents a perspective on language and learning which is founded primarily on the use of literature programs, big books, predictable books, book discussion groups, authentic stories rather than basal readers, acceptance of developmental spelling, and emphasis on the writing process. It is based on the premise that human beings "acquire language through actually using it for a purpose, not through practicing its separate parts until some later date when the parts are assembled and the totality is finally used" (Altwerger, Edelsky, and Flores, 1987, p. 145).

Whole language has emerged as a force in the school curriculum for at least two reasons. One reason is a reaction to the skills-based language programs with their heavy emphasis on the technical (phonics, grammar, correct spelling, etc.) rather than the conceptual aspects of learning. The other reason is that new theories of learning have emerged in recent years, and whole-language advocates have been encouraged by these developments.

Whole language is rooted in part in a learning theory called *constructivism*. Constructivism is based on the premise that the learner constructs all knowledge from previously acquired knowledge, personally, socially, or in combination, and therefore, learning is a more subjective affair than one might imagine (Bransford, Brown, and Cocking, 2000). No two people can or should construct the same knowledge (although it might be quite similar) because each of us has our own unique experiences, our own schema or knowledge structure, our own learning styles, and our own particular motivation to learn.

Because this is so, the thinking goes, it is more appropriate to expose learners to broad ideas than to particularistic skills. The former permits individual accommodation, while the latter assumes that everyone (at least within a group) needs the same thing. And that same thing is a reductionist approach to learning as opposed to a holistic approach to learning. Of course, this is somewhat of an oversimplification because whole-language advocates have rarely said that the teaching of basic reading and grammar skills is always inappropriate; what we are talking about here are points of emphasis.

Some observers have noted the similarities between whole language and an approach that was popular a generation ago called *language experience*. Language experience was based on the premise that reading and writing should come primarily from the child's own experience rather than from predetermined, one-size-fits-all sources such as basal readers. For example, a teacher takes the class for a walk around the environs of the school, and afterward, using large pages of newsprint and felt pen, writes a story that the children tell based on the experience. The children would then practice reading and illustrating their own story. Often, children in language-experience classes would write and illustrate their own "books" which they would share with others or give to their parents or others. The premise was twofold: that reading and writing go together like hand and glove, and that personal experience, interest, and choice are the keys to becoming a reader or a writer.

Noting certain historical similarities while attempting to imply that the ride is or ought to be over, Jeanne Chall (1999) writes, "I propose that it is these views—views that focus on children's interests and choices and the development of their higher mental processes from the start (i.e., student-centered views)—that attracted teachers to the whole word and sentence methods of the 1920s and to whole language in the 1980s and early 1990s" (p. 67).

The ideas of personal experience, of freedom of choice, of interest, of "ownership" as a motivating force have been claimed by more than one group over the years. They were certainly the foundation of the open school movement that swept across the educational landscape in the 1960s and 1970s. The basic idea, which is fundamental to the Doctrine of Interest, proclaimed by the Roman educator Quintilian in the first century, claims that you can force people to learn, but it isn't very effective because people learn best those things that interest them most.

A "Slippery Quarry"

A major problem with the whole-language movement is its variety of definitions. It has been described as a "slippery quarry" and as "something hard to measure" (McKenna, Robinson, and Miller, 1990a). Even whole-language advocates openly admit that the concept is difficult to define and that it defies "a dictionary-type definition." Basically, whole language is a philosophy of teaching and learning that proposes that all language concepts are closely interconnected, that to separate them is artificial, and that they are best learned in a natural or "whole" manner. This description contrasts with the traditional reductionist, skill-focused approach to language in which children begin with letters, sounds, blends, and phonemes, or what more than one proponent of whole language has called, "barking at text." Instead, whole language flows from the child's personal, natural language patterns and with the reading and writing of stories and other forms of literature that draw upon the child's experience. The oft-cited analogy is the natural untaught process of learning to walk. Readers of this book who wish to pursue this issue of definition more deeply are encouraged to read "The Rhetoric of Whole Language," by Moorman, Blanton, and McLaughlin, and "Deconstructing the Rhetoric of Moorman, Blanton, and McLaughlin: A Response," by Goodman. Both articles appear in the October-December 1994 issue of *Reading Research Quarterly*.

Several key terms are closely associated with whole-language learning. One term is *meaning-centered*. A meaning-centered approach seeks relevance and personal meaning and avoids isolated skills as the road to literacy. Another term found in the repertoire of whole-language advocates is *integration*. Because language is the root of much of our learning, whole-language classrooms provide integrated language experiences that touch variously on all parts of the curriculum—art, music, science, social studies, and so forth. And a third term is "natural learning." We don't directly teach people to walk or even to talk. It happens along the way in a supportive environment. Therefore, the argument goes, so should learning to read and write be made as natural as possible. Figure 9.1 illustrates the set of common assumptions and beliefs held by many whole language advocates.

An integral component of whole language philosophy is the nurturing of the natural process by which a child comes to think about language as a result of his or her prior knowledge and life experiences. In this respect, the social and affective components of learning are highly valued and attended to by whole language teachers. Social experiences tend to be holistic and often highly charged effectively, for better or worse. They lend themselves to particularistic analysis only in retrospect. Perhaps in the most fundamental sense of learning, the difference between whole language and traditional language programs is that whole language emphasizes whole-to-part learning whereas traditional forms emphasize part-to-whole learning. In other words, they are diametrically opposing points of view.

WHOLE LANGUAGE IN THE CLASSROOM

In whole language, phonics and word drills were initially downplayed, although this is certainly less so in today's whole-language literature. Instead, students are encouraged to learn to read and write much as they learned to speak—naturally. Emphasis is placed on encouragement with a focus on success in a natural setting rather than on errors, corrections of mistakes, and "word attack" skills. It is believed by whole-language advocates that not only will children more readily learn in a creatively rich literary environment that "nurtures" and "celebrates" reading and writing, but that they will *want* to read and write as a result. Intrinsic motivation and relevance are stressed as the teacher facilitates, rather than directs, the learning process.

Teachers who consider themselves to be users of the whole language approach fall into vaguely defined, often overlapping categories. Purists tend to eschew basic skills approaches altogether, while eclecticists try to accommodate a blend of whole language and traditional phonics-based reading and writing instruction. A more extreme position tends to take whole language to the limits, making it an entire curriculum as the classroom takes on the trappings of open education. But most users of whole language focus its use in the more conventional areas of the language arts curriculum, and increasingly a rapprochement between whole-language approaches and phonics seems to have taken place (Dahl and Scharer, 2000).

FIGURE 9.1. COMMON BELIEFS OF WHOLE-LANGUAGE ADVOCATES

According to whole language theory, teachers should:

- **Focus on meaning, not the component parts of language.** Children learn language from whole to part. Therefore, instruction in reading and writing should begin by presenting whole texts—engaging poems and stories—rather than zeroing in on the "bits and pieces" that make up language.

- **Teach skills in context, not in isolation.** Children learn the subskills of language most readily when these skills are taught in the context of reading and writing activities. Teachers should coach children in skills as the need for the skills arises, rather than marching children in lockstep through a sequenced skills curriculum.

- **Get children writing, early and often.** Reading and writing develop best in tandem. When children write, they master phonics relationships because they must constantly match letters with sounds to write what they want to say.

- **Accept invented spelling.** Whole language teachers do not expect perfect spelling from the beginning. Instead, they encourage children to make their best efforts. "Invented spelling" reveals to what degree the young writers have cracked the phonetic code and over time will improve.

- **Allow pupils to make choices.** When children have some control over their learning, they are more motivated and retain what they learn longer.

- **Child-centered curriculum.** The classroom program focuses on children and their patterns of literacy development and interests. Instruction addresses the learner's processes of reading and writing.

- **Collaborative peer contexts.** Children collaborate as they work on reading and writing projects, exchanging information. Cooperative interactions among students are valued as crucial to language learning and development.

What whole language is not:

- **Breaking language into its component parts.**
- **Teaching skills in isolation or in a strict sequence.**
- **Relying on basal readers with controlled vocabulary.**
- **Using worksheets and drill.**
- **Testing subskills.**

SOURCE: Adapted from the Association for Supervision and Curriculum Development. Whole language: Finding the surest way to literacy. *Curriculum Update* (Fall, 1995), and from Dahl and Scharer (2000).

School districts that adopt whole-language programs often require experienced teachers to take some training designed to move them from the traditional approach to language arts to the whole-language approach. Prospective teachers in such districts are often screened based on their knowledge of and willingness to use whole language. This phenomenon has become somewhat problematic in the wake of the decision by the California State Board of Education to seriously revamp its previously uncritical approach to whole-language reading instruction. The trend now in districts that use literature-based or whole-language approaches is to fully expect that teachers will indeed embed a certain amount of phonics teaching into the curriculum.

Part of the problem concerning the phonics/whole-language debate is that often the combatants are actually defending different territory. Daniels, Zemelman, and Bizar (1999) write, "This battle is an odd one in many ways. To begin, the supposed rivals are not actually claiming the same territory. Decodable-text programs focus only on beginning readers and on just one literary skill: phonics. Whole language offers a comprehensive reading and writing program for all children from prereaders to students throughout their school years" (p. 32).

Figure 9.2 illustrates some of the differences between traditional and whole-language views of the curriculum. A review of the elements of curriculum and instruction found in Figure 9.2 reveal that a fundamental difference is found between the two approaches with respect to learning goals, teacher role, student activities, materials used, methods of assessment, and the very structure of the classroom. Needless to say, any teacher, administrator, or district contemplating such a basic change should be well aware of the implications, and should expect considerable challenge from parents and other interested parties.

POLITICS AND WHOLE LANGUAGE

There is another aspect of the whole-language movement, of which some whole-language enthusiasts are possibly unaware. At the deepest philosophical level, whole language represents something more than another way to teach kids how to read and write. Its source is found in a strong desire for education to play the role of change agent in the social and political fabric not only of schools, but society as a whole. This is hardly a new idea. George Counts, who probably would have approved wholeheartedly of the politics of whole language, wrote *Dare the Schools Build a New Social Order?* (1932) on this very theme in the 1930s. It is this social and political agenda that has fueled much of the debate about whole language. A number of reading researchers and professionals have commented on this phenomenon, but one of the more penetrating analyses is provided by McKenna, Stahl, and Reinking (1994).

FIGURE 9.2. CLASSROOM IMPLICATIONS
FOR CONTRASTING VIEWS OF EDUCATION

	Traditional	*Whole Language*
Learning Goals	Specific objectives in each subject area, usually identified by the school, district, or state. The objectives are hierarchical and tied to textbooks or teacher guides. The focus is on the product, with particular emphasis given to a student's deficits.	Teachers work with students to create a curriculum based on the interests and strengths of the individual student. Learning focuses on the process and learning in a functional context.
Teacher Role	A transmitter of information with major responsibility for determining what and how students should learn.	A facilitator of learning helping the student with the process of learning, sharing responsibility for learning with the student.
Materials	Basal readers, skill books and worksheets, social studies, math, language, science textbooks.	Student-selected reading materials, meaningful projects involving a variety of integrated materials from the various disciplines.
Class Structure and Activities	Students in traditional rows, with direct instruction predominant. Students may be grouped by achievement level. Minimal use of group learning activities. Teaching of skills in isolation from other parts of the curriculum with separate periods of the day for the various subjects.	Variable seating arrangements with considerable flexibility. Subjects integrated with language and reading, with considerable group and cooperative learning activities. Limited direct instruction, or only when the need arises within the context of the learning activities at a meaningful time.
Evaluation	Standardized tests, workbooks, worksheets, teacher-made tests that evaluate isolated skills mastery. The frame of reference for evaluation is an external standard or group norm.	Teacher observations of the learning process, writing samples, student self-evaluation, and portfolios. Students are evaluated against themselves to identify growth in various areas.

They have identified the social-political aspect of the whole-language agenda as spelled out by certain leaders in the movement. They note that some whole-language advocates see "education as a vehicle for individual liberation and the classroom as a model for an egalitarian society" (p. 213). They interpret Kenneth Goodman, a prominent exponent of whole-language teaching, as someone who "appears to see whole language, not as method of teaching reading, but an aspect of an approach to creating a more just world. From this analysis, whole-language advocates do not see the goal of education as improving test scores. Their critique of test scores…is based on…a questioning of the imposition of a standard or norm on an individual child" (p. 214).

Indeed, a number of whole language advocates are very open about these beliefs. Edelsky, Altwerger, and Flores (1991), write that whole language "has a unique potential to be a liberatory pedagogy.…" It is also, they continue, ideally suited for helping "subvert the school's role in maintaining a stratified society." Whole language "devalues the major language-based devices for stratifying people," and "huge chunks of time usually devoted to exercises are freed for projects in which students can analyze social issues like the systemic injustice and inequality that affects all our lives" (pp. 53–54).

The battle lines are sharply drawn. As McKenna et al. noted in their analysis, "to compromise whole language would be to compromise that [political] goal." Critics point out that whole language is built on a theory that may be less about learning to read and write, except as tools of liberation, than about social change and "reorganizing power relationships in schools."

THE RESEARCH BASE FOR WHOLE LANGUAGE

Whole-language advocates claim that "the research base for whole language philosophy is broad and multidisciplinary. It includes research in linguistics, psycholinguistics, sociology, anthropology, philosophy, child development, curriculum, composition, literary theory, semiotics, and other fields of study" (Newman and Church, 1989, p. 20). Movement-leader Kenneth Goodman, who cites such luminaries as Jean Piaget, Lev Vygotsky, Noam Chomsky, and the linguist Michael Halliday as influencing his thinking, has proclaimed that, "Whole language has emerged as a complete pedagogy, rich, diverse, and complex" (1996, p. 135). These claims are daunting, and they might lead one to conclude that such a deeply structured Level I foundation augurs well for the results of this approach. The proof, however, is ultimately found in how or to what extent theoretical contributions are brought together to form a coherent teaching-learning construct or, in more grand terms, a "complete pedagogy."

Other examples of the claims are found in books such as *The Administrator's Guide to Whole Language* (Heald-Taylor, 1989), in which an entire chapter is devoted to whole-language research. Allusions are made to some 50 studies that cover a range of related topics that include writing, oral language, reading, and developmental studies. Prominent among the researchers cited are Kenneth Goodman, Donald Graves, Delores Durkin, Marie Clay, and Frank Smith. This book was published some years ago at a time of largely uncritical enthusiasm and unbridled expansion of the whole-language movement.

More recently, Adams and Bruck (1995) reviewed the whole-language research base, concluding that to the extent to which whole-language proponents equate learning to read with learning to talk (i.e., that it is a "natural" process much like learning to walk), they are wrong. They concluded further that to the extent to which whole-language procedures minimize the role of skilled decoding in reading comprehension, they are wrong. And they conclude that the resulting pedagogical practices of whole language teaching and learning are wrong. Adams and Bruck base their rather strong conclusions on a systematic examination in which they compare whole-language claims with empirical results.

Further, Keith and Paula Stanovich (1995) add that, "[empirical] research has consistently supported the view that reading is not acquired naturally in the same way as speech" (p. 93). Keith Stanovich maintains, "That direct instruction in alphabetic coding facilitates early reading instruction is one of the most well-established conclusions in all of behavioral science. Conversely, the idea that learning to read is just like learning to speak is accepted by no responsible linguist, psychologist, or cognitive scientist in the research community" (*American Educator*, 1995, p. 4).

Thus the conclusion that whole language has indeed a credible pure or basic (Level I) research foundation is certainly debatable, to say the least. Furthermore, that the philosophical basis of whole language is one of a clearly thought-out theory of learning rests on its claim and is clearly challenged by Stanovich when he writes that, "these [theoretical] ideas have unfortunately come into education half-baked and twice distorted. Legitimate philosophy of science was picked up and reworked by scholars in a variety of humanities disciplines who were not philosophers by training and who used the work for their own—often political—agendas" (1993, p. 288). The basic research and the theoretical model of whole language is its primary line of support. It rests, its critics say, on shaky foundations. The theoretical construct has been used to give both inspiration and direction to whole language teaching and learning practices at the classroom level. It is to this level, that of implementation, that we now turn.

The practical questions are: What do students learn in whole-language classrooms? Do students attain higher levels of literacy? Is the learning qualitatively improved in whole-language classrooms? This is the domain of applied research (Level II). The answer to those questions is that evidence is lacking, except where whole language is carefully blended with phonics-based approaches. Let us see why this is so.

HOW DO WE DO IT?

Empirical researchers have observed that investigating the effects of whole-language instruction is difficult because of the lack of an agreed upon definition of whole language. As we suggested previously, people mean different things when they use the term. It should also be noted that a number of whole-language advocates claim that "traditional" methods of assessment are inappropriate when it comes to evaluating this approach to teaching and learning (McKenna, Robinson, and Miller, 1990a, p. 4).

McKenna, Robinson, and Miller (1990a) suggest a cooperative research agenda designed to treat these problems. They propose that these eight steps be taken:

- The concept must be defined to enable researchers to know whether a program represents whole language or not, or at least how to categorize a given program;
- Both experimental and quasi-experimental research is needed;
- Qualitative studies should also be employed;
- The effects on student attitudes should be studied;
- Longitudinal studies should be undertaken;
- Learner characteristics as they interact with traditional and whole-language instruction should be identified;
- Studies should identify the role of teacher variables in instruction;
- Collaborative research partnerships between researchers and whole-language advocates should be developed.

Of course, this very reasonable agenda is needed not merely for whole language program assessment but for program assessment in general.

Some whole-language advocates, however, take strong exception to the idea of an imposed research agenda. In "Whose Agenda Is This, Anyway?," Carole Edelsky (1990) wrote that traditional research forms have little relevance to whole language because "two competing views are more than different 'takes' on language arts instruction; they are conflicting educational paradigms. Each uses different discourse; maintains different values; and emanates from a different educational community" (p. 7). In a response to her response, McKenna et al. wrote, "in essence, people share a system of beliefs and they claim they have evidence to support their beliefs. But, when you look up what [whole-language advocates] cite as evidence, it is often just someone else's published beliefs" (McKenna, Robinson, and Miller, 1990b, p. 12). This has all the earmarks of a stalemate.

The debate about research methodology in the reading profession has obviously been quite rancorous, and suggestions have been made to resolve this dispute that "invoke a spirit of charity" (Stanovich and Stanovich, 1995). The strident nature of the debate is a reflection of how strongly these beliefs are held. As McKenna et al. (1994) have noted, "To compromise whole language would be to compromise that [political] goal." When people have such fundamentally different world views, it would be naive at best, and probably closer to folly, to think that they might readily agree to a research agenda.

In fairness, it should be stated that many whole-language advocates are not necessarily opposed to any form of evaluation research. Rather, they question the appropriateness of the measures used, which are, typically, standardized tests. Such tests, whole-language proponents claim, isolate learning in bits and pieces and ask children to show their knowledge in unnatural settings.

What kinds of program evaluation do whole language proponents advocate? First of all, they would propose that qualitative research, rather than quantitative, be emphasized. They suggest that writing samples that could be judged as process rather than product would be a place to start. Also, they are very interested in determining students' attitudes toward learning to read and write. To get a sense of students' attitudes, it would be necessary to conduct personal interviews and to employ other, similar qualitative data-gathering procedures. Basically, whole-language advocates feel that placing the assessment marbles in the quantitative-product bag is a mistake that leads to irrelevant conclusions about student learning. This leaves the potential consumer in a quandary because we can all appreciate the sensitivity toward attitude development and the employment of more "natural" measures of achievement. On the other hand, it is much easier to compare quantitative achievement results between this reading program and that one when districts are faced with the expensive decisions associated with program adoption and implementation.

Goodman (1996) has argued that, "Reductionist research in reading has inevitably focused on recognition of bits and pieces of language rather than on comprehension of real texts. But we can't assume that perception of letters and words in the process of making sense of real meaningful texts is the same as recognizing letters and words in isolation or in highly reduced contexts. And we can't assume that comprehension follows successive recognition of words" (p. 5). This statement suggests rather strongly that, from Goodman's perspective, what we have are two completely different goal structures and agendas, one empirical-reductionist and the other global-expansionist. To compare them, it would seem to follow, is not merely difficult but less than a good use of one's time. As Goodman writes, "Whole-language teachers have taken control of the body of knowledge about how reading and writing work and have built their own pedagogy on that knowledge—their teaching theory and practice" (p. 117). Such phrases as "have taken control" and "have built their own pedagogy" speak for themselves.

WHAT WE DO KNOW

In spite of all this, what does the research we *do* have say about the effectiveness of whole-language programs? A comprehensive review of the research on whole language effectiveness was conducted by Steven A. Stahl and Patricia D. Miller in 1989, and updated in 1994 by Stahl, Michael McKenna, and Joan Pagnucco. The reviews included both quantitative and naturalistic or qualitative studies. In 1989, Stahl and Miller wrote, "Our review...concludes that we have no evidence showing that whole-language programs produce effects that are stronger than existing basal programs, and potentially may produce lower effects. The alternative, that whole-language programs are too new to evaluate, also suggests a lack of evidence of their efficacy. In short, both views foster doubt as to the prudence of a widespread adoption of such an approach, pending evidence of its effectiveness" (Stahl, 1990, p. 143).

This review of whole-language research outcomes is not without its critics. Many whole-language advocates reject its definitions of whole language and the methodologies of the research itself (Schickendanz, 1990; McGee and Lomax, 1990). The 1994 Stahl et al. review again concluded that whole language did not produce advantages in achievement, and that eclectic programs seemed to produce the most positive effects. They concluded that the evidence suggested that the strongest type of program "might include a great deal of attention to decoding, especially in the early grades, but would give a greater emphasis to the reading of interesting and motivating texts....[S]uch a program would incorporate much from whole language but include more teacher-directed instruction, especially in terms of decoding and comprehension strategies." They also noted, however, that this is not likely to sit well with whole-language people because many of them are convinced that, "one cannot have a little whole language and a little of something else. Partial moves toward whole language are acceptable only as a way station to becoming a true whole language teacher" (p. 182).

Its staunchest critics have called whole language a "disaster," and it is true that the empirical evidence in support of whole-language learning is tenuous to deficient at best. Increasing numbers of professionals and laypersons have concluded that there are major problems and that many children, particularly young children from homes in which little reading takes place as a matter of course, and who need to learn the fundamentals, simply do not learn to read well when whole language is the principal philosophy guiding instruction. The notion put forth by whole-language advocates that learning to read is a naturalistic process much like learning to walk or talk (a notion that is disputed by a large number of linguists and psychologists) breaks down in the absence of home-based role models either of learning to talk using proper grammar or learning to read when little evidence of reading is found in the home.

Responding to the critics, Zemelman, Daniels, and Hyde (1998) note that "a sixty-year body of research on whole language and related literature-based programs shows standardized achievement score gains for students in progressive, whole-language–style programs, not just in regular education but among students with ESL, special education, or disadvantaged backgrounds" (p. 250). They refer critics to Sam Weintraub's *Summary of Investigations Related to Reading (1992–97)*, published by the International Reading Association, which shows strong support for whole-language learning.

Also worth noting is the widely reported success of *Reading Recovery* (Lyons, Pennell, Deford, and Clay, 1993), a tutoring program for young children who are failing at learning to read and which contains whole-language protocols. Marie Clay (1997, 2000), who did much of the early development work of the *Reading Recovery* model, continues to play a leading role in the whole-language movement.

A study that does offer some promise for involving the home, and therefore a more "naturalistic" setting, is one done by Morrow and Young (1997) on the effects of a family home literacy program for inner-city primary school children. Parents were given some training in the use of developmentally appropriate and culturally sensitive literacy activities and materials to use with their children. The results of the study showed both achievement and motivation differences favoring those children in the family program over a comparison group.

And as though the whole-language/phonics debate were not enough, the *connectionist* approach to reading enters the picture in study conducted by Berninger and Abbott (1998). The connectionist method is at least superficially similar to the old "look-say" or whole-word approach to reading instruction, and is based not on rules as phonics is, but on "encounters" with written words in which the learner employs inductive rather than deductive reasoning to learn word meaning. In other words, explicit rules of sounding out words by letter or syllable sound are not taught. This exploratory study conducted with 48 children identified by teachers at the end of first grade as having reading difficulties showed promising results on the basis of standardized test scores and vocabulary development. So, the search for viable methods continues apace.

Reacting to the drumbeat of parent criticism and declining student achievement, the California has modified its earlier embrace of whole language and is currently advocating a more balanced approach with an increased phonics-based emphasis (California Department of Education, 1996, 2000). It should, however, be kept in mind that states and districts embraced whole language in the first place because of the perception that more traditional forms of literacy instruction were not meeting children's needs. So, we have another example of the pendulum swing so recognizable to those who have been in the profession for considerable time. Figure 9.3 presents the highlights of California's new emphasis on phonetic awareness, correct spelling, systematic, explicit phonics approaches, and so on. Especially worth noting is the advocacy of early intervention programs for children at risk of reading failure. The *Report of the California Reading Task Force* contains much of the familiar rhetoric, including the insight that "there is a crisis..." (California Department of Education, 1995, p. 1). Among other things, the California Task Force concluded that "many language arts programs have shifted too far away from direct skills instruction" (p. 1). Statutes instituted in 1995 require that the State Board of Education "adopt materials in grades one through eight that include systematic, explicit phonics, spelling, and basic computational skills" (1996, p. 1).

SO WHERE DOES THIS LEAVE US?

Whole-language advocates continue to tout their approach primarily on the basis of theory, enthusiasm, and testimonials. While these are significant factors which should not be cynically cast aside, they simply are not be enough to go on when it comes to spending big money on new programs and teacher retraining. The fact of the matter is that we simply lack the empirical evidence necessary to state that schools that wish to improve student reading ability and test scores in the areas of the language arts should adopt the whole-language approach. But here's the rub: raising standardized test scores conflicts with the goals and objectives held by whole-language advocates. Their agenda, they state, is more complex than one whose learning outcomes can be captured by the reductionist mentality so pervasive in standard measures. So those who choose to adopt a purely whole-language approach to language arts must do so for reasons they find compelling, and those reasons will have to be sought in sources beyond the empirical record as it exists to date. But this takes us to the far reaches of the debate.

THE SEARCH FOR COMMON GROUND

A study by Dahl and Scharer (2000) points out the efficacy of an approached that combine whole language and phonics. They note that "historically, the phonics versus whole language debate has addressed a

---

FIGURE 9.3. CALIFORNIA'S BALANCED APPROACH TO READING

- ◆ Program components:
  - A strong literature, language, and comprehension program that includes a balance of oral and written language;
  - An organized, explicit skills program that includes phonemic awareness (sounds in words), phonics and decoding skills to address the needs of the emergent reader;
  - Ongoing diagnosis that informs teaching and assessment that ensures accountability;
  - A powerful early intervention program that provides individual tutoring for children at risk of reading failure
- ◆ Instructional Components
  - Phonemic awareness
  - Letter names and shapes
  - Systematic, explicit phonics
  - Programmatic instruction in correct spelling
  - Vocabulary development
  - Comprehension and higher order thinking
  - Appropriate instructional materials

SOURCE: California State Department of Education (1996). *Teaching reading: A balanced, comprehensive approach to teaching reading in prekindergarten through grade three.* Sacramento, CA: Author.

---

deficit argument—that children in whole language classrooms are denied instruction about letter-sound relationships" (p. 584). Their careful investigation into the nature of instruction in whole language classrooms yielded a great deal of evidence of phonics-based teaching. They document instance after instance of combined approaches in the real world of classroom settings they investigated. They present additional evidence of this phenomenon in a previous article reported in *Reading Research Quarterly* (1999).

We want our children to learn to read, to use it as a knowledge-seeking tool, and to enjoy reading, three different, but closely related, outcomes. Growing evidence exists to suggest that both teacher-directed, phonics-based instruction and some student-centered, literature-based learning are needed. What we need is a research agenda that will get us closer to the answers of sequence, balance, and the best use of children's learning time.

REFERENCES

Adams, M. J., & Bruck, M. (1995). Resolving the "great debate." *American Educator, 19*(2), 7–20.

Altwerger, B., Edelsky, C., & Flores, B. (1987). Whole language: What's new? *The Reading Teacher, 41*(2), 144–154.

Association for Supervision and Curriculum Development (1995, Fall). Whole language: Finding the surest way to literacy. *Curriculum Update.*

Berninger, V., & Abbott, R. (1998). Early intervention for reading disabilities: Teaching the alphabetic principle in a connectionist framework. *Journal of Learning Disabilities, 32(6)*, 491–504.

Brophy, J. (2000). Beyond balance: Goal awareness, developmental progressions, tailoring to the context, and supports for teachers in ideal reading and literacy programs. In B. Taylor, M. Graves, & P. Van Den Broek (Eds.) (2000). *Reading for meaning: Fostering comprehension in the middle grades.* New York: Teachers College Press.

California Department of Education (1995). *Every child a reader: The report of the California Reading Task Force.* Sacramento, CA: Author.

California Department of Education (1996). *Teaching reading: A balanced, comprehensive approach to teaching reading in prekindergarten through grade three.* Sacramento, CA: Author.

Cambourne, B. (1988). *The whole story.* Auckland, New Zealand: Ashton Scholastic.

Chall, J. (1999). *The academic achievement challenge: What really works in the classroom?* New York: The Guilford Press.

Clay, M. (2000). *Concepts about print: What have children learned about the way we print language?* Portsmouth, NH: Heineman.

Clay, M. (1997). *Becoming literate: The construction of inner control.* Portsmouth, NH: Heinemann.

Counts, G. (1932). *Dare the schools build a new social order?* New York: Day Publishing.

Dahl, K., & Scharer, P. (2000). Phonics teaching and learning in whole-language classrooms: New evidence from research. *Reading Teacher, 53*(7), 584–595.

Dahl, K., Scharer, P., Lawson, L., & Grogan, P. (1999). Phonics instruction and student achievement in whole language first-grade classrooms. *Reading Research Quarterly, 34*, 312–341.

Daniels, H., Zemelman, S., & Bizar, M. (1999). Whole language works: Sixty years of research. *Educational Leadership, 57*(2), 32–37.

Dole, J. (2000). Explicit and implicit instruction in comprehension. In B. Taylor, M. Graves, & P. Van Den Broek (Eds.) (2000). *Reading for meaning: Fos-*

tering comprehension in the middle grades. New York: Teachers College Press.

Edelsky, C. (1990). Whose agenda is this anyway? A response to McKenna, Robinson, and Miller. *Educational Researcher, 19*(8), 7–11.

Edelsky, C., Altwerger, B., & Flores, B. (1991). *Whole language: What's the difference.* Portsmouth, NH: Heinemann.

Flippo, R. (1997). Sensationalism, phonics, and literacy. *Phi Delta Kappan, 79,* 301–304.

Garcia, G., & Pearson, P. (1990). *Modifying reading instruction to maximize its effectiveness for all students.* Urbana, IL: University of Illinois, Center for the Study of Reading.

Goodman, K. S. (1989). Whole-language research: Foundations and development. *The Elementary School Journal, 90*(2), 207–221.

Goodman, K. S. (1994, October-December). Deconstructing the rhetoric of Moorman, Blanton, and McLaughlin: A response. *Reading Research Quarterly,* 340–346.

Goodman, K. S. (1996). *Ken Goodman on reading: A commonsense look at the nature of language and the science of reading.* Portsmouth, NH: Heinemann.

Goodman, Y. M. (1989). Roots of the whole-language movement. *The Elementary School Journal, 90*(2), 113–127.

Heald-Taylor, G. (1989). *The administrator's guide to whole language.* Katonah, NY: Rich C. Owen Publisher.

Krashen, S. (1999). *Three arguments against whole language and why they are wrong.* Portsmouth, NH: Heinemann.

Learning to read: Schooling's first mission. (1995). *American Educator, 19*(2), 3–6.

Lyons, C., Pennell, G., Deford, D., & Clay, M. (1993). *Partners in learning: Teachers and children in reading recovery.* New York: Teachers College Press.

Manning, G., Manning, M., & Long R. (1990). *Reading and writing in the middle grades: A whole-language view.* Washington, DC: National Education Association.

McGee, L. M., Lomax R. S. (1990). On combining apples and oranges: A response to Stahl and Miller. *Review of Educational Research, 60*(1), 133–140.

McKenna, M. C., Robinson, R. D., & Miller J. W. (1990a). Whole language: A research agenda for the nineties. *Educational Researcher, 19*(8), 3–6.

McKenna, M. C., Robinson, R. D., & Miller J. W. (1990b). Whole language and the need for open inquiry: A rejoinder to Edelsky. *Educational Researcher, 19*(8), 12–13.

McKenna, M. C., Stahl, S. A., and Reinking, D. (1994). A critical commentary on research, politics and whole language. *Journal of Reading Behavior, 26*(2), 211–233.

Moorman, G., Blanton, W., & McLaughlin, T. (1994, October-December). The rhetoric of whole language. *Reading Research Quarterly*, 309–329.

Morrow, L. M. (1992). The impact of a literature-based program on literacy achievement, use of literature and attitudes of children from minority backgrounds. *Reading Research Quarterly, 27*(3), 251–275.

Morrow, L., & Young, J. (1997). A family literacy program connecting school and home: Effects on attitude, motivation, and literacy achievement. *Journal of Educational Psychology, 89*(4), 736–742.

Newman, J. M., & Church S. M. (1989). Myths of whole language. *The Reading Teacher, 44*(1), 20–26.

Pressly, M. (1994). State-of-the-science primary-grades reading instruction or whole language? *Educational Psychologist, 29*(4), 211–216.

Schickendanz, J. A. (1990). The jury is still out on the effects of whole language and language experience approaches for beginning reading: A critique of Stahl and Miller's study. *Review of Educational Research, 60*(1), 127–131.

Stahl, S. (1990). Riding the pendulum: A rejoinder to Schickendanz and McGee and Lomax. *Review of Educational Research, 60*(1), 141–151.

Stahl, S. A., & Miller P. D. (1989). Whole language and language experience approaches for beginning reading: A quantitative research synthesis. *Review of Educational Research, 59*(1), 87–116.

Stahl, S. A., McKenna, M. C., & Pagnucco, J. R. (1994). The Effects of whole-language instruction: An update and a reappraisal. *Educational Psychologist, 29*(4), 175–186.

Stanovich, K. E. (1993). Romance and reality. *The Reading Teacher, 47*(4), 280–291.

Stanovich, K. E., & Stanovich, P. J. (1995). How research might inform debate about early reading acquisition. *Journal of Research in Reading, 18*(2), 87–105.

Watson, D. (1990). Defining and describing whole language. *The Elementary School Journal, 90*(2), 129–141.

Weintraub, S. (Ed.) (1992-1997). *Summary of investigations related to reading.* Newark, DE: International Reading Association.

Zemelman, S., Daniels, H., & Hyde, A. (1998). *Best practice: New standards for teaching and learning in America's schools.* Portsmouth, NH: Heinemann.

10

ELEMENTS OF STYLES: LEARNING, THINKING, TEACHING

Students are not failing because of the curriculum. Students can learn almost any subject matter when they are taught with methods and approaches responsive to their learning style strengths.

Rita Dunn

Like the blind men in the fable about the elephant, learning styles researchers tend to investigate only a part of the whole and thus have yet to provide a definitive picture of the matter before them.

Lynn Curry

Indeed, one of the initial movtivations for studying styles, and which still is a motivation, was the idea that perhaps prediction of achievement could be improved....

Robert Sternberg and Elena Grigorenko

We sometimes pretend something is true not because there's evidence for it but because we want it to be true

Carl Sagan

Style (noun): "A quality of imagination and individuality expressed in one's actions and tastes."

The American Heritage Dictionary
of the English Language (2000).

I had decided to drop the topic of learning styles from this new edition simply because there did not seem to be good evidence of serious theoretical and empirical work behind the many claims attendant to the topic. But some new work by Robert Sternberg of Yale University and his colleagues caused me to reconsider that decision. Sternberg himself has been rather critical of the learning styles movement, claiming that it has failed to distinguish among personality, ability, environmental, and other variables, leading to confusion over the very meaning of the construct. Other criticisms include the failure by many advocates and promoters to adequately conceptualize the theory base and failure to conduct rigorous research studies validating their claims.

The thesis of styles-based education is that individuals vary considerably in their preferences. This is to say that any given person has what are called modality strengths that are, one supposes, determined by a combination of hereditary and environmental influences. These modality strengths, which translate into preferences to think and learn and communicate visually, orally, spatially, tactilely, and so on, in some particular way, are one's style. Beyond that there are some further considerations, for example, whether one functions impulsively or reflectively in solving problems, prefers a formal or relaxed environment, or likes to work together or alone. Because style is supposedly independent of intelligence, it fits the category of preference rather than ability.

All of this is quite intriguing, and it has led to the development of a range of models some of which are quite elaborate. Dunn, Dunn, and Price have noted that their learning style model is predicated on "the manner in which at least eighteen different elements from four basic stimuli affect a person's ability to absorb and retain" (1979). Other equally complex styles models have been developed by Gregorc, McCarthy, and Hunt; Kolb; Renzulli and Smith; and Sternberg and Grigorenko.

It has even been suggested that learning styles, for example, are not merely a phenomenon of individual differences but that differences are also found among and between cultures. Bennett (1990) has noted that Native American students "approach tasks visually, seem to prefer to learn by careful observation which precedes performance, and seem to learn in their natural settings experientially." Bennett suggests further that African-American students tend to be field-dependent learners, which means that they tend to take their cues from the social environment and that much of their motivation comes from factors external to the material to be learned itself. More recently, the term field-dependent appears to have been replaced by the term "field-sensitive" (Swanson, 1995). Added to the cultural dimension is that of social class as a factor in determining how one learns. Given the relatively fluid social and economic mobility one finds in the United States, one wonders whether a person's learning style might change with a corresponding change in class.

If this is all true, what we have is compound interest because the suggestion is that to find a given individual in the vast matrix of teaching and learning, we must determine not merely the person's individual style, but that person's cultural and social context as well. This could lead teachers quickly into a labyrinthine world of diagnosis in the search for style. But it doesn't have to be that complicated, say the purveyors of learning styles.

The National Task Force on Learning Styles and Brain Behavior gives us the following definition of *learning style*:

> Learning style is that consistent pattern of behavior and performance by which an individual approaches educational experiences. It is the composite of characteristic cognitive, affective, and physiological behaviors that serve as relatively stable indicators of how a learner perceives, interacts with, and responds to the learning environment. It is formed in the deep structure of neural organization and personality [that] molds and is molded by human development and the cultural experiences of home, school, and society. (Bennett, 1990, p. 158)

This definition is quite broad and all encompassing, to say the least. Cornett (1983) offers a similar, simplified definition: "[E]ssentially, learning style can be defined as a consistent pattern of behavior but with a certain range of individual variability...." Guild and Garger (1985) point out that the idea of learning style includes cognitive style, teaching style, leadership style, and psychological type. Sternberg (1997) defines cognitive style as an individual's way of processing information. Sternberg identifies four broad styles categories that he calls cognition-centered, personality-centered, activity-centered, and teaching styles.

Cognition-centered styles include Herman Witkin's field-dependent/ independent as well as Jerome Kagan's impulsive/reflective styles. Personality-centered styles include the Jungian categories of introversion/ extroversion, thinking/feeling, intuitive/sensing, and perceptive/judgmental, as well as Anthony Gregorc's concrete/abstract, sequential/random styles. Activity-centered styles include D. A. Kolb's convergent/ divergent and assimilating/accommodating, as well as Dunn and Dunn's environmental, emotional, sociological, and physical styles. And teaching styles include Henson and Borthwick's (1984) styles of task-oriented, cooperative planner, child-centered, subject-centered, learning-centered, and emotionally exciting styles.

Dunn et al. (1995) write that "learning style is the way in which individuals begin to concentrate on, process, internalize, and retain new and difficult academic information." Figure 10.1 illustrates three areas of style characteristics including cognition, conceptualization, and affect. A review of Figure 10.1 will give you a sense of the characteristics of these broad categories and the researchers who have developed ideas related to them.

FIGURE 10.1. THREE AREAS OF STYLE CHARACTERISTICS

Category	Characteristics	Researchers
1. *Cognition*—perceiving, finding out, getting information	sensing/intuition	Jung; Myers-Briggs; Mok; Keirsey and Bates
	field dependent/field independent, abstract/ concrete	Witkin; Gregorc; Kolb and McCarthy
	visual, auditory, kinesthetic, tactile	Barbe and Swassing; Dunn and Dunn
2. *Conceptualizaton*—thinking, forming ideas, processing, memory	extrovert/introvert	Jung; Myers-Briggs; Keirsey and Bates
	reflective observation/ active experimentation	Kolb and McCarthy
	random/sequential	Gregorc
3. *Affect*—feelings, emotional response, motivation, values, judgments	feeler/thinker	Jung; Myers-Briggs; Mok; Keirsey and Bates
	effect of temperature, light, food, time of day, sound, design	Dunn and Dunn

---

It is common to categorize learning styles into some type of taxonomy of human characteristics of learning behavior. The various taxonomies include cognitive, affective, and physiological considerations. Thus, with respect to cognition, a person might exhibit concrete, abstract, sequential, and random learning characteristics. With respect to affect, different persons might find quite different sources for their motivation to learn or they might experience different feelings about how they are responded to as they learn. And with respect to physiological considerations, a person might have preferences for different seating, light, temperature, and room arrangement.

STYLES AND INTELLIGENCE

Most styles advocates stress the idea that each of us receives and processes information differently, and because this is so, teachers should make every attempt to know how students learn best. The logic of this thought dictates to us that although styles are different, they are equal. The argument goes that intelligence and ability are equally but differentially distributed among human beings. Typical school assignments tend to discriminate in favor or against certain learners. But the issue may not be one of ability if one person learns much and another little from, say, a lecture presentation. It may be that the lecture format is simply more suited to one person's learning style (auditory, for example) than to another's. What this implies is that otherwise capable people are left behind in many cases because the approach to learning is inappropriate, not because they are incapable of learning the idea.

The contention that various styles are equal and merely different with respect to ability to learn is not well established. It tends to remain within the realm of speculation. Witkin (1977), a pioneer researcher in this field, maintained that any given style is not superior to another, a proposition that immediately intersects with ideas of the definition of intelligence. However, convincing research has shown that Witkin's field-independent or analytic style (as contrasted with a field-dependent or global style) has been shown to correlate with measures of spatial and verbal ability. Spatial and verbal ability have long been recognized as factors of intelligence.

Compounding the problem is the fact that the very definition of intelligence is being reexamined by such researchers as Howard Gardner (1983, 2000), and the chances are that what we presently mean by intelligence as measured by IQ tests and what we will mean by intelligence in the future are two different things. At present, analytical abilities are considered basic to one's intelligence as measured by IQ tests. Global, intuitive learners tend to score much lower on tests of analytical abilities. Are they therefore less intelligent than analytical thinkers who obviously score higher? Well, it may depend on one's definition of intelligence.

IMPLICATIONS FOR THE CLASSROOM

Styles advocates point to two major areas of concern for the focus of teachers' energies. Those areas are style assessment and style matching. In other words, what we need to do is discover learners' and teachers' styles and somehow match them accordingly. And that, of course, is a matter of assessment.

A variety of styles assessment instruments exist for children as well as for adults. They cover all the areas noted in Figure 10.1. Among the more prominent instruments are the *Myers-Briggs Type Indicator,* the *Learning Styles Inventory,* the *Sternberg-Wagner Self-Assessment Inventories,* and the *Embedded Figures Test.* Because they are tools for assessing an individual's style or preference, the outcome, or test result, is positive no matter what it is. This seems in some ways a rather curious thing. For example, in the *Embedded Figures Test,* if one is unable to identify certain figures against the background in which they are embedded, it is considered not an inability but rather a global, or "field-sensitive" way of looking at things. On the other hand, the ability to identify the various figures merely is meant to indicate that one has an analytical, or field-independent, approach to learning. This may be one of the first instances in the annals of testing where failure to solve a problem merely puts one in a different but equal category. Anyone seriously interested in using one or more of these tests is certainly encouraged to consult the reviews of them found in *Tests in Print,* an updated guide found in most libraries.

In addition to the diagnostic instruments themselves, there are literally dozens of learning styles workbooks with inventories that show learners how to identify their styles. Based on the results, the books offer suggestions for how to approach classes and topics, how to study and prepare for exams, and how to deal with teachers whose own teaching styles vary. Thus, the effort on the part of learners to adapt their style to that of a teacher, or teacher to learner, represents a kind of coping strategy. Whether Sternberg (1997) himself would recommend these over-the-counter workbook inventories is one thing, but he does say that "it is necessary that schools take into account not only fit between teacher and student (or principal and teacher) style, but also the way a subject is taught and the way a student thinks" (p. 111).

This second major issue, *matching* teachers and students with respect to style, becomes crucial once people have been properly diagnosed. This brings to mind images created by the old insight that somewhere out there is the ideal learning environment. Maybe for some it brings to mind thoughts of Abraham Lincoln studying by firelight in a crude log cabin. Or one can imagine Aristotle walking through the shaded groves of ancient Athens speaking for the Ages while eager disciples follow in his wake taking in his every word. Or imagine a little child sitting in his or her mother's lap being told, for the *n*th time, a certain story. Then there is the kid who is simply great at arcade games but who has little interest in or seemingly little ability to do paper-and-pencil work. Recently a friend of mine told me he has a distinct preference for being near a refrigerator while studying.

This could go on, but you get the idea. Each of us probably has some sense of the optimum conditions that make learning more appealing and meaningful for us. However, a style preference, for example, a preference to listen to music while studying, does not necessarily translate into higher achievement. This is an often overlooked issue, and certainly one for which empirical evidence matching style with achievement is lacking.

The challenge for the teacher is to be sensitive to student differences, to use different modalities, such as stories, explanations, projects, and activities, to reach all the different learners in the class effectively, and to use special techniques to meet different styles, such as overviews for global learners and linear explanations for analytical learners. The challenge for all of us as learners is to accommodate to different situations, some of which match our styles and some of which do not. But, of course, it is not that simple. As Sternberg has pointed out, each teacher, perhaps without even thinking about it, does have a dominant teaching style, favoring this way or that of going about things. This tends to favor students who either have a similar style or who are able to adapt readily to the teacher's style. The result is that those who don't may achieve less well regardless of their innate abilities.

Advocates propose a number of teaching strategies that encompass the variety of learning styles. One might say that this is the essence of good teaching anyway. Here is a list of some of the ways to reach different styles:

+ Using questions at a variety of levels of thinking;
+ Providing an overview of material before proceeding to specifics;
+ Allowing sufficient time for information to be processed adequately;
+ Using examples and activities directed to both left and right hemispheres of the brain;
+ Providing set induction and closure activities;
+ Setting clear purposes before any listening, viewing, or reading experience;
+ Using spaced practice;
+ Using multisensory means to convey ideas to be learned;
+ Using a variety of teaching and learning approaches, including projects, inquiry, stories, individualized work, and cooperative learning;
+ Allowing some student choices in method of demonstrating learning, for example, writing, drawing, or presenting.

These strategies would quite possibly benefit most learners in most learning situations, and would, according to learning styles advocates, reach, differentially, all types of learners. However, as good as they might seem, most of the strategies just enumerated have little empirical evidence behind them to show that they do indeed benefit students' academic progress, and more pointedly to show which type of learners benefit most from them.

On more narrow grounds, specific strategies are thought to work better with certain styles. Figure 10.2 is an example of instructional strategies designed to meet the needs of one type of learner, field-dependent (global-intuitive) learners. Schools have long been thought to discriminate against field-dependent learners, for example. Textbooks, workbooks, lectures, and verbal explanations tend traditionally to be quite linear and analytical in their approaches to knowledge. To overcome this, teachers are urged to use the strategies illustrated in Figure 10.2 because they are particularly appropriate and helpful to global thinkers. Supposedly, lists could be generated appropriate for each style.

FIGURE 10.2. INSTRUCTIONAL STRATEGIES FOR FIELD-DEPENDENT LEARNERS

---

1. Present learning in a global way: focus on the "big picture"; give an overview and the concept.

2. Make connections among content, integrate learning, and identify relationships among subjects.

3. Provide a context for learning and a sense of the purpose of the learning.

4. Provide structure, clear expectations, direction, and organization.

5. Personalize content. Give frequent illustrations relating to students' and teachers' experiences.

6. Emphasize a positive class climate and helpful relationships with others.

SOURCE: Guild, P. (1990). *Using learning styles to help students be successful*. Seattle, WA: Seattle Public Schools.

THE RESEARCH BASE FOR LEARNING STYLES

The learning styles literature is related to the literature of brain research, but the two movements are certainly not synonymous.

Brain research investigators tend to focus on medical research as well as research in such areas as cognitive science as the source of their learning theories. Learning styles advocates allude to brain research, but seem to base their position more on psychological research such as the work done by Witkin of *Embedded Figures Test* fame. They cite brain research because it is obviously related more and more to psychological research, but for these people, brain function research is not the primary focus.

There are two types of Level I research on which learning styles is supposedly based. The first is represented by brain-mind research, including, for example, ways in which different people approach problem solving and intellectual tasks, and the implications of growth spurts and gender difference in learners. The basic brain research at the frontiers of knowledge indicates that certain gene functions may have implications for learning styles, but to this date most of the work has been done with animals, mainly insects, in laboratory settings (APA *Monitor*, 1997).

The second type of basic research is the psychological research on individual differences conducted throughout the twentieth century. Because of his work on personality types, Carl Jung is cited as one of the pioneers in this area. Jerome Kagan's (1966) work in impulsivity/reflectivity in learners is also considered seminal. Witkin's work in the development of the *Embedded Figures Test*, and I. B. Myers and Leslie Briggs' work in the development of their types indicator, have served to operationalize the definition of differences in styles found among human beings. D. A. Kolb's (1978) work emphasizes convergent/divergent, assimilating/accommodating styles. But in this brief enumeration alone one encounters much of the source of confusion. Some of this work is based on personality type, some on cognitive functioning, some on activity. Clearly, all these can and do interact with one another.

A host of instruments that purport to diagnose learning styles has been derived from the works of Jung, Kagan, Witkin, Kolb, and Myers and Briggs. In most cases, developers cite the pioneering work of these investigators as providing the foundation of a specific learning styles instrument. A problem with these instruments has been their close association with intelligence measures. Kagan's work in which reflective problem solvers are distinguished from impulsive problem solvers provides an example. If you were to ask teachers who is likely to be more intelligent, a reflective person or an impulsive person, the answer seems obvious. Impulsive types have been shown, for example, to have lower motivation to master academic tasks and tend to have relatively lower performance standards (Kagan, 1965, 1966; Kagan and Messer, 1975).

Another problem with these assessment inventories, however, is that they are plagued by troubles of validity and reliability. In other words, do they really measure what they claim to measure (validity) and are they stable measures of someone's style over time (reliability)? A significant and troubling issue with the research at this level can be traced to the ambiguities of the meaning of learning style. For example, a factor analysis of four such instruments showed that each instrument was measuring distinctly different characteristics (Ferrell, 1983). So much for agreed-on definition and construct validity.

Other criticisms include the fragile or even missing link between theo-retical work, assessment, and practice. Writing about the Dunn and Dunn learning styles theory and accompanying model, Sternberg (1997) con-cludes, "it is hard to say exactly how the 18 different styles were chosen, or even why they are called styles. They refer more to elements that affect a person's ability to learn than to ways of learning themselves" (p. 146). If it is true that we are talking about abilities rather than preferences, then we are back to square one.

THE SEARCH FOR EMPIRICAL FINDINGS: LEVELS II AND III

The Level II research on learning styles has been quite weak to say the least. However, with the entry of Sternberg and Grigorenko (1997) into the arena, things seem more promising. Certain proponents of learning styles maintain that style-based instruction increases learning (Dunn et al., 1995). The most far-reaching claims appear to be made by Rita Dunn and Marie Carbo, both of whom do research and teach workshops for teachers around the country on the topic of learning styles, and both of whom have materials for teachers and school districts to purchase. Thus, they each play the triple role of theorist-researcher, developer, and pur-veyor of learning styles ideas, instruments, and materials, something that if it were done in the medical profession would raise the proverbial red flag. But this is, of course, not the medical profession.

Both Dunn (1995, 1999) and Carbo (1992, 1997) tout the importance of the social-physical-emotional-intellectual learning environment, claim-ing that such variables as temperature, light, body position, and so on, should be accommodated to the individual's style. They make further claims about the necessity of matching instructional techniques between teacher and learner. They cite various research studies and sources to sup-port these claims while buttressing their positions with everything from allusions to unpublished graduate student theses and dissertations to anecdotal accounts of great teachers, breakthrough classrooms and lead-ing-edge–school success.

Many outside the movement are critical of the research used to sup-port learning styles (Kavale, Hirshoren, and Forness, 1997; Adams and Engelmann, 1996; Curry, 1990). The criticisms include these points:

- The validity and reliability of the instruments are question-able; many learning styles theorists have not distinguished learning styles constructs from intelligence (Curry, 1990).

- The experimental designs employed in classroom-based learning styles research are weak to nonexistent and have inadequate controls. Robert Slavin states: "What has never been studied, to my knowledge, is the question of whether teachers who adapt to students' styles get better results than those who don't" (O'Neil, 1990).

♦ Bias on the part of the researchers, possibly due to "mercenary" interests (Kavale and Forness, 1990; Kavale, Hirshoren, and Forness, 1997), in learning styles results.

♦ The Hawthorne Effect generated by the enthusiasm of doing something new may explain some of the results (Kavale, Hirshoren, and Forness, 1997).

♦ Many studies in the learning styles literature have been conducted by graduate students preparing their dissertations under the direction of faculty members who have a vested interest in substantiating a particular learning styles conceptualization (Curry, 1990; Kavale, Hirshoren, and Forness, 1997).

With respect to these concerns, let us turn to a meta-analysis (Dunn et al., 1995) of the most ubiquitous learning styles model, that of Dunn and Dunn. The authors note efficacious outcomes favoring styles-based teaching as reported in 10 published (and 1 unpublished) research articles representing investigations that range from elementary to college levels. They also note positive results for special education and learning-disabled students. Further, their meta-analysis included 36 different studies with a database of 3181 participants. They conclude that "students whose learning styles are accommodated would be expected to achieve 75% of a standard deviation higher than students who have not had their learning styles accommodated" (p. 353). This would represent an effect size of .75, which is considered to be high and impressive.

A closer look, however, at Dunn et al.'s meta-analysis raises several questions. The 11 studies alluded to in the previous paragraph were, with two or three exceptions, reported in journals that have little or no reputation for publishing carefully refereed, empirical studies—*Teaching K–8, Principal, Educational Leadership, Journal of College Student Development.* Furthermore, of the 36 studies included in the meta-analysis itself, only one was to be found in a published journal. Unpublished research is basically evidence that (a) has not been evaluated by expert jurors and (b) is difficult to access. The 35 unpublished studies were doctoral dissertations, a source known to be notoriously deficient and uneven in quality. Twenty-four of the cited dissertation studies were done at St. John's University under the direction of Dunn and her colleagues, raising serious issues of conflict of interest, but also raising the question of why the studies are unpublished, uncritiqued, and difficult to access. The *Annotated Bibliography of Research* (1992, 1995) cited by Dunn et al. is also unpublished. The St. John's University Center for the Study of Teaching and Learning issues it. More recently, Dunn and Debello (1999) edited a book citing improved test scores, attitudes, and behaviors in school settings as a result of the use of learning styles approaches.

Kavale et al. (1997) cite numerous methodological and interpretive problems with the Dunn et al. meta-analysis. They raise serious questions about the procedures used to derive the large effect size. Also, even if one were to accept the questionable effect size that Dunn et al. claim, there is the relatively easier task of introducing other teaching procedures (e.g., reinforcement, homework) that have large, well-established effect sizes. They conclude that:

> The Dunn et al. (1995) meta-analysis has all the hallmarks of a desperate attempt to rescue a failed methodology. The weak rationale, curious procedures, significant omissions, and circumscribed interpretation should all serve as cautions to the educational community before accepting the findings as truth when, in reality, they remain far removed from the truth. (p. 23)

In spite of these claims of efficacious outcomes, one needs to look closely at the quality and availability of the research. In addition, the entire construct continues to have a dubious theoretical base. It suffers greatly from lack of definition, from issues of test validity and reliability, and from over-promotion. For teachers and administrators to invest time and effort in these pursuits is probably not a productive thing.

At this point you may be thinking that there is no good news. However, the work of Robert Sternberg and Elena Grigorenko in thinking styles seems to offer considerable promise. Sternberg (1997a) writes, "In school, children who are viewed as stupid often suffer from nothing more than a style that mismatches that of their teacher." Sternberg makes it clear that a style is a preferred way of thinking, not an ability. He describes the typical person as having not *a* style, but a *profile* of styles. He and his colleagues have gone on to document and empirically validate a set of instruments that assess one's style profile in the following categories: functions, forms, levels, scope, and leanings. See Figure 10.3 for an explanation of the categories. It is Sternberg's contention that if we really want to reach all our students we must take their styles into account. He notes that so-called gifted students are most likely those whose styles match their patterns of abilities. In other words, their styles match up with the abilities valued at school.

Openly admitting that differences do exist among theorists, he nevertheless makes clear his own viewpoint on findings from his styles research with the general conclusions shown in Figure 10.4 (p. 160). Sternberg says that those educators interested in styles-based teaching and learning would do well to begin with these assumptions.

FIGURE 10.3. A SUMMARY OF STERNBERG'S THINKING STYLES CATEGORIES

- ◆ Functions: Legislative, Executive Judicial
- ◆ Forms: Monarchic, Hierarchic, Oligarchic, Anarchic
- ◆ Levels: Global, Local
- ◆ Scope: Internal, External
- ◆ Leanings: Liberal, Conservative

Sternberg categorizes his own styles work as a "mental self-governance" theory. His careful theorizing has led Sternberg and his colleagues to the conclusion that individuals govern their thoughts and actions in ways that add up to a kind of composite style, based on the following factors: functions, forms, levels, scope, and leanings (see Figure 10.3, p.). The operational definitions of a person's style is derived from a series of tests, each of which is designed to address one of the five factors, called the *Sternberg-Wagner Self-Assessment Inventories.* The tests are available in versions for both students and teachers, and can be found along with explanations of categories, and so on, in Sternberg's *Thinking Styles* (1997). Sternberg and his colleagues have conducted a number of carefully crafted empirical studies in school settings designed to validate the instruments (Sternberg & Grigorenko, 1997a).

An interesting study by Oakland et al. (2000) compared temperament-based learning styles of gifted and nongifted students. Using the *Student Styles Questionnaire* (Horton and Oakland, 1996) to determine the learning styles preferences of 1554 students aged 8 to 17, they found certain significant differences between identified gifted and nongifted students. Students identified as gifted showed a stronger preference for imaginative styles, while nongifted students showed preference for practical styles. On other dimensions such as extroversion/extroversion showed no differences. Regarding gender differences among gifted students, girls showed a much stronger preference for imaginative styles than did boys.

At Level III, there appear to be no published accounts to indicate that any large-scale program evaluation has ever been conducted to determine whether an inservice program or a districtwide intervention in learning styles changes anything. In spite of this disquieting finding, learning styles inservice training and preservice training continues apace as though there were compelling evidence of its positive contribution to school life.

FIGURE 10.4. PRINCIPLES OF THINKING STYLES

1. Styles are preferences in the use of abilities, not abilities themselves.
2. A match between styles and abilities creates a synergy that is more than the sum of its parts.
3. Life choices need to fit styles as well as abilities.
4. People have profiles (or patterns) of styles, not just a single style.
5. Styles are variable across tasks and situation.
6. People differ in the strengths of their preferences.
7. People differ in their stylistic flexibility.
8. Styles are socialized.
9. Styles can vary across the life span.
10. Styles are measurable.
11. Styles are teachable.
12. Styles valued at one time may not be valued at another.
13. Styles valued in one place may not be valued in another.
14. Styles are not, on average, good or bad—it's a question of fit.
15. We confuse stylistic fit with levels of abilities.

SOURCE: Sternberg, R. J. (1997). *Thinking Styles*. Cambridge: Cambridge University Press.

FIGURE 10.5. STERNBERG AND GRIGORENKO'S LEARNING STYLE MODEL

Aspects of the Model	Specific Styles for the Aspect	Characteristics of Each Style
Functions	Legislative	Creates one's own rules, formulates one's own structures and approaches; avoids the prestructured
	Executive	Is an implementer: follows rules; relies on existing structures and predefined rules
	Judicial	Prefers to evaluate, judge, and analyze existing rules and ideas
Forms	Monarchic	Focuses on single goal or task until it is completed
	Hierarchic	Has multiple goals with varying priorities: is comfortable with systematically getting things done
	Oligarchic	Has multiple goals with equal priorities; has difficulty setting priorities for getting things done
	Anarchic	Does not like to be tied down to the current way of doing things; tends to be opposed to existing systems or ways without always having an alternative; has a random approach that often leads to unusual connections
Levels	Local	Prefers specific, concrete details that require precision in execution
	Global	Prefers general problems that require abstract thinking and conceptualization in the world of ideas
Scope	Internal	Prefers working alone, independently of others and on one's own
	External	Prefers to work with and interact with other people
Leanings	Liberal	Goes beyond the current way and permits change from traditional methods (as opposed to the Legislative style, the new ideas do not have to be one's own)
	Conservative	Prefers to follow the traditional and the familiar (may think up one's own ideas, but they are consistent with custom)

CONCLUSION

The concept of styles is appealing. Who wouldn't want to think that everyone has equal ability and that it is merely given to each of us in different ways? Howard Gardner's pioneering work in the development of a theory of multiple intelligences offers great hope for education because it gives us a reality base for considering a wide range of behaviors and abilities within the scope of that elusive word, "intelligence." But his work could be translated into learning styles applications only tangentially. Who wouldn't want to try to find the best way for a child to learn? We all recognize the bias inherent in a school system where so much of the learning reward structure is devoted to reading print and writing answers. Many of the strategies identified for teaching and learning by learning styles advocates make perfect sense, not because of the validity of the learning styles construct, but because they contain elements of strategies for which there is empirical support. However, at this point in time, the burden is still on the learning styles advocates to provide a clearer sense of the beneficial outcomes of a styles-based approach, something we feel they have not done. Certainly, a decision to change methodologies or to do wholesale retraining of teachers based on the research in this area would be a mistake because neither the quantity nor the quality of the evidence is there. The most promising styles area seems to be thinking styles as developed by Sternberg and his colleagues. As the work continues, one would hope to see numbers of Level II studies in the way that such numbers have developed in cooperative learning. Level III work seems to be another matter yet to be undertaken.

REFERENCES

Adams, G. L., & Engelmann, S. (1996). *Research on direct instruction: 25 years beyond DISTAR*. Seattle, WA: Educational Achievement Systems.

Barbe, W. B., & Swassing, R. H. (1979). *Teaching through modality strengths*. Columbus, OH: Zaner-Bloser.

Bennett, C. I. (1990). *Comprehensive multicultural education: Theory and practice*, 2nd ed. Boston: Allyn and Bacon.

Bransford, J., Brown, A., & Cocking, R. (Eds.) (2000). *How people learn: Brain, mind, experience, and school*. Washington, DC: National Academy Press.

Carbo, M. (1992). Giving unequal learners an equal chance: A reply to a biased critique of learning styles. *Remedial and Special Education 13*(1), 19–29.

Carbo, M. (1997). *What every principal should know about teaching reading: How to raise test scores and nurture a love of reading*. Washington, DC: National Reading Styles Institute.

Cornett, C. E. (1983). *What you should know about teaching and learning styles.* Bloomington, IN: Phi Delta Kappa Educational Foundation.

Curry, L. (1990). A critique of the research on learning styles. *Educational Leadership 48*(2), 50–56.

Dunn, R., & Debello, T. (1999). *Improved test scores, attitudes, and behaviors in america's schools: Supervisors success stories.* Westport, CT: Bergin and Garvey.

Dunn, R. (1990). Rita Dunn answers questions on learning styles. *Educational Leadership 48*(2), 15–21.

Dunn, R., Beaudry, J., & Klavas, A. (1989). Survey of research on learning styles. *Educational Leadership 46*(6), 50–58.

Dunn, R. S., Dunn, K. J., & Price, G. (1979). Learning styles/teaching styles: Should they...can they...be matched. *Educational Leadership 36*(4), 238–244.

Dunn, R., Griggs, S., Olson, J., Beasley, M., & Gorman, B. (1995). A meta-analytic validation of the Dunn and Dunn model of learning-style preferences. *Journal of Educational Research 88*(6), 353–362.

Ferrell, B. G. (1983). A factor analytic comparison of four learning styles instruments. *Journal of Educational Psychology 75*(1), 33–39.

Gardner, H. (1983). *Frames of mind: A theory of multiple intelligences.* New York: Basic Books.

Gardner, H. (1993). *Multiple intelligences: The theory in practice.* New York: Basic Books.

Gardner, H. (2000). *The Disciplined Mind.* New York: Penguin Books.

Guild, P. (1994) The culture/learning style connection. *Educational Leadership 51*(8), 16–21.

Guild, P. B., & Garger, S. (1985). *Marching to different drummers.* Alexandria, VA: Association for Supervision and Curriculum Development.

Gregorc, A. F. (1982). *An adult's guide to style.* Maynard, MA: Gabriel Systems.

Henson, K., & Borthwick, P. (1984). Matching styles: A historical look. *Theory into Practice, 23,* 1, 3–9, 31.

Horton, C., & Oakland, T. (1996). *Student styles questionnaire: Star qualities in learning, relating, and working: Classroom applications booklet.* New York: The Psychological Association.

Kagan, J. (1965). Individual differences in the resolution of response uncertainty. *Journal of Personality and Social Psychology, 2,* 154–160.

Kagan, J. (1966). Reflection-impulsivity: The generality and dynamics of conceptual tempo. *Journal of Abnormal Psychology, 71,* 17–24.

Kagan, J., & Messer, S. (1975). A reply to "some misgivings about the matching familiar figures test as a measure of reflection-impulsivity." *Developmental Psychology, 11,* 244–248.

Kavale, K. A., & Forness, S. R. (1987). Substance over style: Assessing the efficacy of modality testing and teaching. *Exceptional Children 54*(4), 228–239.

Kavale, K. A., & Forness, S. R. (1990). Substance over style: A rejoinder to Dunn's animadversions. *Exceptional Children 56*(4), 357–361.

Kavale, K., Hirshoren, A., & Forness, S. (1997). *Meta-analytic validation of the Dunn and Dunn model of learning-style preferences: A critique of what was Dunn.* Unpublished manuscript. Iowa City, IA: Department of Special Education, University of Iowa.

Keefe, J. (1986). *Profiling and utilizing learning style.* Reston, VA: National Association of Secondary School Principles.

Kolb, D. A. (1985). *The learning style inventory.* Boston: McBer & Co.

McCarthy, B. (1987). *The 4MAT system: Teaching to learning styles with right/left mode techniques.* Barrington, IL: Excel.

McCarthy, B., & Morris, S. (1995). *4MAT in action: Sample units for grades K–6,* (3rd ed.). Barrington, IL: Excel.

McCarthy, B., & Morris, S. (1995). *4MAT in action: Sample units for grades K–12,* (3rd ed.). Barrington, IL: Excel

MacLeod, C., Jackson, R., & Palmer, J. (1986). On the relation between spatial ability and field dependence. *Intelligence, 10(2),* 141–151.

Myers, I. B. (1962). *Introduction to type.* Palo Alto, CA: Consulting Psychologists Press.

Oakland, T., Joyce, D., Horton, C., & Glutting, J. (2000). Temperament-based learning styles of identified gifted and nongifted students. *Gifted Child Quarterly, 44(3),* 183–189.

O'Neil, J. (1990a). Findings of styles research murky at best. *Educational Leadership 48*(2), 7.

O'Neil, J. (1990b). Making sense of style. *Educational Leadership 48*(2), 4–9.

Snider, V. E. (1990). What we know about learning styles from research in special education. *Educational Leadership 48*(2), 53.

Snider, V. E. (1992). Learning styles and learning to read: A critique. *Remedial and Special Education, 13*(1), 6–18.

Sternberg, R. (1997a). *Thinking styles.* Cambridge: Cambridge University Press.

Sternberg, R. (Ed.) (2000). *Handbook of intelligence.* Cambridge: Cambridge University Press.

Sternberg, R., & Grigorenko, E. (1997b). Are cognitive styles still in style? *American Psychologist, 52(7),* 700–712.

Swanson, L. J. (1995). *Learning styles: A review of the literature.* (ERIC Document Reproduction Service No. ED387067.)

Witkin, H., & Goodenough, D. (1981). *Cognitive styles: Essence and origins.* New York: International Universities Press.

11

CURRICULUM
INTEGRATION

*Whether it is called best practice, or whole language, or inte-
grated learning, or interdisciplinary studies, by some other
name, or by no name at all, this movement is broad and deep
and enduring.*

Steven Zemelman, Harvey Daniels,
and Arthur Hyde

*Herein lies one of the problems with the notion of integrated
curriculum: Do theory and practice converge to produce more
thorough or comprehensive learning experiences for students,
or do teachers run the risk of leaving wide gaps in students'
understanding of important concepts and subject matter?*

Terrance Mason

All things are connected.

Chief Seattle

The nationwide reform movement has led schools in a multitude of
cases to consider the implementation of integrated curricula. The main
arguments for integrated curricula or interdisciplinary studies as they are
sometimes called, are threefold: (a) the knowledge explosion is very real
and there is simply too much information to be covered in the curriculum;
(b) most school subjects are taught in isolation, and students never are
able to make the connections; and (c) curriculum integration is designed
around problems and concerns students have about themselves and their
world.

One idea behind integration is that by combining subjects around
themes or projects, a certain economy is achieved because much of the
repetitive material that occurs from subject to subject is eliminated.

Flowing from the first idea is a second, which posits that when subjects are connected, students begin to see meaningful relationships because the subject matter serves as a vehicle for learning rather than as an end in itself. And to this can be added the idea that a subject-matter-driven curriculum, particularly one based on separate subjects, fails to address students' concerns about themselves and the world around them. These are among the primary claims of the advocates of curriculum integration. A summary of the rationale for the integration of the curriculum, along with some of the problems with doing so is presented in Figure 11.1.

Heightened teacher collaboration, greater student involvement, increased relevance, greater learner motivation and achievement, higher-level thinking, better content mastery, real-world applications, and fewer fragmented learning experiences are among the improvements that supposedly follow suit when a change to integrated curriculum is made. Most teachers and administrators dream of these outcomes, so the claims tend to be rather attractive.

Integrating the curriculum is not a new idea. The learning done in most "natural" situations including apprenticeships, for example, tends to be seamless. But in school settings, the idea of integrated learning and teaching came to the fore as part of the progressive educational movement of the early twentieth century. In ways that modern educators may not even realize, the progressive movement achieved much in this regard. Language arts and social studies, "subjects" taken for granted in today's elementary curriculum, are themselves interdisciplinary versions of several former separate subjects. And at the secondary level, many districts have for several years integrated their mathematics programs, shucking off the old algebra-geometry-advanced algebra sequence. There are many other examples of progressive influence, including the growing tendency to do "real world" investigations, which by definition are problem-focused rather than being on a single academic discipline.

The current trend, however, goes somewhat further than the prior attempts to coalesce, say, history, geography, and civics into something called social studies. Today, the movement is dedicated to crossing new frontiers between and among school subjects. It should be noted, however, that the philosophical premise remains the same as that advanced during the original progressive movement. Let's take a moment to examine that premise.

ALL THINGS ARE CONNECTED

"Traditional" school programs tend to be subject-centered. That is, the organizing focus in teaching and learning is on separate school subjects, or academic disciplines. In most cases, those subjects are offered separately, even in elementary classrooms. At the secondary level, the distinc-

FIGURE 11.1. ARGUMENTS FOR AND AGAINST INTEGRATING THE CURRICULUM

Arguments for integrating the curriculum

♦ **Psychological/developmental**—Research in developmental and cognitive psychology suggests that individuals learn best when encountering ideas connected to one another.

♦ **Sociocultural**—The current curriculum, especially in the secondary school, is fundamentally obsolete and does not address the needs, interests, and capacities of today's students.

♦ **Motivational**—The integrated curriculum deemphasizes rote learning and content coverage, and because it is often organized around student-selected themes and provides for choice, it will enhance student interest and motivation.

♦ **Pedagogical**—The traditional curriculum is so vast and intractable that educators cannot hope to cover all the so-called essentials for productive living, and therefore they should focus their efforts on providing experiences leading toward internalization of positive attitudes toward learning.

Obstacles to successful curriculum integration

♦ **The trivialization problem**—It is sometimes appropriate for teachers to address ideas within a single content area, and that some ideas are best understood without introducing confusing or inconsequential subject matter.

♦ **The "skills" problem**—A number of educators maintain that students can attempt interdisciplinary work only after they have mastered some elements of disciplinary knowledge, and if integration activities dominate the curriculum, there will be inadequate time to teach these skills.

♦ **The teacher knowledge problem**—If teachers lack knowledge and skills within multiple disciplines, their ability to integrate those disciplines is highly problematic.

♦ **The school structure problem**—Many teachers have never experienced subject integration themselves, being products of discipline-based schooling throughout their lives, which means that vast retraining and reconceptualizing must take place.

♦ **The assessment problem**—The mode of assessment in most school systems is not able to effectively assess students' attainment of deep understanding, the stated goal of integrated learning.

SOURCE: Adapted from Mason, T. C. (1996). Integrated curricula: Potential and problems. *Journal of Teacher Education*, 47(4), 263–270.

tion is even clearer, as signaled by the organization of the school faculty into departments based on academic disciplines. Each subject has a sequence to it, one that generally becomes more technical and abstract through the succeeding years. Each subject also has a scope within a given grade level. The scope of a subject has to do with how broad or wide-ranging the treatment is. The scope and the sequence tend to represent the boundaries of a given subject. But the point is that the focus is always on the subject and its domain of knowledge and skills. The best way to understand the traditional curriculum is to think of its dominant form, the textbook. This is so because most textbooks are written for a particular subject at a particular level, for example, fourth grade mathematics. You could search far and wide for a textbook on, say, seventh grade mathematics and music, but it is doubtful that you would find it, and if you did, how many schools are ready to adopt it?

Curriculum integration, on the other hand, takes a quite different approach to teaching and learning. It is far more than a mere blending of separate subjects. It represents a philosophy of student-centered, often socially relevant learning. By placing the learner rather than the subject matter at the center of gravity, projects and activities take precedence over academic disciplines. This is so because this seems to be the way children and adolescents learn when given a choice. In other words, it is closer to the "natural" way that people learn. The academic disciplines, from such a perspective, are regarded as tools for learning rather than as ends in themselves. If they are tools, so the argument goes, why not blend them wherever it makes sense to do so?

Integrated programs typically eschew textbook treatments. Thus, the curriculum is changed in more ways than one. Most curriculums in American schools are textbook-driven. Textbooks tend to configure and control both scope and sequence. But integrated curriculums focus on group activities and projects; textbooks, if they are used at all, are relegated to the status of resource material. The curriculum still has to come from somewhere, and if it is not to come from textbooks, what are its sources?

The curriculum in integrated settings tends to be site-based. This is disconcerting to commercial publishers because generic textbooks published for use everywhere are simply not applicable. Integrated curriculums are often tied to local issues, especially when those local issues have global connections. Examples include studies of local water supplies, wetlands, and pollution. Or, equally often, units will be constructed around a compelling theme such as local architecture, patterns in nature, or cultural heritage.

Teachers and students are generally involved together in the planning and development of the theme or issue chosen for study. Often, a study begins with a brainstorming session where the teacher leads students through the construction of a "webbing" similar to that shown in Figure

11.2. The webbing, or map, gives focus and structure to the unit, project, or investigation while allowing many avenues of individual or group work. This stage is considered to be very crucial, apparently, because the sense of "ownership" or investiture in the curriculum is thought by advocates to be a motivating force throughout the study. See Figure 11.3 (p. 173) for a step-by-step approach to developing such a unit.

A criticism of integrated or interdisciplinary curriculums is one that is obvious to any essentialist. Because the units are teacher-student developed, they tend to have a seemingly random flavor. The essentialist's need for an orderly scope and sequence of knowledge and skills is often not met, to say the least. To integrated studies advocates, who mostly tend to be progressives, this is the beauty of such a curriculum. It is fair to say, however, that integrated curriculums often tend to favor social studies, language arts, and the arts, though not necessarily in any systematic way, while slighting mathematics—and this is a serious problem. It is not insoluble, but it is difficult to overcome.

There is also a phenomenon known as "the tyranny of integration." Sometimes teachers become so committed to integrated studies that they find themselves trying to integrate everything they teach. This can quickly lead to a different kind of artificiality. The fact of the matter is that not everything probably can or should be integrated. Matters of discretion become paramount when such factors are weighed. The simple idea that is too easily lost sight of is that integration is a *means* to an end and not an end in itself.

THE RESEARCH BASE FOR CURRICULUM INTEGRATION

REMEMBER JOHN DEWEY?

The primary theoretical basis of curriculum integration is found in progressive educational philosophy. The progressive movement, which included such luminaries as John Dewey, William Kilpatrick, George Counts, and Harold Rugg, reached its zenith earlier in the twentieth century. It is a child-centered approach to learning that places great emphasis on creativity, activities, "naturalistic" learning, real-world outcomes, and, above all, experience.

Progressive education came to be known for what it opposed as much as what it advocated. This was a matter of great concern to Dewey and others. Progressives were opposed to the factory-like efficiency model on which schools depended (and still do). They decried the artificial instruction and learning driven by textbooks and written exams. They said that school learning was so unlike the real world that it has little or no meaning to the average child. Robert Hutchins, not a progressive, said it best: "Students resort to the extracurriculum because the curriculum is so stupid."

FIGURE 11.2. AN EXAMPLE OF WEBBING

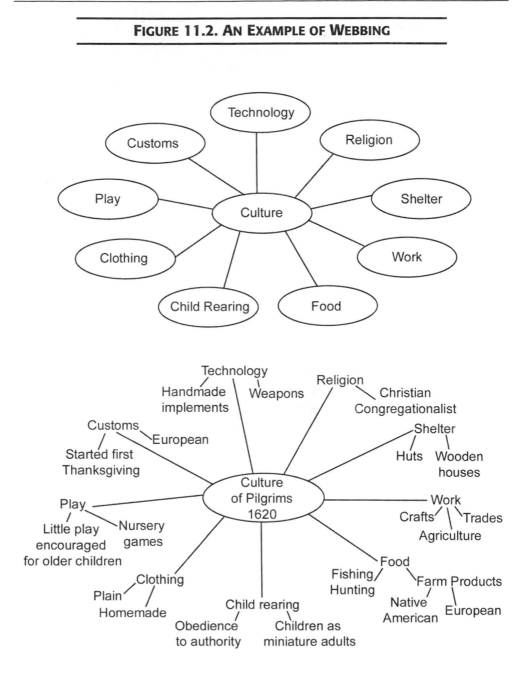

SOURCE: Ellis, A. K. (2001). *Teaching and learning elementary social studies,* 7th ed. Boston: Allyn and Bacon.

FIGURE 11.3. A PROCEDURE FOR
DEVELOPING INTEGRATED UNITS OF STUDY

Step 1—Selecting an organizing center. The "organizing center" is the focus of the curriculum development (i.e., theme, topic of study, concept). Once parameters are explored, the topic must be broadened to provide a base for investigation from various points of view in preparation for the next developmental step.

Step 2—Brainstorming associations. A graphic device (i.e., planning wheel) is useful as teachers and students begin to explore the theme from the perspectives of various discipline fields. The organizing center for the theme is the hub of the wheel; each spoke is a discipline area. The open-ended technique of brainstorming is used to generate spontaneous ideas that will be recorded on the wheel.

Step 3—Establishing guiding questions to serve as a scope and sequence. This step takes the array of brainstormed associations from the wheel and organizes them. Now the course of study begins to take shape. A framework for the unit of study will develop naturally as scope and sequence-guiding questions are developed.

Step 4—Writing activities for implementation. Guiding inquiry questions have been formulated, now the means for exploring them must be developed. Activity design is crucial because it tells what students will be doing. Bloom's taxonomy is a good guideline for activity design, as it will help ensure the cultivation of higher-level thought processes.

SOURCE: Jacobs, H. H. (Ed.) (1989). *Interdisciplinary curriculum: Design and implementation*, pp. 63–56. Alexandria, VA: ASCD.

In his classic work *Interest and Effort in Education,* Dewey wrote eloquently, establishing the thesis of progressivism and therefore of integrated studies:

> Our whole policy of compulsory education rises or falls with our ability to make school life an interesting and absorbing experience to the child. In one sense, there is no such thing as compulsory education. We can have compulsory physical attendance at school; but education comes only through willing

> attention to and participation in school activities. It follows that
> the teacher must select these activities with reference to the
> child's interests, powers, and capacities. In no other way can
> she guarantee that the child will be present. (Dewey, 1913, p. ix)

Such theorizing about the nature of education is foundational to integrated curricular efforts.

The other, more recent theoretical basis for integrated curriculum is found in constructivist theory. As we noted in an earlier chapter, constructivism is a theory of learning that states that each person must construct his or her own reality. The constructivity principle states that "construction should always precede analysis" (Post et al., 1992, p. 10). Put another way, this means that experience is the key to meaningful learning; not someone else's experience abstracted and condensed into textbook form, but one's own direct experience. The current interest in the contributions to thought and language made by the Russian psychologist Lev Vygotsky (1962; see also Moll, 1993) has especially bolstered the argument for the social interactionist aspects so readily prevalent in the group projects associated with integrated and interdisciplinary teaching and learning. So, in this sense, the traditional curriculum of learning alone and doing mainly seatwork is not merely turned around, it is stood on its head. Although the work done in constructivist thought is quite recent, it is essentially in harmony with the earlier thinking of the progressives.

Advocates of integrating the curriculum also cite Level I research in the area of brain function (see Chapter 5). They point to research that indicates that the brain seeks patterns and that this is a basic process. They believe that the brain actually resists learning that is fragmented, personally meaningless, and presented in isolation. Contrariwise, they note that knowledge is learned more quickly and remembered longer when constructed in a meaningful context in which connections between and among ideas are made. (Beane, 1997)

But not everyone agrees. The author Thomas Sowell is particularly critical of interdisciplinary teaching and learning, calling it "another popular buzzword." He notes that much of what passes for interdisciplinary is in fact "*nondisciplinary,* in that it simply ignores boundaries between disciplines." He states further that, "academic disciplines exist precisely because the human mind is inadequate to grasp things whole and spontaneously, or to judge 'the whole person.' Thus mathematics must be separated out for special study, even though it is an ingredient in a vast spectrum of other activities" (Sowell, 1995, p. 205). Sowell's point of view is shared by many who feel that depth of subject matter, crucial coverage, the sequencing of important skills, and other related concerns are inevitably shortchanged in interdisciplinary efforts. Further, this point of view holds that there are indeed many opportunities to relate any single discipline to other spheres of knowledge, and that good teachers have always done that while preserving the integrity of their discipline.

BOLD CLAIMS—LITTLE EVIDENCE

Research at Levels II and III is somewhat dependent on investigations of highly related topics such as block scheduling, team teaching, and self-contained programs, where, by inference, one might conclude that these approaches at least lend themselves to integration. This may be explained by the observation that curriculum integration is itself a large holding company of educational variables that, put together, defies classic research methods. There would simply be too many variables to control if one set out to do traditional controlled studies of the topic as a whole. Often curriculum integration is "integrated" into other reform efforts, for example, block scheduling, which make the task of isolating the curriculum as a treatment variable difficult, to say the least. Additionally, assessment of the outcomes most sought after by advocates of this type of curriculum arrangement is problematic because of the tendency of advocates to challenge the validity of traditional paper and pencil testing.

A qualitative study by Hargreaves and Moore (2000) addressed the relationship between curriculum integration and "classroom relevance" in the practices of 29 seventh- and ninth-grade teachers in Ontario, Canada, schools. Hargreaves and Moore interviewed the teachers, resulting in excess of 1000 pages of text. In addition, they held several group meetings with the teachers and conducted in depth classroom observations of up to 10 days each in 4 of the teachers' classrooms. The purpose of the study was essentially to document the planning, actions, and reflections of a group of teachers committed to integration. The descriptions they provide of the teachers' reflections about their work with students are indeed useful to anyone contemplating the implementation of an integrated curriculum. Hargreaves and Moore concluded that "successful and stimulating integration, we have learned, is most likely when teachers put students and what is relevant and meaningful for students first, and when they have the knowledge and imagination to draw widely on their own and others' subject expertise to make that relevance into an experience that is also rigorous for students" (p. 111).

Hargreaves and Moore also reach another conclusion, one that seems rather curious in light of the fact that they provide no related achievement data to accompany their claim that the teachers' work involved "the use of higher-order thinking skills, the exercise of problem-solving capacities, the application of knowledge to real problems, the valuing of creativity and invention, the embedding of learning in real time and real life, and the importance of learning collaboratively as well as individually" (p. 111). One might reasonably expect that in the light of such claims, some empirical means of validation might be presented.

Kathy Lake (1994) examined the available research and concluded that there are "no detrimental effects on learning when students are involved in an integrated curriculum" (p. 7). How one can conclude that there are no detrimental effects is not clear, but perhaps Lake means that there have been no documented or discernible detrimental effects. She was able to locate a few studies dating back as far as 1965 to show that some students actually learned more in the integrated curriculum, and she noted some educational advantages such as teacher cooperation. However, she was cautious about reaching conclusions about the benefits of integrated studies because of the limited amount of research.

Morrow, Pressley, and Smith (1995) report the interesting results of a well-crafted study of the effects of integrating literacy and science programs. Their results indicate "clear support for integrating literacy and science instruction at the third-grade level with respect to the development of language arts competencies," which "did not come at a cost to science content learning"(p. 25). If advocates of integrating the curriculum wish to substantiate their enthusiastic claims with empirical data, additional studies will have to be conducted. At this stage, the number of empirical studies remains so small that any kind of meaningful meta-analysis that might point to some generalized findings is precluded.

Czerniak, Weber, Sandmann, and Ahern's (1999) review of the literature offers one of the best recent surveys of research findings in curriculum integration. They note that virtually every one of the major professional organizations supports the idea of curriculum integration. This same assertion is made as well by Zemelman, Daniels, and Hyde (1998). Czerniak et al., however, observe that "few empirical studies exist to support the notion that an integrated curriculum is any better than a well-designed traditional curriculum" (p. 421).

A problem that Czerniak et al. cite as not incidental is the lack of any agreed-on operational definition of curriculum integration. Like whole language, the term means many things to many people. Terms often used interchangeably include interdisciplinary, fused, thematic, connected, nested, transdisciplinary, multidisciplinary, and sequenced. As they point out, this only compounds the confusion when it comes to talking about effectiveness. Lederman and Niess (1997) make the same two charges, namely the lack of empirical evidence and confusion over the meaning of terms.

Czerniak et al., searching for supportive evidence cite the following:

> Beane (1995) reported that, on traditional measures of school achievement, students who experience an integrated curriculum do as well as if not better than students who experience a separate-subjects curriculum. Stevenson and Carr (1993) re-

ported increased student interest and achievement in integrated instruction as did Greene (1991).

So in fairness, while it may be said that little empirical evidence exists, there is in fact some. Czerniak et al. note the irony of discipline-based standards set forth by the various professional organizations while those same organizations at the same time advocate integrated curricular approaches.

Vars (1996) notes that "more than 100 studies" have shown that students in interdisciplinary programs "do as well as, and often better than students in so-called conventional programs" (p. 148). His review of the research in interdisciplinary curriculum and instruction is actually more a summary and synthesis of findings than a critical, analytic examination of the quality of the research. In this light, one ought to be reluctant to conclude that the research base is convincingly supportive of integrated or interdisciplinary efforts. A reasonable assessment is that the number of confounding variables and rival hypotheses is sufficient to warrant caution. Still, Vars' contribution is considerable, and interested readers are advised to examine the many published studies he cites. Vars wisely concludes, "In short, research on the effects of interdisciplinary curriculum and instruction affirms the benefits of these approaches, but warns against raising unrealistic expectations in the minds of teachers, students, or parents" (p. 159).

The difficulties inherent in conducting good Level II research have not kept enthusiasts from making wide-ranging claims of the efficacious outcomes of interdisciplinary curriculums. The following six claims are presented in the name of "research" done in this area. While the claims are intriguing and possibly accurate, they seem to go well beyond any sound empirical base at this time.

The first claim is that *interdisciplinary curriculum improves higher level thinking skills.* Here the term *metacurriculum* is invoked. Metacurriculum refers to the larger, more transcendent ideas that emerge when people focus on problems to be solved rather than on the reductionist, bits-and-pieces activities that occupy so much of school life. The suggestion is that students will become more skilled in flexible thinking as they are placed in learning situations that address connections rather than the kinds of computation, workbook, and seatwork skills of the traditional separate subjects curriculum. The evidence that exists to substantiate this claim seems to be missing.

This leads to the second claim that *learning is less fragmented.* Students are provided with a more coherent set of learning experiences and, therefore, with a more unified sense of process and content. If, for example, a theme such as "patterns in the environment" is selected for study, then knowledge and skills from the various disciplines must "cohere" or integrate because they are merely means to a more relevant end, rather than being ends in themselves. This thought has considerable appeal. Who wants to argue against coherence? It is, however, based on a logical discontinuity which could lead one to conclude that a teacher who uses an interdisciplinary curriculum is more likely to present a more connected, coherent world view of learning than does a teacher assigned to teach a single subject. In fact, connections are what any good, well-informed teacher attempts to make, and it is just possible that teacher knowledge, both subject-specific and general, may have as much to do with the making of connections than anything else.

Claim number three is that *interdisciplinary curriculum provides real-world applications, hence heightening the opportunity for transfer of learning.* It is often the case that interdisciplinary units have real-world connections built into them. However, that could be said as well of units taught within the frame of a separate subject. However, the probability is greater that real-world applications will take place in interdisciplinary curriculum settings than in traditional school circumstances. There may well be something to the claim that interdisciplinary efforts with their real-world emphasis lead to learning transfer, but in light of the scant evidence it is more a matter of speculation than conclusion. It is, after all, possible that a real-world emphasis may get in the way of some of the reflective, long-term work necessary to fit people for careers in, for example, physics or the arts. Most skilled pianists, for example, had to spend many hours studying music theory and practicing piano, delaying "relevance" often for years.

The fourth claim is that *improved mastery of content results from interdisciplinary learning.* The case is made in the literature for better understanding, greater retention, and even academic gains as demonstrated by test scores. Perhaps so, but the evidence is not sufficiently in place. More often the case can be made that no evidence is present to lead us to conclude that interdisciplinary curriculum and instruction causes harm to student achievement when compared to other approaches.

Claim number five is that *interdisciplinary learning experiences positively shape a learner's overall approach to knowledge.* The idea is that students will develop a heightened sense of initiative and autonomy in their thinking conduct. Related to this is the idea that students improve their moral perspective by learning to adopt multiple points of view on issues. This is an interesting hypothesis, and one that should be tested empirically.

Claim six in the literature is that *motivation to learn is improved in interdisciplinary settings.* Students become engaged in "thoughtful confrontation" with subject matter. More students are reached because of the greater need for different perspectives and learning styles in solving broad-based problems. Teachers themselves become more motivated because teacher-to-teacher contact is enhanced as team efforts are called for in planning, teaching, and evaluating. It is difficult to make the counterclaim that such an assertion is false; however, the claim itself is unsupported by evidence.

To conclude that because these claims are at present largely unsupported, does not mean that they should be dismissed out of hand. Rather they should be treated as important hypotheses for some focused Level II research. If the claims are changed to hypotheses, we have before us an excellent research agenda that should keep investigators busy for several years, much as good Level II research has been successfully conducted for the cooperative learning agenda.

There appears to be a minimal amount of activity at Level III, with some notable exception. *Humanitas,* an interdisciplinary humanities program for secondary students, was evaluated in the Los Angeles Unified School District using what appears to be a very careful design (Aschbacher, 1991). The program evaluation, carried out by the Center for the Study of Evaluation at UCLA, could well serve as a model for this type of sorely needed research. Achievement comparisons of *Humanitas* students and other students from comparison groups showed that the program had very positive effects on students' writing and history content knowledge during the first year. The improvement continued as students stayed in the program, which they did in greater percentages than did their counterparts in four comparison schools. Other sophisticated aspects of the evaluation included surveys of students, teachers, and administrators, observations in classrooms, analyses of teachers' assignments and examinations, reviews of student portfolios, and an examination of such "educational indicators" as school attendance, discipline problems, and "college-oriented" behaviors by students. Classroom observation, for example, showed that *Humanitas* students spent more time per day in thoughtful discussions with a greater number of students contributing than did comparison groups. And even though *Humanitas* students received assignments judged to be harder than those given to comparison group students, the *Humanitas* students liked school better than did comparison students. I recommend a careful reading of the evaluation study (Aschbacher and Herman, 1989) by personnel in any district interested in doing serious program evaluation. It is a sophisticated, penetrating analysis that serves not only as a guide for meaningful program assessment but as a guide for planning and implementing programs.

Going back more than half a century, one encounters what is generally considered to be the most celebrated program evaluation study ever conducted. It was called "The Eight Year Study," sponsored by the Progressive Education Association, now defunct, but then still a force in education. The purpose of the Eight Year Study (begun in 1933 and reported in 1942) was to determine whether a curriculum designed to meet the "needs and interests" of students is as effective at preparing students for college as is a traditional, subject-centered program. The study involved 30 progressive or experimental high schools that were matched as closely as possible with traditional comparison schools. Much of the curricular experience in the progressive schools was interdisciplinary in nature. The results of the Eight Year Study indicated that students from the progressive schools were as well prepared for college as their traditional counterparts with regard to academics and were more involved in such social and extracurricular activities as yearbook, student government, and clubs. In spite of the evidence, the many pressing issues of World War II obscured the results, and as Decker Walker writes, "the reforms of this period survived only in isolated places and as the seeds of further reforms" (Walker, 1990, p. 72).

We realize that it is stretching things a bit to claim the Eight Year Study as a program evaluation of interdisciplinary curriculums. However, many of the curricular offerings in the progressive schools were what are called "core curriculum," which is a way of combining subjects like English and history, for example, into a single offering called "Social Living." In fact, much of middle school philosophy emerged from the progressive movement, and one of the middle school tenets is to coalesce subjects into integrated studies using block scheduling.

OTHER RESEARCH

Finally, there are some emergent research findings that offer tentative support to the use of an integrated curriculum. One source of such research is the updated effective schools findings. Effective schools research has been conducted for several decades, yielding a variety of lists of school characteristics that distinguish "more effective" schools from schools that are less so. These characteristics are thought by some to have a cause-and-effect relationship with respect to learning. However, please bear in mind that correlations derived by this type of research are not the same as cause-and-effect findings. Such attributions can really only be considered hypotheses, yet to be tested empirically. Still, these characteristics do point toward possibilities of why some schools may be better than others. The most recent effective schools research (Cotton, 1995) identified the following among a long list of classroom and school attributes:

- ♦ Teachers provide instruction that integrates traditional school subjects, as appropriate.
- ♦ Teachers integrate workplace readiness skills into content-area instruction.
- ♦ Administrators and teachers integrate the curriculum, as appropriate.

A second body of research is emerging from the many restructuring efforts currently under way across the nation. Lee and Smith's study of 820 secondary schools led them to conclude that, "the consistent pattern of findings allows us to make quite unequivocal statements about the organizational structure of high schools: students learn more in schools which are restructured" (Lee & Smith, 1994a, p. 23). About 25% of these restructured schools were using "interdisciplinary teaching teams" (Lee & Smith, 1994b).

We recognize the limitations inherent in any hard-and-fast attempt to apply this research to interdisciplinary teaching and learning. But the results reported in this chapter do give us a place to begin, a kind of port of entry to this intriguing landscape. What is needed now is a systematic way in which to enlarge both the quality and quantity of the findings derived from carefully crafted qualitative and quantitative research studies. Perhaps what it will take is the establishment of some sort of center for the study of interdisciplinary curriculum.

CONCLUSION

The idea of approaching the school curriculum from an integrated perspective rather than that of separate subjects is a compelling idea. All of us have been told that separating academic disciplines for scholarly purposes probably makes sense, but even that premise can be questioned in light of the crossing of frontiers in, for example, biology and psychology or genetics and linguistics. But for children and adolescents who are still in the process of adapting, organizing, and otherwise constructing their own schema, such an artificial separation seems to make little sense. On the other hand, students can readily understand the purpose of a project or an activity based on an interesting theme or issue. However, such reasoning would be stronger if it were more fully supported by empirical evidence.

It is also the case that schools are often curious places where large numbers of people congregate but are expected to work separately and only rarely to collaborate. Obviously, integrated studies are a way of bringing people together. Teachers who have become involved in integrated efforts will often remark that they are really getting to know some of their colleagues for the first time even though they may have worked next door to them for years. Students, too, because of the project nature of integrated studies, are given greater opportunity to work with each other. Such experiences surely work to the greater benefit of teachers and students.

On the other hand, the claims made in the name of interdisciplinary curriculum are expansive and may only raise hopes beyond reasonable expectations. If you decide to approach the curriculum from an integrated perspective, you ought to do so for reasons of collegiality and real-world applications. But if you are expecting that such a move will result in higher test scores, well the evidence is tentative at best.

Perhaps this is the time and place to say that higher test scores, a very admirable goal, are not alone a sufficient reason for having schools. School is also about social intelligence, citizenship, participation, and decision making. Please don't misunderstand the intent of this remark. It is not an argument for ignoring test scores. To do so would be folly. So, of course, the best answer is to raise test scores and to meet participatory needs as well. This is the spirit in which you ought to consider curriculum integration. Professional judgment, whether in education or in some other field, is always a difficult, complex enterprise.

REFERENCES

Altshuler, K. (1991). The interdisciplinary classroom. *The Physics Teacher*, *29*(7), 428–429.

Anderson, K. (1991). Interdisciplinary inquiry. *School Arts*, *91*(3), 4.

Aschbacher, P. R. (1991). Humanitas: A thematic curriculum. *Educational Leadership*, *49*(2), 16–19.

Aschbacher, P. R., and Herman, J. L. (1989). *The Humanitas program evaluation final report, 1988–1989*. Los Angeles: UCLA Center for the Study of Evaluation.

Beane, J. (1997). *Curriculum integration: Designing the core of democratic education*. New York: Teachers College Press.

Brophy, J., and Alleman, J. (1991). A caveat: Curriculum integration isn't always a good idea. *Educational Researcher*, *49*(2), 66.

Busshman, J. H. (1991). Reshaping the secondary curriculum. *The Clearing House*, *65*(2), 83–85.

Cotton, K. (1995). *Effective schooling practices: a research synthesis 1995 update*. Portland, OR: Northwest Regional Educational Laboratory.

Czerniak, C., Weber, W., Sandmann, A., and Ahern, J. (1999). A literature review of science and mathematics integration. *School Science and Mathematics, 99(8)*, 421–431.

Dewey, J. (1913). *Interest and effort in education*. Boston: Houghton Mifflin.

Ellis, A. (2001). *Teaching and learning elementary social studies*, 7th ed. Boston: Allyn & Bacon.

Everett, M. (1992). Developmental interdisciplinary schools for the twenty-first century. *The Education Digest*, *57*(7), 57–59.

Hargreaves, A., and Moore, S. (2000). Curriculum integration and classroom relevance: A study of teachers' practice. *Journal of Curriculum & Supervision, 15(2)*, 89-112.

Jacobs, H. H. (Ed.) (1989). *Interdisciplinary curriculum: Design and implementation.* Alexandria, VA: ASCD.

Jacobs, H. H. (1991). Planning for curriculum integration. *Educational Leadership, 49(2)*, 27–28.

Lake, K. (1994). *School improvement research series VIII: Integrated curriculum.* Portland, OR: Northwest Regional Educational Laboratory.

Lee, V. E., and Smith, J. B. (1994a). *Effects of high school restructuring and size on gains in achievement and engagement for early secondary school students.* Madison, WI: Center on Organization and Restructuring of Schools.

Lee, V. E., and Smith, J. B. (1994b). High school restructuring and student achievement. *Issues in Restructuring Schools: Issue Report No. 7.* Madison, WI: Center on Organization and Restructuring of Schools.

Mason, T. C. (1996). Integrated curricula: potential and problems. *Journal of Teacher Education, 47(4)*, 263–270.

Moll, L. C. (Ed.) (1993). *Vygotsky and education: Instructional implications and applications of sociohistorical psychology.* New York: Cambridge University Press.

Morrow, L. M., Pressley, M., and Smith, J. K. (1995). *The effect of a literature-based program integrated into literacy and science instruction on achievement, use and attitudes toward literacy and science.* Reading Research Report No. 37. Athens, GA: National Reading Research Center.

Post, T. R., Ellis, A. K., Humphreys, A. H., and Buggey, L. J. (1997). *Interdisciplinary approaches to curriculum: Themes for teaching.* Upper Saddle River, NJ: Merrill/Prentice-Hall.

Sowell, T. (1995). *The vision of the anointed.* New York: Basic Books.

Spady, W. G., and Marshall, K. J. (1991). Beyond traditional outcome-based education. *Educational Leadership, 49(2)*, 67–72.

Vars, G. (1991). Integrated curriculum in historical perspective. *Educational Leadership, 49(2)*, 14–15.

Vars, G. (1996). The effects of interdisciplinary curriculum and instruction. In Hlebowish, P., and Wraga, W. (Eds.). *Annual review of research for school leaders.* New York: Scholastic.

Vygotsky, L. S. (1962). *Thought and language.* Cambridge, MA: MIT Press.

Walker, D. (1990). *Fundamentals of curriculum.* Orlando, FL: Harcourt Brace Jovanovich.

Zemelman, S., Daniels, H., and Hyde, A. (1998). *Best practice: New standards for teaching and learning in America's schools,* 2nd ed. Portsmouth, NH: Heinemann.

12

COOPERATIVE LEARNING

*An essential instructional skill that all teachers need is
knowing how and when to structure students' learning
goals competitively, individualistically and cooperatively.
Each goal structure has its place; an effective teacher
will use all three appropriately.*

David and Roger Johnson

*The future of cooperative learning is difficult to predict. My
hope is that even when cooperative learning is no longer the
"hot new method," schools and teachers will continue to use
it as a routine part of instruction. My fear is that cooperative
learning will largely disappear as a result of the faddism so
common in American Education.*

Robert Slavin

*Cooperative learning as it is generally applied puts
the very concept of real learning at risk.*

Vicki Randall

Cooperative learning is one of the most durable, if not *the* most durable, educational innovations of our time. It has permeated all levels of teacher training from preservice to inservice. It has been estimated that more that 35,000 teachers and would-be teachers have been trained at the Minneapolis-based Cooperative Learning Center alone. There are more than 900 research studies validating the efficacy of cooperative learning over competitive and individualistic learning (Johnson, Johnson, & Stanne, 2001). And cooperative learning is not a peculiarly American educational phenomenon. It is touted worldwide, from Israel to New Zealand, from Sweden to Japan.

The research claims that detail the elements of cooperative learning are more elaborate and documented than those of any other movement in education today. Study after study finds its way into the scholarly journals. Beyond the numbers of research studies, literally hundreds of articles on application and practice appear annually on this topic. The major professional subject matter associations have all published special editions showing how cooperative learning can be used in mathematics, social studies, language arts, science, and other subject areas. In spite of this, citing what they call the "discrepancy" between the research findings and actual practice, Johnson and Johnson (1999) write, "With the amount of research available, it is surprising that classroom practice is so oriented toward competitive and individualistic learning and schools are so dominated by competitive and individualistic learning structures" (p. 218).

The claims made on behalf of cooperative learning are legendary. Seemingly, it can solve any educational problem. Some years ago, researcher Robert Slavin (1989/1990), himself a recognized authority in the field of cooperative learning, warned:

> Another danger inherent in the success of cooperative learning is that the methods will be oversold and under trained. It is being promoted as an alternative to tracking and within class grouping, as a means of mainstreaming academically handicapped students, as a means of improving race relations in desegregated schools, as a solution to the problems of students at risk, as a means of increasing prosocial behavior among children, as well as a method for simply increasing the achievement of all students. Cooperative learning can in fact accomplish this staggering array of objectives, but not as a result of a single 3-hour inservice session. (p. 3)

Of course, Slavin is perfectly correct that a brief introduction to such a complex idea is hardly sufficient to accomplish anything more than a sense of what cooperative learning is. But note his agreement with the wide range of educational problems that cooperative learning can productively address! If it could do half these things, it would be the pedagogical equivalent of a cure for cancer.

What is this apparently wonderful thing called cooperative learning? How does it work? Can it really bring about fundamental changes for the better in classroom life? Let's take a closer look at it so that you can begin to decide for yourself.

COOPERATIVE-LEARNING MODELS

Cooperative learning takes on many different forms in classrooms, but they all involve students working in groups or teams to achieve certain educational goals. Beyond the most basic premise of working together, students must also depend on each other, a concept called *positive interdependence*. From here cooperative learning takes on specific traits advocated differentially by different developers. In some cases, cooperative learning is conceived of as a generic strategy that one could use in practically any setting or in any course of study. In other cases, cooperative learning is conceived of as subject-matter–specific strategy.

Five or more major models of cooperative learning exist. They have much in common, but the differences among them provide useful distinctions. All five represent training programs for teachers who, having taken the training, should be equipped to implement the various attendant strategies in their classrooms.

David and Roger Johnson (1999) of the University of Minnesota are the authors of the Learning Together model. The model is based in a generic group process theory applicable to all disciplines and grade levels. Students are placed in formal or informal base groups which are charged with solving problems, discussing issues, carrying out projects, and other tasks.

The Johnson and Johnson model is built on five elements, which trace back to the theories of Morton Deutsch (1949), mentioned in Chapter 1. The first element is positive interdependence in which students must believe that they are linked with other students to the point that they cannot succeed unless the other students also succeed. The second element is that of face-to-face interaction in which students must converse with each other, helping one another with the learning tasks, problems, and novel ideas. The third element is individual accountability in which each student must be held accountable for his or her performance with the results given to both the individual and the group. The fourth element is social skills in which students are taught and must use appropriate group interaction skills as part of the learning process. The fifth element is group processing of goal achievement in which student groups must regularly monitor what they are accomplishing and how the group and individuals might function more effectively. Obviously, teachers must be trained in these elements, and they must be able to teach them to their students in turn.

Robert Slavin (1994, 1999) of Johns Hopkins University has developed a cooperative learning model called Student Team Learning. His model is less generic than that of the Johnsons. In fact, it has at least four permutations, each of which is specifically designed to address different concerns. For example, his Cooperative Integrated Reading and Composition (CIRC) model is specifically designed for learning reading and writing in grades 3 through 6. His Team-Assisted Individualization (TAI) model is designed for mathematics learning in grades 3 through 6. Slavin's approach to cooperative learning represents a sophisticated set of strategies which, as he has stated, cannot be acquired in a three-hour workshop session.

Other notable models include that of Shlomo and Yael Sharan (1999) of Israel, which is a general plan for organizing a classroom using a variety of cooperative tactics for different disciplines; that of Spencer Kagan (1998), whose Structural Approach includes such intriguing procedures as *Roundrobin, Corners, Numbered Heads Together, Roundtable,* and *Match Mine;* and Elliot Aronson's *Jigsaw* (1978), composed of interdependent learning teams for academic content applicable to various age groups. Figure 12.1 illustrates the several models which we have described.

In addition to these major models, a number of other cooperative learning approaches have been developed, including DeVries and Edwards' *Teams-Games-Tournaments (TGT)* and Cohen's *Complex Instruction.*

Johnson, Johnson, and Stanne (2001) note that methods of cooperative learning can be placed on a continuum comprised of two large, overarching categories: *direct cooperative learning methods* and *conceptual cooperative learning methods.* Direct methods consist of well-defined procedures that teachers and their students are supposed to follow in lock-step fashion. Conceptual methods are based on frameworks that teachers can adapt as templates to use with lessons and activities which they and their students structure.

Used properly, cooperative learning is designed to supplement and complement direct instruction and the other teaching and learning activities typical of classroom life. Its main function is to replace much of the individual, often competitive, seatwork that so dominates American classrooms. John Goodlad's (1984) research showed that students on average initiate talk only 7 minutes per day. In cooperative-learning environments, that figure changes dramatically.

It should be noted, as well, that the advocates of cooperative learning are not necessarily opposed to individualistic and competitive learning. Their opposition is to its near-complete dominance. Most cooperative learning advocates will say that there is a time and a place for each type of learning, but that there must be considerably more cooperative learning in classrooms than is presently the case.

Slavin's perspective is typical of the movement when he states that "cooperative learning methods share the idea that students work together to learn and are responsible for one another's learning as well as their own" (Slavin, 1991, p. 73). Slavin's well-stated phrase sums up the essence of cooperative learning. Read it carefully.

FIGURE 12.1. MAJOR COOPERATIVE-LEARNING MODELS, THEIR ADVOCATES AND THEIR FOCUS

Researcher/ Educator	Model	Focus
David Johnson & RogerJohnson	*Learning Together* ♦ Formal, Informal, and Cooperative Base Groups	Generic group process theory and skills for the teacher for developing a cooperative classroom. Applicable to all levels and disciplines.
Robert Slavin & Associates	*Student Team Learning* ♦ Student Teams-Achievement Divisions (STAD) ♦ Teams-Games-Tournament (TGT) ♦ Team-Assisted Individualization (TAI) ♦ Cooperative Integrated Reading and Composition (CIRC)	STAD & TGT—general techniques adaptable to most disciplines and grade levels. TAI—specifically for grades 3–6 mathematics. CIRC—specifically for grades 3–6 reading and writing.
Shlomo Sharan & Yael Sharan	*Group Investigation*	A general plan for organizing a classroom using a variety of cooperative strategies for several disciplines.
Spencer Kagan	*Structural Approach* ♦ Roundrobin ♦ Corners ♦ Numbered Heads ♦ Together ♦ Roundtable ♦ Match Mine	"Content-free" ways of organizing social interaction in the classroom and for a variety of grade levels.
Eliot Aronson	*Jigsaw*	Interdependent learning teams for academic material that can be broken down into sections; for varying age groups.

THE CRITICS CORNER

It might seem that everyone is pleased with cooperative learning. Actually, this is not the case. Parents, especially paraents of gifted and talented students, often express their incredulity with the process, sometimes because they do not understand cooperative learning and sometimes because they do. Vicki Randall (1999), an adjunct faculty member at Brigham Young University, expresses several concerns over cooperative learning, questioning its benefits and speculating that it places uneccesary burdens on students.

Randall cites "three weaknesses" of cooperative learning that she thinks teachers and parents ought to be aware of. The first weakness relates to the matter of group members' responsibility for one another's learning. She feels this creates a "heavy responsibility" for young people, noting that "even experienced teachers seldom wish to be held accountable for learning failures in their classrooms" (p. 15). She raises the profound philosophical question, "Can you ultimately be responsible for anyone's learning besides your own?" (p. 15).

A second weakness, as Randall sees it, is found in the design of the cooperative learning group. Groups are typically structured with students of mixed abilities. Randall cites complaints from higher-ability students who grow weary of "going over and over the same material they have already learned or having to explain it to those who could care less" (p. 15). She also points to a study (Mulryan, 1994) that showed low-achieving students in mixed groups become passive and do not focus on the task at hand. She calls these problems "a formula for frustration."

The third flaw is more subtle according to Randall. She notes that cooperative groups typically focus on routine skills, facts, and lower-order thinking, putting the very concept of real learning at risk. She speculates that indeed groups could engage in projects that require higher-order thinking, but that the evidence shows this is seldom the case.

Randall concedes that cooperative learning does have a place in our classrooms, but that it has been oversold and overused. But given the weaknesses she cites, she concludes that users ought to proceed with caution. Not everyone, of course, would agree with her analysis of cooperative learning's inherent weaknesses, but nevertheless she makes a compelling case for its careful, judicious use.

THE RESEARCH BASE FOR COOPERATIVE LEARNING

The Level I research can be traced back to the theories of group dynamics and social interaction developed in the 1930s and 1940s by pioneer researcher Kurt Lewin (1947). As Slavin (1986, p. 276) notes: "A long tradition of research in social psychology has established that group discussion, particularly when group members must publicly commit themselves, is far more effective at changing individuals' attitudes and behaviors than even the most persuasive lecture."

Lewin's ideas were further refined by the social psychologist Morton Deutsch (1949), who derived a theory of group process based on shared goals and rewards. Deutsch postulated that when a group is rewarded based on the behavior of its members, the group members would encourage one another to do whatever helps the group to be rewarded.

The work of Lewin, Deutsch, and others led to new perceptions about the power of truly integrated groups to get things done, to sanction and support members, and to create a different social fabric. It is, of course, in one form or another, an old idea, and to their credit, cooperative learning advocates admit this rather freely. Socrates, for example, used cooperative dialogue between teacher and pupil to advance learning. The Gestalt movement in psychology, which arose in Europe late in the nineteenth century, furnishes much of the original paradigm. Its famous epigram, that "the whole of something is greater than the sum of its individual parts," is fundamental to cooperative efforts. The pioneering work in perception and structural wholeness of such legendary psychologists as Max Wertheimer led to new insights regarding the strengths of collaboration in problem solving. What may have been felt or even known intuitively by some over the centuries (King Arthur's legendary Round Table comes to mind), now had a basis of well-grounded theoretical support. This set the stage for researchers to focus on the efficacy of cooperative group learning in school settings.

At Level II, the sheer amount of empirical evidence that has accumulated from research studies in cooperative learning is staggering. There are literally hundreds of published individual studies as well as numerous reviews, syntheses, and meta-analyses. There appears to be no review, synthesis, or meta-analysis that concludes that cooperative learning is deficient as a means to raise student achievement. In general, the conclusions are the same, and all tend to be mainly supportive.

Slavin's (1991) synthesis of the research on cooperative learning yields four main conclusions, each of which is consistent with the pure or basic research and theoretical model derived from Wertheimer, Lewin, Deutsch, and others. The conclusions are rather sweeping, but they certainly have a sound empirical foundation:

♦ For enhancing student achievement, the most successful approaches have incorporated two key elements: group goals and individual accountability; that is, groups are rewarded based on the individual learning of all group members.

♦ When group goals and individual accountability are clear, achievement effects of cooperative learning are consistently positive; 37 of 44 experimental/control comparisons of at least 4 weeks duration yielded significant positive effects, and none favored traditional methods.

♦ Positive achievement effects of cooperative learning have been found to about the same degree at all grade levels from 2 to 12, in all major subjects of the curriculum, and in urban, rural, and suburban schools. Effects are equally positive for high, average, and low achievers.

♦ Positive effects of cooperative learning have been documented consistently for such diverse outcomes as self-esteem, intergroup relations, acceptance of academically handicapped students, attitudes toward school, and ability to work with others.

A meta-analysis was conducted by Z. Qin and David and Roger Johnson (1995) in which these researchers examined the effects of cooperative learning on problem solving. Having examined research studies done between 1929 and 1993, they concluded that cooperative learners outperformed their individualistic and/or competitive counterparts in all four of the problem-solving areas examined: linguistic, nonlinguistic, well-defined, and ill-defined. These researchers concluded, "The practical implications of the finding that cooperation generally improves problem solving are obvious: On the job and in the classroom, cooperative groups will be better able to deal with complex problems than will competitors working alone" (p. 140).

The most recent meta-analysis of cooperative learning was conducted by Johnson, Johnson, and Stanne (2001). They reviewed 148 studies that yielded 188 separate comparisons of cooperative vs. control methods. In the vast majority of situations, the control groups were based on individualistic learning, although some were competitive. The independent variable, obviously, was cooperative learning, and the dependent variable of their investigative synthesis was student achievement. It is worth noting that 50% of the studies were of a duration of 30 or more lessons, 7% were of a single lesson, and 43% lasted for periods of 2 to 29 sessions.

The results of this meta-analysis clearly favor cooperative learning over both individualistic and competitive approaches. In the case of the Johnson and Johnson (1999) model *Learning Together*, the effect sizes were quite large: 1.03 in favor of cooperative over individualistic learning and .85 in favor of cooperative over competitive learning. Positive effect-size differences were found favoring cooperation in comparisons with individualistic and competitive learning for all the other major models, ranging from .18 to .66. It should be noted that certain models have been studied far more systematically than others. In fact, no studies appear to have been done on Kagan's *Cooperative Learning Structures* model, whereas 86 studies were reported in this meta-analysis alone for Johnson and Johnson's *Learning Together* model.

At Level III, Stevens and Slavin (1995a; 1995b) conducted an impressive school evaluation study, the results of which indicated that cooperative learning could be effective in changing the school and classroom organization and instructional approach. Their research also shows that such large-scale implementation can be done effectively, and that learning can be enhanced for a variety of types of students when cooperative learning is used appropriately. They concluded their evaluation with this commentary:

> This study is the first and only evaluation of a cooperative elementary school. It is not merely another study of cooperative learning; it is the only study to evaluate cooperative learning as the focus of schoolwide change, the only study to evaluate cooperative learning in many subjects at once, and one of the few to show the effects of cooperative learning over a multiyear period. (p. 347)

This appears to be the only such published Level III research. This level of research is greatly needed by the profession, and, unfortunately, it is seldom present in the annals of innovation. The hope is that this will be the first of many such studies on not only cooperative learning, but on all of the innovations mentioned in this book.

CONCLUSION

Of all the educational innovations reviewed in this book, cooperative learning has the best and largest empirical base. It is not a perfect base, and as Slavin (1989/1990) pointed out, more research is needed at senior high school levels as well as at college and university levels. This in fact appears to be happening increasingly (Johnson, Johnson, & Stanne, 2001). It is also instructive to note that a good beginning has been made in the conduct of much-needed program evaluation or Level III research. Slavin also notes that the appropriateness of cooperative-learning strategies for the advancement of higher-order conceptual learning is yet to be established firmly. However, the Qin, Johnson, and Johnson research mentioned earlier is certainly a start in that direction.

For the administrator or teacher who wishes to bring about positive change in a more or less traditional school environment, cooperative learning would seem to be well worth exploring. To do it well takes considerable training and motivation. And to convince some parents and other community members that it is more than kids sharing answers with each other will take some doing. These are comments one could make about any innovation, but in this case, the innovator will have little trouble finding supportive evidence.

Cooperative learning has been used in school settings for more than three decades now, and the question might arise whether it has hit its peak. Actually, the number of studies that Johnson, Johnson, and Stanne (2001) reference in their meta-analysis shows far more studies from the 1990s than from the 1980s and 1970s combined. Perhaps it is safe to say about cooperative learning that it has become a staple of school life.

REFERENCES

Aronson, E., Blaney, N., Stephan, C., Sikes, J., and Snapp, M. (1978). *The Jigsaw classroom.* Beverly Hills, CA: Sage.

Deutsch, M. (1949). A theory of cooperation and competition. *Human Relations, 2,* 129–152.

Gilles, R. (1999). Maintenance of cooperative and helping behaviors in reconstituted groups. *The Journal of Educational Research, 92*(6), 357–363.

Goodlad, J. (1984). *A place called school.* New York: McGraw-Hill.

Johnson, D., and Johnson, R. (1989). *Leading the cooperative school.* Edina, MN: Interaction Book Company.

Johnson, D., and Johnson, R. (1994). *Cooperative learning in the classroom.* Alexandria, VA: Association for Supervision and Curriculum Development.

Johnson, D., and Johnson, R. (1999). *Learning together and alone. Cooperative, competitive, and individualistic learning, 5th edition.* Boston: Allyn and Bacon, Inc.

Johnson, D., and Johnson, R. (2001). *Cooperation and competition: Theory and research,* 2nd ed. Edina, MN: Interaction Book Company.

Johnson, D., Johnson, R., and Holubec, E. (1988). *Cooperation in the classroom.* Edina, MN: Interaction Book Co.

Johnson, D., Johnson, R., and Stanne, M. (2001). *Methods of cooperative learning: What can we prove works?* Minneapolis, MN: University of Minnesota Cooperative Learning Center. (This study was completed as part of a research project for the Florida State Department of Education.)

Kagan, S. (1989). *Cooperative learning resources for teachers.* San Juan Capistrano, CA: Resources for Teachers.

Kagan, S. (1989/90). The structural approach to cooperative learning. *Educational Leadership, 47*(4), 12–16.

Kagan, S. (1997). *Cooperative Learning.* Kagan Cooperative.

Lewin, K. (1947). *Field theory in social sciences.* New York: Harper and Row.

Mulryan, C. (1994). Perceptions of intermediate students' cooperative small-group work in mathematics. *Journal of Educational Research, 87,* 280–290.

Qin, Z., Johnson, D. W., and Johnson, R. T. (1995). Cooperative versus competitive efforts and problem solving. *Review of Educational Research, 65*(2), 129–143.

Randall, V. (2000, March/April). Cooperative learning: Abused and overused? *Gifted Child Today,* 14–16.

Sharan, S. (Ed.) (1990). *Cooperative learning: Theory and research.* New York: Praeger.

Sharan, S. (Ed.) (1999). *Handbook of cooperative learning methods.* New York: Praeger.

Slavin, R. (1994). *Cooperative learning: Theory, research, and practice.* Boston: Allyn and Bacon.

Slavin, R. (1989/1990). Research on cooperative learning: Consensus and controversy. *Educational Leadership, 47*(4), 52–54.

Slavin, R. (1991). Synthesis of research on cooperative learning. *Educational Leadership, 48*(5), 71–82.

Slavin, R. (1995). Synthesis of research on cooperative learning. In Page, J. A. (Ed.) *Beyond tracking: Finding success in inclusive schools.* Bloomington, IN: Phi Delta Kappa Educational Foundation.

Slavin, R. (1999). *Educational psychology: Theory and practice.* Boston: Allyn and Bacon.

Slavin, R., et al. (Eds.) (1985). *Learning to cooperate, cooperating to learn.* New York: Plenum Press.

Stevens, R. J., and Slavin, R. (1995a). Effects of a cooperative learning approach in reading and writing on academically handicapped and non-handicapped students. *The Elementary School Journal, 95*(3), 241–261.

Stevens, R. J., and Slavin, R. (1995b). The cooperative elementary school: Effects on students' achievement, attitudes, and social relations. *American Educational Research Journal, 32*(2), 321–351.

13

SUCCESS FOR ALL AND
SCHOOLWIDE REFORM

*Research-based, school-by-school reform is in its
infancy, but it shows great potential. To abandon it
because a few schools failed or because a few teachers
don't like it would be like abandoning aviation in the
1920's because a few airplanes crashed. Success for All
is one of the greatest success stories of educational
research and reform.*

Robert Slavin and Nancy Madden

*The issue of whether the use of Success for All (SFA)
is supported by valid research is probably the most
important and relevant research discussion for
practitioners in recent years.*

Stanley Pogrow

Honest disagreement is often a sign of progress.

Mohandas K. Gandhi.

In 1999, the American Institutes for Research, commissioned by five
leading education groups to review the research evidence behind major
educational innovations, gave its "seal of approval" to just three programs. *Success for All,* a schoolwide reform program developed at Johns
Hopkins University by Robert Slavin and his associates, was one of the
three programs. *Success for All,* a program that originated in the late 1980s,
is a schoolwide restructuring effort designed to ensure early school success in reading and other related curricular areas.

Recent Congressional funding trends have reformulated Title I policy
away from programs with a specific curricular/instructional focus and
toward "schoolwide" reform programs. At this point, *Success for All* is the

single largest recipient of funds from the U.S. Department of Education. This is so in good measure because *Success for All* has shown evaluation outcomes that have impressed officials of such influential agencies as the American Institutes of Research and the Thomas Fordham Foundation.

Success for All has indeed been successful if school adoptions were the criterion. Slavin (2000) estimates that more than 1800 schools serving about a million children are enrolled in *SFA*. It has also been successful by another account, dollars raised for research, development, and dissemination. Stanley Pogrow (2000) estimates that *SFA* and related projects undertaken at Slavin's Center for Research on the Education of Students Placed at Risk at Johns Hopkins received 35% of the total federal dollars allocated for the dissemination of schoolwide models in a recent funding round. Progrow concludes that "the lion's share of the new grants go to Slavin and his associates" (p. 599).

What is *Success for All*? Why has it become *the* schoolwide reform model across the country? Why have the Congress and the Department of Education looked on it so favorably? Why have so many school districts adopted it? Why are certain other researchers and program developers so upset over *SFA*'s ascendancy? And of course, what does the research say?

THE SUCCESS FOR ALL MODEL

Success for All is a schoolwide reform model composed mainly of a reading program designed to improve basic reading skills. The *SFA* philosophy calls for a comprehensive, balanced reading program that combines phonics skills development in the context of language-rich and literature-rich learning environments. The focus is on early intervention and the prevention of reading difficulties. Vocabulary building, auditory discrimination, sound blending, and other phonics-based activities are emphasized, but within cooperative group settings. Its companion program, *Roots and Wings*, emphasizes reading, mathematics, social studies, and science for students beyond primary levels. According to *Atlantic Monthly* writer Nicholas Lemann (1998), it has been described as "prescriptive," "highly structured," even "teacher proof."

Slavin et al. (1996) describe *SFA* as a comprehensive restructuring program for elementary schools "designed to make the idea that all children can learn a practical, daily organizing principle for schools, especially those serving many children placed at risk" (p. xii). The authors go on to note that the typical approaches used in elementary schools are not supportive of prevention and early intervention, something that *SFA* is designed to do. They note that although kindergarten and first grade often appear to go pretty well for many students, in fact what begins to occur is a noticeable falling behind, often resulting in eventual remediation, special education, or retention. A key assumption of *SFA* is that every child can learn, even those who are so often written off as incapable, poorly motivated, or otherwise at risk for school success. The authors say that, yes, some children need more help than others and may even need different approaches to teaching and learning, but the idea remains that every child can become a successful reader.

Schools that elect (faculty must approve with an 80% favorable vote) to use *SFA* are exhorted to use it according to the script. The developers say its probabilities of working well are in direct proportion to the extent that school personnel follow its protocols faithfully. Like so many other programs that have had their share of successes and failures, untoward outcomes are often traced directly to failure to follow the prescription. The authors write,

> The most important idea in *Success for All* is that the school must relentlessly stick with every child until that child is succeeding. If prevention is not enough, the child may need tutoring. If this is not enough, he or she may need help with behavior or attendance or eyeglasses. If this is not enough, he or she may need a modified approach to reading. The school does not merely provide services to children, it constantly assesses the results of the services it provides and keeps varying or adding services until every child is successful. (Slavin, et al, 1996, p. 3)

The major elements of *Success for All* are detailed in Figure 13.1.

FIGURE 13.1. MAJOR ELEMENTS OF SUCCESS FOR ALL

Success for All is a schoolwide program for students in grades pre-K through 6 that organizes resources to attempt to ensure that virtually every student will reach the third grade on time with adequate basic skills and build on this basis throughout the elementary grades and that no student will be allowed to "fall between the cracks." The main elements of the program follow.

Tutors. In grades 1–3, specially trained certified teachers and paraprofessionals work one-to-one with any students who are failing to keep up with their classmates in reading. Tutorial instruction is closely coordinated with regular classroom instruction. It takes place 20 minutes each day during times other than reading periods.

Schoolwide Curriculum. During reading periods, students are regrouped across age lines so that each reading class contains students who are all at a single reading level. Use of tutors as reading teachers during reading time reduces the size of most reading classes to about 20. The reading program in grades K–1 emphasizes language and comprehension skills, phonics, sound blending, and use of shared stories that students read to one another in pairs. The shared stores combine teacher-read material with phonetically regular student material to teach decoding and comprehension in the context of meaningful, engaging stories. In grades 2–6, students use novels or basals but not workbooks. This program emphasizes cooperative learning activities built around partner reading, identification of characters, settings, problems, and problem solutions in narratives, story summarization, writing, and direct instruction in reading comprehension skills. At all levels, students are required to read books of their own choice for 20 minutes at home each evening. Classroom libraries of trade books are provided for this purpose. Cooperative learning programs in writing/language arts are used in grades K–6.

Preschool and Kindergarten. The preschool and kindergarten programs in Success for All emphasize language development, readiness, and self-concept. Preschools and Kindergartens use thematic units, language development activities, and a program called Story Telling and Retelling (StaR).

Eight-Week's Assessments. Students in grades 1–6 are assessed every eight weeks to determine whether they are making adequate progress in reading. This information is used to suggest alternative teaching strategies in the regular classroom, changes in reading group placement, provision of tutoring services, or other means of meeting students' needs.

Family Support Team. A family support team works in each school to help support parents in ensuring the success of their children, focusing on parent education, parent involvement, attendance: and student behavior. This team is composed of existing or additional staff members, such as parent liaisons, social workers, counselors, and vice principals.

Facilitator. A program facilitator works with teachers to help them implement the reading program, manages the eight-week assessments, assists the family support team, makes sure that all staff members are communicating with one another, and helps the staff as a whole make certain that every child is making adequate progress.

In summary, *SFA* is a structured reading program that emphasizes story telling and retelling along with such skill development activities as phonics, vocabulary building, auditory discrimination, and sound blending using cooperative learning strategies. For students at grades 1 to 3, the daily reading period is scheduled for 90 minutes with students grouped into homogeneous cross-grade ability groups. One-on-one tutoring for students reading below grade level is provided by specially trained certified teachers. Assessments take place every eight weeks in order to determine individual student progress, adjust reading group placements, and assign tutoring to those who need it. Teachers and tutors are given special training in *SFA* curriculum and instruction prior to the start of the year and throughout. In addition, family support teams provide parent education and assist families in helping their children with the school experience. A facilitator works with school staff in order to ensure program implementation, and an advisory committee comprised of the school principal, facilitator, teacher and parent representatives, and family support staff meets regularly to review the program. (Adapted from Weiler, 1998.)

LEVEL I THEORY AND RESEARCH

Not much has apparently been written about the theoretical dimensions of *Success for All.* In fact the program has been criticized on those grounds among others. It does seem to contain elements of behaviorism, essentialism, with certain qualities of progressivsm. It is behavioristic in that it invokes the technical interest in learning based on observable outcomes. Reductionism plays a key role. For example, the "Tutoring Diagnostic Assessment Checklist" (Slavin et al., 1996, pp. 76–77) is a scripted guide, broken down into 35 skills that the tutor must verify the child has mastered or not. By using the checklist, the tutor is able to determine whether the child is having problems pronouncing words, recognizing letters, or comprehending text, or whether the child has even more basic problems. On the basis of such a diagnosis, the tutor then makes a plan tailored to the specific needs of the learner. The program also contains elements of progressivsm to be sure, particularly in the form of cooperative learning reading activities. But the theoretical and empirically documented elements of behaviorism, including reinforcement, frequent testing, repetition, feedback, record keeping, and incentives are all there.

Greeno (1998) writes, "A key assumption of behaviorist educational practice is that complex skills are learned by acquiring simpler components followed by combinations of these into more complex behavioral abilities" (p. 16). This reasonably describes *SFA*'s approach. Lessons, tasks, and assessments are organized and sequenced according to this concept from simple to increasingly complex expectations.

As for essentialism, many of its familiar arguments are implicit in *Success for All*. Increasing numbers of our children are not learning basic, essential skills; they will not be prepared for the increasingly complex world they will inherit. This leaves us with the untold costs of leaving certain people behind, of letting an entire generation slip through our fingers. The social and economic benefits of educating all cannot be denied. These arguments are well known but compelling nonetheless. And in keeping with the essentialist tradition, there is a willingness to use certain progressive methods if they are perceived to be useful to the goals, in this case of basic literacy and numeracy.

So, it is probably safe to say that *Success for All* is eclectic in that it draws on several psychologies and world views of education. Without doubt it is rooted in empirically-validated findings from a number of quarters. But of course, when a new construct is fashioned, it becomes incumbent on the developers to point to empirically-validated claims, not of the original and often separate pieces of which it is built, as so often has been the case when purveyors make "research-based" claims.

It is certainly conventional wisdom to assume that a well-founded innovation ought to have a sound theoretical, or Level I, construct. That assumption is one of the recurring themes of this book. Nevertheless, two of the programs showing the most consistently positive empirical findings, Direct Instruction and SFA, are lacking such a clear construct. Reviews by the Thomas Fordham Foundation (Traub, 1999) and by the American Institutes of Research (Herman, 1999) both concluded that DI and SFA met the highest standards of evaluation rigor and produced most efficacious academic outcomes. And in fairness certainly to SFA, one could make an inferential case for theory pretty much as I have attempted to do by citing elements of essentialism, behaviorism, and progressivism as deep structure.

LEVEL II AND LEVEL III RESEARCH

In an article titled "Research on Achievement Outcomes of Success for All: A Summary and Response to Critics (2000)," Slavin and Nancy Madden, CEO and president of the Success for All Foundation, cite the numerous empirical findings validating the success, as defined primarily by academic achievement, of *SFA*. They point out that research has been conducted not only by the developers themselves, but by a number of third-party investigations. In fact, they name the names of 52 different researchers who have investigated *SFA* (Slavin & Madden, 2000, p. 66). They go on to state that all of the research they cite has compared *SFA* to matched control school settings using standardized tests of reading ability.

The standard approach used to ascertain the effects of *SFA* is to match an *SFA* school with a "control" school having a similar academic, ethnic, and socioeconomic profile. That accomplished, the next step is to assess and compare reading scores using standardized reading measures as pre- and posttests. The term "control" is probably misapplied because the studies are obviously not controlled experiments. It seems to me a better term would be "comparison" schools. Nonetheless, this approach where comparisons of achievement are used under reasonably controlled circumstances is far better than that which is found (more typically not found) when innovative programs are adopted.

Robert Slavin (1998) describes *SFA* as "without any doubt the most extensively researched whole-school reform model in existence." He may be right. He notes that dozens of American Educational Research Association (AERA) papers and technical reports have been written and articles published in leading education research journals. He goes on further to say that almost all of the studies conducted on the effects of *SFA* have shown favorable results. He claims that of the 52 researchers mentioned above, 47 found results favorable to *SFA*. Further, he notes that *SFA*, unlike so many other educational innovations, has been studied in the context of carefully crafted comparisons with schools using other approaches.

Slavin's research done with colleagues on the effects of *SFA* has been criticized by a few other researchers on the grounds that the developer is also the assessor. Well, yes, that could be a problem, and it is in those cases where the developer depends upon essentially unpublished research to make the case. But this is not necessarily the situation here. The research of Slavin and colleagues has been published in the most prestigious educational research journals, well known for their high gatekeeping standards. In other words, there is "third party" assessment in the form of jurors who decide on a submitted article's fate. If only all program developers would research their own products to the extent that Slavin has, there would be some hope for progress. Further, Slavin has consistently made his own data available to others who for reasons of their own may wish to utilize or review it.

Beyond that, there has been considerable research activity on *SFA* done by investigators other than Slavin and colleagues. Let us look at some of that.

Richard Venezky of the University of Delaware studied *SFA*'s implementation in the Baltimore, Maryland, Public Schools from 1987 to 1993. He observed that *SFA* students had fallen below grade level on standardized tests by grade five. Venezky challenged the citing of *SFA* student gains over control group classes in Baltimore by Slavin as a valid indicator of success, but it does seem, in Slavin's defense, that given the extreme poverty conditions of the *SFA* and control group schools, such gains have to be taken into account. That the *SFA* stduents did not on average attain grade level, while unfortunate, should not diminish what was accomplished.

An evaluation study of reading achievement by bilingual primary-age students conducted by investigators at the Southwest Regional Laboratory (1995) found results consistent with other evaluations showing "substantial positive effects on reading achievement for children who start the program in first grade or earlier." The study's authors conclude that these results add to a "growing research base attesting to *Success for All's* effectiveness with English language learners."

Jeanne Weiler (1998) of Teachers College writes, in her summary of evaluations of *SFA*, that "results from research conducted by the program developers, as well as by external evaluators, have shown the *SFA* program to be effective in enhancing the reading achievement of economically disadvantaged and nonnative English speaking students" (p. 1). Weiler cites numerous program evaluation studies of *SFA*, the majority of which are supportive. She notes that the research indicates that students in the bottom quartile appear to derive the greatest benefits from *SFA,* and that it is less clear whether average and above average students do benefit from it. She notes as well that longitudinal studies have shown that former *SFA* students do not maintain their early reading superiority over non-*SFA* students in middle grades. This troublesome finding seems to be a problem across the board and not necessarily specific to *SFA*. Weiler provides wise counsel to would-be adopters: "Practitioners considering implementing the *SFA* model would be well advised to delve more deeply into the existing research to determine whether such an approach would be suitable for their students."

An evaluation study by Madden et al. (1993) reported outcomes based on 3 to 4 years of implementation of *SFA* in Baltimore schools. The investigators found rather large effect sizes (from .51 to 1.00) favoring the reading abilities of *SFA* students over comparison schools students. They also reported reduced retention rates and improved attendance on the part of *SFA* students over comparison schools. They do note the considerable cost to a school of *SFA* as an issue to be considered, but balance that against the costs of retaining students, of special education placements, and so on. These achievement results show some measure of contrast with the conclusions reached by Venezky, whose conclusions about the Baltimore *SFA* results were less supportive.

The Houston, Texas, Independent School District (HISD) issued the findings of a program evaluation of *SFA* for the 1997-98 school year. The program was utilized at 66 schools in the district, serving 43,329 students, including all first graders in those schools. The questions posed for evaluation included: How consistently was the model implemented? What were teacher and facilitator perceptions and recommendations? and Did the program succeed in bringing students to grade level?

Survey results indicated that the *SFA* model was not always maintained for a variety of reasons. Reading test score results were mixed and not easily interpreted. According to the report, the passing rate for *SFA* students on *reading* subtests of the Texas state assessment ranged from 83% to 85% for grades 3, 4, and 5, and 67% at grade 6. The Stanford 9 percentile ranks indicated that, overall, *SFA* students who had just entered first grade were reading at the same level as the normative sample. However, students in the remainder of the grades (2 to 6) in which *SFA* is found in the district were ranked below average. The Houston summary made no mention of comparison or control schools, so it is difficult to derive any firm conclusions from this evaluation.

The studies cited above tend to be exemplary of the kind of research devoted to *SFA*. To enumerate them all is beyond the scope and purpose of this book. To the extent that you are interested in reading any or all of them, you are referred to the reference section of this chapter which will more than get you started.

THE CONTINUING CONTROVERSY OVER SUCCESS FOR ALL

Stanley Progrow (1998, 1999, 2000, 2000a) is one of *SFA*'s most outspoken critics. He cites innumberable problems ranging from his objection to *SFA*'s "lion's share" of Title I grant funds to conflicts of interest on the part of Slavin and his fellow developers/researchers. Pogrow points to what he believes are highly biased research methods "that make failure look like success," citing instances where control schools were not appropriately selected, were dropped for inexplicable reasons, were not taught proper curriculum content, or simply were not given equal instructional time. These are serious charges in view of the time, money, and hopes at stake. Progrow's criticisms are literally too many to mention, but here are a few more:

♦ Why is *SFA* receiving dissemination grant money when it is already more than 15 years old and does $44 million of business annually?

♦ What is *SFA*'s definition of success? Title I programs have nearly always shown K–3 achievement gains, but inevitably encounter serious problems through the middle grades and beyond, just as *SFA* has.

♦ In spite of test score gains, *SFA* offers no convinicing evidence that it works in the "real world" of urban schools where high student and faculty turnover, absenteeism, and so on, are always a reality. (This is basically Pogrow's rejoinder to Slavin's comments that where schools did not achieve up to expectation, it was because the *SFA* model was not faithfully followed.)

- ♦ *SFA* teaches to particular criterion tests so actual gains compared to control schools may not have occurred.

Pogrow may be *SFA*'s most published and most persistent critic, but he is not alone in his discontents. The eminent researcher Herbert Walberg and his doctoral student Rebecca Greenberg (1999a, 1999b) have also weighed in. One of their main concerns is the issue that inevitably arises when developers of a program or product are also its researchers. (They don't mention the issue of developers not merely as researchers, but as purveyors as well.) They write, "Program designers who evaluate their own program, however, may have conflicts of interest." They express their "suspicion" of unconscious bias, a problem "long recognized in the sciences."

Walberg and Greenberg point to the care taken in the medical profession to avoid bias through the technique of double-blind experiments designed to eliminate investigator and experimenter effects. This, they conclude, has hardly been the case with *SFA*. They note "that Slavin's claims for *SFA* are extraordinary, but the independent evaluations show negative effects of the program" (Greenberg & Walberg, 1998).

They cite the work of Richard Venesky (1998) as well as an outside evaluation conducted by Jones et al. (1998) as evidence that *SFA* simply does not produce the results claimed by Slavin and his associates. Further, they list numerous threats to the internal and external validity of those studies that do show positive effects of *SFA*. Among those threats are achievement gains on tests due to practice testing not available to control schools, an irrelevant theoretical framework, inappropriate choice of researchers, noncomparable comparison groups, and inaccurate recording of data, among others. Again, these are serious claims that cannot be taken lightly considering the source.

ENTER THE WEB

As you might have guessed in these days of breakthrough technologies, a Web site has been developed the purpose of which is to keep folks updated on *SFA*. In this case, what we have is a Web site for the disaffected, one started and maintained by disenchanted teachers in *SFA* schools. Here it is: http://www.alt.sfa.com Anyone wishing to find attack after attack on *SFA* might well begin here. The Web site carries everything from copies of published articles, such as those written by Pogrow and Walberg and Greenberg, to teacher, principal, and parent comments on the negative effects of *SFA*. Mainly the complaints are that *SFA* is too controlling and teacher-proof; that it reduces professionals to monitors; that *SFA* promotes misleading claims about its effectiveness; that the record keeping associated with the program is exhorbitant; and that the expenses incurred by adopting *SFA* could be better used otherwise. Obviously, anyone in this day and age can start a Web site, so one ought not to infer widespread dissatisfaction on the basis of its establishment alone. We all know that the disaffected are proportionately far more likely to take action, speak up, write letters, etc., than are those who support efforts. Ask any political figure or school administrator should you doubt this. As Slavin and Madden have pointed out, "He [Pogrow] carries on about two teachers who started a web site criticizing Success for All, but fails to cite three studies that found the great majority of teachers in experienced [sic] schools continue to support the program (and fails to note that 80% of teachers have to support the program in a secret ballot in the first place). If 20% of teachers dislike SFA, that's 10,000 unhappy teachers, enough to fill up many web sites. But it's 40,000 happy ones." (2000a, p. 1).

ANSWERS TO CRITICS

These criticisms have naturally left Slavin and *SFA* on the defensive, a position he may not have anticipated in the wake of the many positive outcomes reported by him and his colleagues in highly reputable journals. Calling *SFA* "one of the greatest success stories of educational research and reform" (2000, p. 38), Slavin cites in his own and *SFA*'s defense that contrary to published accusations:

- His studies do utilize control group designs.
- The reading achievement effect sizes favoring SFA over control groups in the period 1988–1999 range from .39 at grade 3 to .62 at grade 5 (see Figure 13.2).
- The tests used to measure reading achievement are high profile standardized tests, including the Woodcock Reading Mastery Test, the Durrell Oral Reading Scale, and the Gray Oral Reading Test.
- SFA has substantially reduced both absenteeism and special education placements in those schools where it has been implemented effectively.
- SFA has been primarily evaluated by third-party investigators.
- SFA has outperformed other school reform models in head-to-head comparisons, including Accelerated Schools and Reading Recovery.

**FIGURE 13.2 COMPARISON OF SUCCESS FOR ALL AND
CONTROL SCHOOLS IN MEAN READING GRADE
EQUIVALENTS AND EFFECT SIZES, 1988–1999**

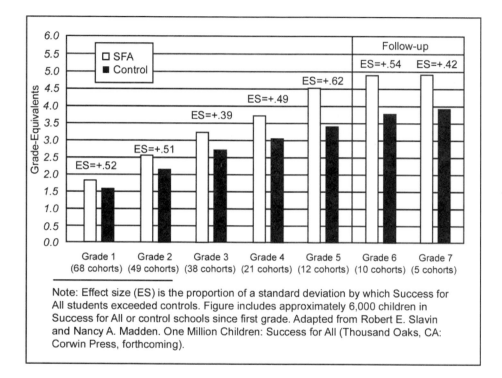

Note: Effect size (ES) is the proportion of a standard deviation by which Success for All students exceeded controls. Figure includes approximately 6,000 children in Success for All or control schools since first grade. Adapted from Robert E. Slavin and Nancy A. Madden. One Million Children: Success for All (Thousand Oaks, CA: Corwin Press, forthcoming).

Slavin admits that there are scattered instances in which *SFA* has not performed up to expectations, but he says that this is more often than not the case when the program has not been faithfully implemented and carried out. One example he mentions, a humorous one if it were not for all that is at stake, is a school in South Carolina where Hurricane Hugo disrupted the program by blowing the roof off the school. Such an act of God surely represents a threat to both the internal and external validity of a study!

If he has his detractors, he also has his supporters. Bruce Joyce (1999), in a curious article worthy of the annals of the "with friends like these..." tradition, offers no evidence but much sympathy on behalf of *SFA*. He cites *SFA* "as one of the best current efforts to tackle our common problem of too many students with low levels of literacy" (p. 131). Setting aside the possibility that this is a healthy academic debate, Joyce ventures the opinion, one more often left to the courts to decide, that certain of Walberg and Greenberg's less than flattering assertions represent "slander, pure and simple..." (p. 131). Joyce reaches the conclusion that "our great literacy task requires developers who will face squarely the terrific obstacles that we must overcome as we struggle to create a fully literate society" (p. 131). Well, perhaps developers of innovative programs are the key, but the record of hopes and promises suggests otherwise. At any rate, we could probably use a few independent researchers to investigate the effects of the developers' heroic efforts.

WHERE DOES THIS LEAVE US?

The claims found on either side of this issue could well make up the stuff of a lively seminar devoted to critical reading in the interpretation of educational research. Certainly, both Slavin and his detractors agree on one thing: much is at stake. This is an extremely important debate, one of significance well beyond *SFA*. It strikes at the heart of the matter of the ability of educational innovations, in this case schoolwide innovations, to deliver on their promises. A recurring theme through three editions of this book is that they mainly do not. The record of most innovations is one that Slavin (1989) himself so accurately chronicled: initial enthusiasm based on anecdotal accounts, word spreading rapidly that here is something that works, large-scale adoptions, research findings that tend to be ambivalent, and eventual abandonment and an embracing of the next fad.

SFA has demonstrated a fair amount of success, obviously enough to win the favor of the "education establishment" in the form of the Congress, the Department of Education, the largest professional organizations, and several research institutes. Certainly in comparison with other schoolwide reform programs and with most educational innovations in general, *SFA* has a track record of published research. Furthermore, most of the research findings show favorable results. It is, however, expensive, time-consuming, difficult to carry out faithfully, and off-putting to some teachers and parents. Curiously, not much has been written about what students think of it. And finally, the case against it made by numerous detractors cannot be simply ignored, especially the contrary research evidence. With all this said, the published research showing favorable achievement outcomes where SFA is dutifully carried out far outweighs the less favorable findings. Further, the research base on SFA is among the most developed and sophisticated of the innovations considered in this book. With respect to the sheer numbers of studies and from the standpoint of the quality of the research, SFA must be given good marks.

CONCLUSION

This chapter is titled "Success for All and Schoolwide Reform." *SFA* has served as a kind of case study because it is easily the most visible, most adopted, most funded, most researched, and most controversial of all schoolwide reform efforts. But I wish to conclude with some remarks on schoolwide reform in general. This movement raises a number of significant questions, more questions in fact than it answers if we are truly to make progress. Specifically, let us look at five such questions.

Is schoolwide reform the best route to take? Students learn alone and in groups. They don't learn as a school even though it is possible to average the academic progress that way. Instruction and other learning experiences simply do not happen schoolwide, nor should they. We know that individual teacher effects are considerable and that good results are realized most predictably when good teachers use good curricula. To blanket a school with a highly-touted program will inevitably leave as many teachers disgruntled as pleased. Especially when a program is scripted and must be followed carefully, certain teachers feel that their unique professional abilities and attributes are given short shrift.

Are the additional expenses of schoolwide reform programs justified? This question is problematic given that we are already among the world's leaders in per pupil expenditures but not in achievement. One could argue that it is more expensive to allow the problems of illiteracy to grow unchecked than to spend money to make readers out of the nation's children. But when evidence of the academic outcomes of schoolwide program interventions is either lacking or not sufficiently persuasive, and it generally is, what does one conclude? And even where early gains are shown (K–3), little progress has been made to sustain them through the middle grades and beyond.

Is it healthy to put schools into academic receivership? When a faculty either elects or is assigned to adopt a schoolwide reform program conceived and developed by an outside agency, the message is often that the faculty were not able to do the job themselves. It is all too easy to pronounce failure and to say "let someone else take over." It is also all too easy to forget or more likely never to have known just how difficult teaching is in certain situations. But what are the long-term effects of asking professionals to follow someone else's script, to feel that they must faithfully execute the program when they might wish to be doing other things with their students, things that they feel in their judgement are just as worthwhile or more so?

What is the role of the school principal in all of this? It is quite possible that far too much emphasis has been placed in recent years on "vision," "managing change," "leadership," and "strategy," rendering the school principal an empty suit when it comes to knowledge of curriculum and instruction. Principals have been asked to spend so much time chasing such will o' the wisps as total quality management, strategic planning, and other ideas dubiously borrowed from business. When principals know less and less about teaching and learning, they become ready prey to the siren call of outside rescue, forgetting or not even knowing that we have a considerable body of good research about what works in classrooms.

At what point do educational research findings become compelling? The *SFA* controversy is sure to leave the well-read professional scratching his/her head. First of all, it is well to remember the questions posed at the beginning of this book relative to the statement, "the research says." What research, done where, under what conditions, compared to what? Are there replication studies? Have meta-analyses or research reviews been published? A comment made in passing by Walberg and Greenberg is of great importance. They challenge *SFA* on a number of grounds, but one question they pose has to do with the theoretical (Level I) construct of the model. This issue should always be raised by professionals who are consdering an adoption. Only when we are satisfied at this level should we even bother to go on asking questions about empirical studies (Level II) or large-scale program evaluations (Level III).

There is the old story from the days of the space race between the United States and the former Soviet Union. A problem that both countries had was that of figuring out a way that people aboard the space stations could write in conditions of zero gravity. The United States spent millions of dollars in an attempt to develop a ball-point pen that could function in zero gravity. The Russians, strapped for cash, simply used pencils. Maybe there is a lesson here.

REFERENCES

Greenberg, R., and Walberg, H. (1999). *The Diogenes effect: Why program evaluations fail.* http://www.alt-sfa.com/diogenes_effect.htm.

Greeno, J. (1998). The situativity of knowing, learning, and research. *American Psychologist, 53*(1), 5–26.

Herman, R. (1999). *An educator's guide to schoolwide reform.* Arlington, VA: Educational Research Service.

Houston, Texas, Independent School District (1997/1998). *Success for All: 1997-98 executive summary.* Source: http://www.houston.isd.tenet.edu.

Joyce, B. (1999). The great literacy problem and success for all. *Phi Delta Kappan, 81,* 129–131.

Lemann, N. (1998, November). Ready, read! *Atlantic Monthly.*

Pogrow, S. (1998). What is an exemplary program, and why should anyone care? A reaction to Slavin and Klein. *Educational Researcher, 27,* 22–29.

Pogrow, S. (1999). Rejoinder: Consistent large gains and high levels of achievement are the best measures of program quality: Pogrow responds to Slavin. *Educational Researcher, 28,* 24–26, 31.

Pogrow, S. (2000). The unsubstantiated "success" of success for all: Implications for policy, practice, and the soul of our profession. *Phi Delta Kappan, 82,* 596–600.

Pogrow, S. (2000). Success for all does not produce success for students. *Phi Delta Kappan, 82,* 67–80.

Ross, S., Smith, L, Slavin, R., and Madden, N. (1997). Improving the academic success of disadvantaged children: An examina tion of success for all. *Psychology in the Schools, 34*(2), 171–180.

Ruffini, S., Feldman, B., Edirisooriya, G., Howe, L., and Borders, D. (2000). Assessment of success for all: School years 1988–1991. Department of Research and Evaluation, Baltimore City Public Schools. Source: http://www.alt-sfa.com/ruffini.htm.

Slavin, R. (1997). Design competitions and expert panels: Similar objectives, very different paths. *Educational Researcher, 26,* 21–22.

Slavin, R. (1998, April 29). Slavin responds to essay's "ad hominem" critique. *Education Week.*

Slavin, R. (1999). Rejoinder: Yes, control groups are essential in program evaluation: A response to Pogrow. *Educational Researcher, 28,* 36–38.

Slavin, R., and Madden, N. (2000). Research on achievement outcomes of success for all: A summary and response to critics. *Phi Delta Kappan, 82*(1), 38–40, 59–66.

Slavin, R., and Madden, N. (2000a). *Success for all works.* Baltimore: Success for All Foundation.

Slavin, R., Madden, N., Dolan, L., and Wasik, B. (1996). *Every child, every school: Success for all.* Thousand Oaks, CA: Corwin Press.

Southwest Regional Laboratory (1995). Effects of success for all on the reading achievement of first graders in California bilingual programs. (ERIC Document No. ED 394 327.)

Traub, J. (1999). *Better by design? A consumer's guide to schoolwide reform.* Washington, DC: Thomas Fordham Foundation.

Venesky, R. (1999). An alternative perspective on success for all. In K. Wong (ed.). *Advances in educational policy.* Greenwich, CT: JAI Press.

Walberg, H., and Greenberg, R. (1999). Educators should require evidence. *Phi Delta Kappan, 81,* 132–135.

Walberg, H., and Greenberg, R. (1999). The Diogenes factor. *Phi Delta Kappan, 81,* 127–128.

Weiler, J. (1998, December). Success for all: A summary of evaluations. *ERIC Clearing House on Urban Education, No. 139.* EDO-UD-98-9.

14

DIRECT INSTRUCTION

D.I. interventions have been shown to produce superior performance with preschool, elementary, and secondary regular and special education students and adults. They have produced superior results with various minority populations, including non-English speakers.

Gary L. Adams

It's a matter of balance…and Direct Instruction may in fact be limiting for some people in that it doesn't allow them to be as creative as they might….It prescribes, it's limiting, it's structured, it tells you exactly how it should be done…. Classrooms ought to be more than worksheets, ought to be more than multiplication facts….It's got to be reading plus and reading for a purpose.

Bertha Pendleton

"What if somebody could come up with a method of teaching children how to read that was simple and worked every time. That sounds like the impossible dream to parents and school kids. But we found there is such a method. And you may be shocked to find out that most schools refuse to try it." This was how Hugh Downs of ABC-TV began a 1996 episode of *20/20*, the long-running TV news magazine. During Downs' interview with Professor Siegfried Engelmann, the originator and developer of Direct Instruction (D.I.), Engelmann claimed that in his 30 years of working with D.I. he has never found a student who couldn't learn to read.

Now take a moment to consider this: *An Educators' Guide to Schoolwide Reform* (1999), published by the Washington, DC-based American Institutes for Research, gave Direct Instruction highest marks (along with two other programs) for evidence of positive effects on student achievement. The study was sponsored by the National Education Association, American Federation of Teachers, National Association of Elementary School

Principals, National Association of Secondary School Principals, and the American Association of School Administrators.

Consider this statement by Janice Dole (2000): "…Clearly the direct and explicit instruction models of reading have been shown to demonstrate improved reading comprehension for many students, especially lower-achieving readers. This research is largely quantitative in nature, and it is certainly robust" (p. 65).

Given the problems with basic literacy that this country faces, could this be the miracle cure we have all been looking for? It sounds too good to be true. The never-ending quest for a silver bullet seems for once to have been satisfied. Advocates say search no more—it is just a matter of applying the principles of D.I. in classrooms. And yet, Direct Instruction has its detractors, critics, and opponents. Why is this so? In this chapter, we examine the evidence in support of and against D.I., and let you reach your own conclusion. We will define it, search for theory building and empirical evidence, and see whether program evaluations tend to support its use or not.

What Is Direct Instruction?

There is some confusion over the terminology, so let us begin there. First of all, it is useful to distinguish between direct instruction (d.i.), and Direct Instruction (D.I.), although there is a relationship. D.I. refers to a range of about 60 instructional programs, developed by Engelmann and his colleagues, that set standards of learning based on specific techniques and teacher-directed sequences, whereas d.i. refers to the work of Barak Rosenshine (1979, 1986), and others, which is based on a highly organized and structured, teacher-directed, task-oriented approach to instruction. Obviously, there is common ground here, the commonality being primarily that of a basic skills, linear, teacher-directed approach to instruction. Philosophically, both are, roughly speaking, educational manifestations of a point of view known as essentialism.

Linda Darling-Hammond and Jon Snyder (1992) quote Rosenshine's description of direct instruction as occurring in:

> academically focused, teacher directed classrooms using sequenced and structured materials. It [d.i.] refers to teaching activities where goals are clear to students, time allocated for instruction is sufficient and continuous, coverage of content is extensive, the performance of students is monitored, questions are at a low cognitive level…and feedback to students is immediate and academically oriented. In direct instruction, the teacher controls instructional goals, chooses materials appropriate for the student's ability, and paces the instructional episode. The goal is to move the students through a sequenced set

of materials or tasks. Such materials are common across class-rooms and have a relatively strong congruence with the tasks on achievement tests. (p. 65)

Jere Brophy (2000), a distinguished researcher who notes that his own work is "sometimes cited as supportive of explicit instructional methods," writes that "demonstration, guided practice with feedback, and independent practice are the essential features of direct instruction. Note that these components are not significantly different from modeling, coaching, scaffolding, and transfer of responsibility from teacher to student, the components that are commonly identified as essential features of socially mediated situated learning" (p. 176).

In an attempt to clear the air, Adams and Engelmann (1996) write that "the most common confusion is that Direct Instruction is simply teacher-directed instruction, the opposite of the so-called 'child-centered' approaches (such as the open classroom or discovery method) in which the teacher is supposed to act as a facilitator for students. Traditional teacher-directed instruction is not Direct Instruction; it is just direct teaching or teacher-directed instruction" (p. 1). While this statement oversimplifies Rosenshine's rather elaborate description, it does draw attention to the useful idea that direct instruction is more generic, a larger tent so to say, than Direct Instruction. D.I. is a specific instructional approach consisting of (a) "Direct Instruction techniques and sequences that set standards by documenting what students can achieve," or (b) "commercial Direct Instruction sequences and materials that are designed for use by people who have not been trained directly by Engelmann and his colleagues" (p. 2). As we shall see, commercial variants of D.I. appear under different labels applied to reading, math, and language.

It is thus safe to say that D.I. is a specific example of d.i. To return to Rosenshine's description, D.I. fits into it rather well. D.I. proponents are quick to point out that their programs are not representative of many of the aspects of generic direct instruction. Lecture, for example, is a type of direct instruction, and D.I. programs are virtually lecture-free. Wide-ranging, teacher-directed class discussions are also examples of direct instruction not found in Direct Instruction. So, like any variant of a larger set, there is commonality as well as divergence between it and other members of the set. This attempt at likenesses and differences on our part may seem laborious, but without it confusion reigns. Our focus in this chapter is primarily on D.I. because D.I.'s research claims are manageable within the constraints of a chapter, while to assess the research findings in d.i. would take us into such labyrinthine corridors as lecture, seatwork, textbooks, teacher-led class discussion, and a range of variables rather numerous to say the least.

Direct Instruction was first implemented in 1968 as part of the U.S. Office of Education's Project Follow Through and has continued in use in a variety of states, districts, and schools around the country since that time. The first series in reading and arithmetic was known as DISTAR (Direct Instruction System for Teaching Arithmetic and Reading, later changed to Direct Instruction System for Teaching and Remediation). These and other instructional programs have been published commercially and have a variety of names (see Figure 14.1). In addition an entire series of instructional programs is available on videodisc and aimed at adult learners.

FIGURE 14.1. DIRECT INSTRUCTION COMMERCIAL PROGRAMS

Reading	*Language Arts*	*Mathematics*
◆ Reading Mastery I, II	◆ Reasoning and Writing: Levels A–F	◆ Connecting Math Concepts: Levels A–F
◆ Reading Mastery: Fast Cycle	◆ DISTAR Language I, II	◆ Arithmetic I, II
◆ Reading Mastery III, IV, V, VI	◆ Cursive Writing Program	◆ Corrective Mathematics
◆ Corrective Reading: Decoding	◆ Expressive Writing 1, 2	◆ Mathematics Modules
◆ Corrective Reading: Comprehension	◆ Spelling Mastery	
	◆ Corrective Spelling Through Morphographs	

SOURCE: Adams, G., and Engelmann, S. (1996). *Research on direct instruction: 20 years beyond DISTAR.* Seattle, WA: Educational Achievement Systems.

DISTAR was designed for use with K–3 children, particularly in compensatory school settings with lower achievers. It "emphasizes frequent teacher-student interactions guided by carefully sequenced, daily lessons in reading, arithmetic, and language" (Engelmann et al., 1988). The developers describe the underlying assumptions of the Direct Instruction Model: "(a) all children can be taught; (b) the learning of basic skills and their application in higher-order skills is essential to intelligent behavior and should be the main focus of a compensatory education program; (c) the disadvantaged must be taught at a faster rate than typically occurs if they are to catch up with their middle-class peers" (p. 303).

The Direct Instruction Model is guided by two major rules (Figure 14.2) and includes carefully designed curriculums in reading, arithmetic, and language. These curriculums are basic skills, to say the least: phonics and decoding skills, grammar rules, arithmetic operations, logical processes, and problem solving. The model also stresses increased teaching time, with at least 2 hours a day devoted to these specific skills. "Efficiently teaching" means "scripted presentation of lessons, small-group instruction, reinforcement, corrections, and procedures to teach every child by giving added attention to the lower performers (Engelmann et al., pp. 306–307). Basically, there is a lot of oral drill, recitation, and memory work. The scripted lessons include exactly what the teacher will say and do during the instructional time using procedures that have been field-tested and revised for effectiveness. This also permits a supervisor to identify deficiencies quickly and to provide appropriate remedies. Critics at the time quickly labeled such approaches to education as "teacher proof," meaning that the procedures were so tightly scripted that even the worst of teachers could hardly go wrong. The idea, so critics claimed, was that "at last here is a method that even *you* can't screw up."

The D.I. model ideally requires extensive staff development and training. Teachers can, and have, used D.I. without formal training, but there is much they might miss by doing so. The equation is far more complex than merely putting a teacher in front of a group of students, even with the materials at hand, and allowing him or her to interpret along the way. Among its elaborate features, for example, is a procedure for keeping track of and coordinating all services given to an individual student, including nutrition, health, psychological, social, and guidance and counseling services. The major components of the program are presented in Figure 14.3 (p. 221).

Since 1968, then, Direct Instruction programs have been used nationwide by a very dedicated, but relatively small, number of teachers and professionals who claim great success with it. The tenets have changed little since its inception 30 years ago, although it has probably become even more associated with teaching directed at low achievers and disadvantaged children than with high achievers. Its proponents say this is simply because the system works with low performers where other methods do not. They claim that it works equally well with average and high achievers, but obviously with fewer repetitions, shorter time needed for learning, and so forth.

FIGURE 14.2. THE TWO MAJOR RULES
OF DIRECTION INSTRUCTION

I. Teach more in less time:

 ♦ The model uses a teacher and an aide at levels 1 and 2 of the programs, usually in kindergarten and first grade. The aides are trained to teach and function fully as teachers and, thus, increase the amount of teacher-student interaction time.

 ♦ Programs are designed to focus on teaching the general use of information and skills where possible, so that through teaching a subject, the whole set is learned. For example, by teaching 40 sounds and skills for hooking them together students learn a generalized decoding skill that is relevant to one-half of the more common English words.

II. Control the details of what happens:

 ♦ Daily lesson scripts are provided that tell the teacher exactly what to say and do. All teachers and aides use the DISTAR programs in reading, language, and arithmetic developed by Engelmann and his associates.

 ♦ Training is provided so that the staff knows how to execute the details of the program.

 ♦ Student progress and, indirectly, teacher implementation are monitored through the use of criterion-referenced "continuous progress tests" on the children every 2 weeks.

 ♦ Supervisors (1 for each 10 to 15 classrooms) are trained to spend 75% of their time actually in classrooms working with teachers and aides.

 ♦ Procedures for teachers, supervisors, administrators, and parents are detailed in implementation and parent coordinator manuals.

SOURCE: Engelmann, S., Becker, W. C., Carnine, D., and Gersten, R. (1988). The direct instruction follow through model: Design and outcomes. *Education and Treatment of Children, 11*(4), 303–304.

FIGURE 14.3. MAJOR COMPONENTS
OF THE DIRECT INSTRUCTION MODEL

+ Consistent focus on academic objectives.

+ High allocations of time to small-group instruction in reading, language, and math.

+ Tight, carefully sequenced DISTAR curriculum, which includes a task analysis of all skills and cognitive operations, and numerous opportunities for review and practice of recently learned skills.

+ Ongoing inservice and preservice training that offers concrete, "hands on" solutions to problems arising in the classroom.

+ A comprehensive system for monitoring both the rate at which students progress through the curriculum and their mastery of the material covered.

SOURCE: Adapted from Meyer, L. A., Gersten, R. M., and Gutkin, J. (1983). Direction instruction: A project follow through success story in an inner-city school. *The Elementary School Journal, 84(2)*, 243.

THE CRITICS

There is surprisingly little criticism in the literature, at least that we could find, of Direct Instruction. That does not mean there are no critics. Indeed, there are many. Curiously, however, D.I. has been largely unacknowledged except by its advocates. Perhaps the old saw "ignore it and it will go away" obtains here. The following mention of the D.I. approach, aimed primarily at phonics-based reading instruction, is offered by Zemelman, Daniels, and Hyde (1998). They write: "'Scientific' study of human behavior, however, is never simple. Studies of the effectiveness of phonics, phonemic awareness, or the highly structure approach called 'direct instruction' also showed positive results—five large-scale studies in all, in our tally over the five-year period" (p. 251). The comment was made as a point of contrast/comparison with the following which they cite:

+ Fifteen studies that validate the comparative effectiveness, at a statistically significant level, of one or another particular element used in progressive and Whole-Language classrooms.

+ Five studies showing statistically significant higher test scores in broader Whole-Language classrooms than in traditional classrooms using basal texts and worksheets.

+ Two smaller case studies showing effectiveness of Whole-Language strategies.

- ♦ One study showing no difference between a Whole Language and traditional classroom, and two showing no difference in effectiveness of a particular Whole-Language element.

Zemelman, Daniels, and Hyde obviously have found more evidence supporting Whole Language than they found supporting D.I., but some in favor of each. They explain these seemingly contradictory results by noting that "teachers and researchers have differing definitions of 'reading,' and consequently test differing aspects of it. Studies of progressive strategies usually test children's reading *comprehension*. Researchers who believe separate decoding skills are more important understandably use tests that check those skills" (p. 251). Given this insight, the mixed results certainly seem more understandable.

In an earlier edition of their book, Zemelman, Daniels, and Hyde (1993) noted that because of the heavy and insistent emphasis given to decoding, "most Americans stopped reading the moment they escaped from school" (p. 22). There is, however, more than one way to "escape" from school. A study by Meyer et al. (1983) of high school graduation rates for three cohort groups in the New York City schools showed that the dropout rates were statistically significantly lower among students taught by Direct Instruction than were those of a comparison group. And the percentages of those applying to and accepted by colleges were statistically significantly higher among the D.I. group than among the comparison group.

One does find in the writings of D.I. enthusiasts allusions to the objections of the critics. Critics, they say, argue that D.I. is "old-fashioned," that it is too much work for the teacher, that it is more tiring, too regimented, promotes passive and rote learning, and stifles teacher creativity. To rebut these charges, to the extent that they are even made, there is no evidence offered; in fact, one seldom finds *any* written criticism from the critics. It seems to be basically ignored, much like broccoli, primarily based on personal distaste.

It is not at all unusual when teachers talk about D.I. to hear them point out that it is so regimented that it stifles their creativity. This is an interesting statement, to say the least. They reject it not because it doesn't work, but because it stifles teacher creativity. That is, they feel limited. But it could at least be argued that teacher creativity is not the end product or purpose of schooling, student learning is. Imagine doctors rejecting a treatment, not because it didn't work, but because it cramped their style, or stifled their creativity, or was too boring and tedious for them to use. Admittedly, this is a problem because teacher happiness and fulfillment is important. But perhaps one could put forth the scarcely novel idea that there is a time for everything—a time to be creative and a time to be didactic—especially if that didacticism is shown to work in the teaching of basic skills. As to the criticism of rote learning, there may be some degree of truth to it, although D.I. proponents say that that is only part of what is learned. On the other hand, rote learning is quite necessary in the form of number facts, letter sounds, and so on, in order to provide the building blocks of higher learning.

Janice Dole (2000) writes, "Despite the success of DISTAR and additional research on the effectiveness of direct instruction, many educators had—and still have—a difficult time accepting the direct instruction model....Many educators rejected the rote drill-and-practice approach of the direct instruction model and questioned its utility with average learners and in ill-structured domains such as comprehension" (p. 55). Dole goes on to cite teachers' objections to direct instruction because of their perceptions that it diminishes reading enjoyment and focuses on "small, unimportant skills."

THE RESEARCH BASE FOR DIRECT INSTRUCTION

LEVEL I RESEARCH

The theoretical basis of both direct instruction and Direct Instruction is represented by a seemingly ad hoc mixture of behaviorism, cognitive science, and reductionism. When one peels away the layers and reaches the core, however, one encounters a clearly behaviorist/essentialist philosophy. Consider, for example, this ambiguity-reducing statement by Adams and Engelmann, authors of *Research on Direct Instruction: 20 Years Beyond DISTAR* (1996): "The first job of the teacher, therefore, is to teach basic skills and knowledge" (p. 27). Many, of course, would agree with this thought, but it does clearly put some distance between those who sympathize with it and those who advocate progressive education. Essentialism is largely a twentieth-century phenomenon that rose to prominence based on its drumbeat attacks on progressivism. Educational essentialists of prominence include William Bagley, Arthur Bestor, and, more recently, E. D. Hirsch, Jr. Basically, essentialism promotes fundamental skills and knowledge, standards, testing, and mastery learning, while eschewing such approaches as nondirective learning, personalized curriculum, open-concept education, and developmentally appropriate practice.

That D.I. is behaviorist in orientation is clear. Emphasis is placed on objective and observable behaviors; reinforcement theory is promoted in the form of rapid feedback; the teacher (not the student) is expected to arrange the conditions of learning; and carefully planned, sequentially-ordered teaching is carried out. Thus, one could reasonably find the theories of Pavlov, Watson, Skinner, and other giants of this movement as forming much of its backcloth. However, just as behaviorism has modified its stance against mental processes that cannot be observed, so does one find elements of cognitive science imbedded here. The type of cognitive science one encounters in D.I. is that branch related to information processing rather than to the developmental, environmental perspective advocated by Jean Piaget. Reductionism suggests that learning can be broken down into constituent parts, and that simpler parts of whole complex ideas are more manageable for the learner when they are taught in some meaningful sequence that leads toward comprehension of the whole. This certainly describes D.I.

D.I. in fact represents something close to pure empiricism. In this respect, it emerges as an atheoretical model. Over the past three decades, D.I. researchers have systematically sought for evidence of its efficacy, paying little attention to theory building or to matters of abstract philosophy Study after study has been conducted in such curricular areas as reading, language, and mathematics. D.I. researchers have asked the pragmatic question, "Does it work?" The sheer weight of the evidence published in respected journals is impressive. This is remarkably different from the many innovations that claim (often dubiously) a profound theoretical basis, but that offer little published evidence to substantiate academic or other effects. It is this very strength that may contain the elements of its weakness. Why, advocates and empirical researchers ask, is D.I. so little acknowledged and so reluctantly accepted? There may be a number of reasons, including a built-in bias toward progressive education on the part of teachers. But if that were all, how does one explain the phenomenal acceptance by teacher training institutions and school districts of such behaviorist-essentialist protocols as instructional objectives, Madeline Hunter's ITIP, and mastery learning? Clearly, ours is a field that is more than willing to embrace eclecticism, with few qualms about a mixed progressive-essentialist agenda. Madeline Hunter was an extremely effective promoter of ITIP, an innovation that may have been more widespread and used in schools than any other innovation of our time. She communicated a vision of ITIP that teachers, administrators, and professors in schools of education eagerly subscribed to in spite of the fact that the empirical evidence one might wish for really never was there. We suggest that even *good* evidence is not easy to sell in the absence of a well-communicated vision. Regarding D.I., this is unfortunate, because what we seem to have here, to paraphrase Cool Hand Luke's chain-gang boss, is a failure to communicate.

LEVELS II AND III RESEARCH

An impressive research agenda has been carried out over the last 30 years on D.I. instructional programs. Studies have been conducted on both small- and large-scale usage, for short periods of time, and in the form of longer-term follow-up evaluations. Because of the nature of D.I. instructional programs, the research tends more often than not to be a combination of quasi-experimental and program evaluation designs, and for this reason we will discuss Level II and Level III research together.

Return with us for a moment to those thrilling days of yesteryear, to the 1960s and Lyndon Johnson's Great Society, when there seemed to be a lot more money for educational research than there is today. It was during this time that the U.S. Office of Education initiated Project Follow Through to the tune of $59 million, the most expensive education research project ever funded. The project, which involved some 170-plus communities, was designed to evaluate different approaches to educating economically disadvantaged students. "A wide array of instructional approaches were included in Follow Through, ranging from open classroom models, to cognitive models based on the theories of Piaget, to highly structured programs utilizing principles of contemporary learning theory" (Meyer et al., 1983). One of these instructional approaches was the Direct Instruction Model.

The Stanford Research Institute and Abt Associates were contracted to evaluate the effectiveness of the various models in the areas of basic skills, and cognitive and affective behaviors. To make a long story short, the Direct Instruction Model produced the most desirable results in all three areas. This included results superior in the cognitive areas to those instructional programs designed specifically to focus on cognitive outcomes, and results superior in the affective areas to those instructional programs designed specifically to focus on affective outcomes (Stebbins et al., 1977). The regimented protocols of D.I. are certainly at odds with the progressive educational wisdom of the day, and as far as educational practice is concerned, these findings seemed to have been basically ignored.

Apparently convinced that there must have been a mistake, officials of the Ford Foundation funded an evaluation of the evaluation that (not surprisingly) questioned certain conclusions drawn by the evaluators (House, Glass, & McLean, 1978). This critique resulted in several more in-depth analyses of the data generated by Project Follow Through, in which D.I. looked even better (see Adams & Engelmann, 1996, pp. 67–98, for a summary of these reports). If the research stopped at this point, we would say that the controversy surrounding the Follow Through studies could pose some reasonable threat to the research base. In the world of education, where such a premium is placed on the "new," this is, after all, ancient history. There was, however, much more to come.

In the wake of Project Follow Through, research on the effectiveness of D.I. continued at both Levels II and III. Project Follow Through itself generated numerous follow-up studies of the long-term effects, the great majority of which supported the efficacy of D.I. Having found results similar to those noted by Meyer et al. (mentioned earlier in this chapter), Gersten and Keating (1987) noted that high school students who received

Direct Instruction in primary grades had lower school dropout rates, higher test scores, and a higher percentage of college applications and acceptance. Finally, Gersten, Keating, and Becker (1988) conducted two longitudinal studies on the effects of Direct Instruction and found that the results consistently favored D.I. in educational outcomes such as graduation rates, dropout rates, and college acceptance, as well as in measures of achievement, especially reading.

Apart from Project Follow Through, scores of studies were conducted during the 1970s, 1980s, and 1990s probing the effects of D.I. in the areas of language, math, problem solving and reasoning skills, reading, and spelling. A number of research reviews and meta-analyses have been conducted over the years, but it will serve the point to mention just a few. Cotton and Savard (1982) reviewed 33 relevant documents that supported Direct Instruction as improving basic skills achievement and affective development, but they did not conclude that D.I. was appropriate for older students. White (1988) conducted a meta-analysis reviewing 25 studies with special education populations, which showed very favorable results for D.I., including the observation that not one research study favored the comparison group. They noted that the effects of D.I. were independent of such variables as handicapping condition, age group, or skill area. Adams and Engelmann (1996) conducted the most thorough review of the research. This very impressive analysis of the literature, Project Follow Through publications, and meta-analysis of scores of Level II and Level III studies on the effects of D.I. are very solid evidence of its efficacy, providing educators with a formidable research base.

One other note on the research on D.I. seems appropriate. Since its inception, D.I. has had a loyal group of adherents, and their names are very prevalent in the D.I. literature, including the research studies. Among those are Becker, Carnine, Engelmann, Maggs, and Gersten. One rightfully becomes skeptical when the proponents of a program, and in this case a commercial program, are also the primary researchers. A conflict of interest is always a strong possibility. In this case, however, this does not appear to be an issue for several reasons. First, there are a number of other researchers who have studied D.I. who are not connected to its commercial aspects, and their findings are basically the same. Second, the research by prominent D.I. advocates is published in prestigious, peer-reviewed journals, an extremely important quality control point. Third, no sustained or focused criticism can be found that challenges the quality of the research.

CONCLUSION

It is difficult to know how to conclude a chapter devoted to a topic that has such a solid record of supportive evidence behind it but which is not particularly liked by large numbers of teachers. Such is the case with Direct Instruction. Well, broccoli has a pretty solid record, and yet it is easy to find people who don't like and who won't eat that green stuff. Human nature is such that we seem to pick and choose our research findings. Smoking and unprotected sex have been shown to be potentially harmful to one's health, but this does not stop large numbers of people who have heard the message from engaging in those practices. One could go on to mention other contradictions between what we know and what we do, such as tv watching and exercise. Maybe Direct Instruction is the broccoli of educational practice, good for you but not everybody's favorite dish.

That said, the evidence seems compelling. Citing a number of research syntheses in beginning reading instruction, the late Jeanne Chall (1999), a renowned reading researcher, wrote:

> These syntheses found, in general, that classic approaches to beginning reading instruction (e.g., direct, systematic instruction in phonics—a code emphasis) were more effective than the various innovative approaches with which they were compared (e.g., a meaning emphasis, no phonics, incidental phonics, phonics only as needed, or a whole-language approach). (p. 62)

The concerns are obvious. The 1998 National Assessment of Educational Progress (NAEP) showed that only 31% of fourth graders, 33% of eighth graders, and 40% of twelfth graders achieved a *proficient* level in reading (Donahue et al., 1999). Any school or district interested in improving reading and mathematics scores certainly ought to carefully consider the Direct Instruction model. This is especially so if the situation is one where there are numbers of children in remedial programs or large numbers of underachieving students. Meanwhile, the debate between essentialists and progressives, one which has gone on for years and which finds concrete locus in this discussion, will no doubt continue.

REFERENCES

Adams, G., and Engelmann, S. (1996). *Research on direct instruction: 20 years beyond DISTAR*. Seattle, WA: Educational Achievement Systems.

American Institutes for Research (1999). *An educators' guide to schoolwide reform*. Washington, DC: NEA, AFT, NAESP, NASSP, AASA. The full text is available at: http://www.aasa.org.

Bracey, G. (2000). "Diverging" American and Japanese science scores. *Phi Delta Kappan, 81*(10), 791–792.

Brophy, J. (2000). Beyond balance: Goal awareness, developmental progressions, tailoring to the context, and supports for teachers in ideal reading and literacy programs. In B. Taylor, M. Graves, and P. Van Den Broek (Eds.). *Reading for meaning: Fostering comprehension in the middle grades.* New York: Teachers College Press.

Carnine, D. (1996). *Direct instruction reading.* Englewood Cliffs, NJ: Prentice-Hall.

Chall, J. (1999). *The academic achievement challenge: What really works in the classroom.* New York: The Guilford Press.

Cotton, K., and Savard, W. G. *Direct instruction. Topic summary report. Research on school effectiveness project.* Portland, OR: Northwest Regional Educational Laboratory.

Dole, J. (2000). Explicit and implicit instruction in comprehension. In B. Taylor, M. Graves, and P. Van Den Broek (Eds.). *Reading for meaning.* New York: Teachers College Press.

Ellis, A. K., and Fouts, J. T. (1996). *Handbook of educational terms with applications.* Larchmont, NY: Eye On Education.

Engelmann, S., Becker, W. C., Carnine, D., and Gersten, R. (1988). The direct instruction follow through model: Design and outcomes. *Education and Treatment of Children, 11*(4), 303–317.

Gersten, R., and Keating, T. (1987). Long-term benefits from direct instruction. *Educational Leadership, 44,* 28–31.

Gersten, R., Keating, T., and Becker, W. (1988). The continued impact of the direct instruction model: Longitudinal studies of Follow Through students. *Education and Treatment of Children, 11(4),* 318–327.

House, E. R., Glass, G. V., and McLean, L. D. (1978). No simple answer: Critique of the Follow Through evaluation. *Harvard Educational Review, 48,* 128–160.

Meyer, L. A., Gersten, R. M., and Gutkin, J. (1983). Direction instruction: A project Follow Through success story in an inner-city school. *The Elementary School Journal, 84*(2), 241–252.

Moore, J. (1986). Direct instruction: A model of instructional design. *Educational Psychology, 6,* 201–229.

Rosenshine, B. (1979). Content, time, and direct instruction. In P. Peterson, and H. Walberg (Eds.). *Research on teaching: Concepts, findings, and implications,* pp. 28–56. Berkeley, CA: McCutchan.

Rosenshine, B. (1986). Synthesis of research on explicit teaching. *Educational Leadership, 43*(7), 60–69.

Stallings, J. (1987). *Longitudinal findings for early childhood programs: Focus on direct instruction.* (ERIC Document Reproduction Service No. ED297874.)

Stebbins, L. B., St. Pierre, R. G., Proper, E. C., Anderson, R. B., and Cerva, T. R. (1977). *Education as experimentation: A planned variation model. Vol. 4A–D. An evaluation of Follow Through.* Cambridge, MA: Abt Associates.

Taylor, B., Graves, M., and Van Den Broek, P. (Eds.) (2000). *Reading for meaning.* New York: Teachers College Press.

White, W. A. T. (1988). A meta-analysis of the effects of direct instruction in special education. *Education and Treatment of Children, 11*(4), 364–374.

Zemelman, S., Daniels, H., and Hyde, A. (1993). *Best practice: New standards for teaching and learning in America's schools.* Portsmouth, NH: Heinemann.

Zemelman, S. Daniels, H., and Hyde, A. (1998). *Best practice: New standards for teaching and learning in America's schools,* 2nd ed. Portsmouth, NH: Heinemann.

15

AUTHENTIC AND PERFORMANCE ASSESSMENT

The only way to improve schools...is to ensure that faculties judge local work using authentic standards and measures....[I]t means doing away with the current extremes of private, eccentric teacher grading, on the one hand; and secure standardized tests composed of simplistic items on the other.

Grant Wiggins

...[A]lternative assessment's rising tide has overflowed most of education's shoreline, and the schools are increasingly being flooded with calls for more direct assessment of student performance....Many practitioners are unsure whether to venture into the torrents of unfamiliar assessment strategies or to drift quietly in education's backwaters, waiting to see if this movement crests and ebbs as quickly as have dozens of others.

Blaine R. Worthen

Standardized tests are still the bread and butter of statewide assessment. But in all regions—north and south, liberal and conservative—alternative assessments have been added to the menu, if not as the main course, then at least as a side dish.

Lee Sherman Caudell

THE MOVEMENT

As Ashton Trice (2000) notes, "Tensions in American education about assessment are likely to be with us for a long time…" (p. 16). Partly as a cause and partly as a result of these tensions, alternative assessment strategies have emerged as a key element of the school restructuring movement. Like so many of the varied pieces of the vast and often contradictory school-restructuring puzzle, alternative assessment represents a frontal attack on the status quo. At the energizing source of the alternative assessment paradigm is a deep and abiding dissatisfaction with traditional evaluation procedures, both standardized tests and teacher-made achievement tests. But it doesn't stop there; the alternative assessment movement has produced a number of nontraditional ideas for taking into account student learning.

As one might expect, an entire range of terms and phrases has emerged. The significant vocabulary includes authentic assessment, performance assessment, practical testing, and direct testing. Whatever the terminology, the move to alternative assessment practices is reaching epic proportions. To place this movement into some kind of meaningful context, it is necessary to develop a contrasting image of more traditional assessment patterns and their effects on students.

TRADITIONAL MEASURES

Student progress is traditionally assessed and reported along a feedback continuum which incorporates everything from daily marks and test scores to semester grades and standardized test results. These marks take on a life of their own, creating a sense of reality in the minds of teachers, students, and parents. In fact, this "reality" may or may not have curriculum content validity; that is, the tests and, therefore, the grades that flow from them may or may not be very well connected to the curriculum that is taught to students. There is, in fact, a long history of discontent with both standardized and teacher-made tests for this reason alone.

From another viewpoint, just as teacher-made tests furnish teachers with comparative information about their students' progress, so do standardized tests furnish communities, districts, states, and the nation with benchmarks of comparative scores over time and with one another. Thus we can compare any given district with its own past performance and with other districts; we can compare Vermont, say, with Nevada, and so on. For all its perceived shortcomings, it is a relatively efficient system, one that has been around for at least 50 years. Still, the criticisms have become increasingly strident, and they cannot simply be ignored.

In the early days of the movement and up to the present time, Thomas Toch (1991, 2000) has taken standardized tests to task. He cited the many standardized tests that states have put in place as a means of holding teachers accountable. Thinking that such tests will lead to improved classroom performance because teachers will "know" that they have to prepare their students more adequately, state legislators have enacted legislation requiring tests in nearly every state. But Toch sees this as nothing more than a return to "minimum competency testing," a movement that was tried and that failed in the 1970s. In a very thoughtful passage, Toch writes,

> Yet there is an immense paradox in the recent surge in standardized testing. Despite the key role standardized tests are playing in the reformers' accountability campaign, the bulk of the new tests are severely flawed as measures of the excellence movement's progress. One major reason is that the tests do not measure the sorts of advanced skills and knowledge that the reformers have argued all students should master....It is largely impossible to gauge from the results of such tests whether students are mastering the intellectual skills that have been the focus of the reform movement: the abilities to judge, analyze, infer, interpret, reason, and the like. Nor do the majority of the tests gauge students' more advanced knowledge of literature, history, science, and other disciplines. Indeed, the recent surge in standardized testing amounts to little more than an extension of the minimum basic-skills testing movement of the 1970s. (1991, p. 207)

This very vexing problem carries with it yet another twist, as though it weren't enough: that of the ongoing critique that standardized tests (and teacher-made tests as well) tend to measure mainly lower-register thinking and knowledge. Several decades ago, in an article in the *American Psychologist*, David McClelland, a noted researcher and theoretician, criticized standardized testing in the most basic sense. He proposed (a) teaching people how to raise their test scores, (b) testing abilities rather than aptitudes, (c) designing tests so that people's scores would rise as they learned more, and (d) abandoning multiple-choice formats—all of which is yet to happen. But his most fundamental suggestion for change was his idea that we need to stop ranking millions of people on their perceived knowledge and skills and start building tests that tap into people's motivations for learning, something that could actually be used to shape instruction for individuals (McClelland, 1973; Lehman, 1994; Goleman, 1998).

Teacher-made tests are yet another story. Consider this comment by Mehrens and Lehmann (1991): "Students sometimes complain that they are fed up with tests that are ambiguous, unclear, and irrelevant. Student comments such as 'I didn't know what the teacher was looking for' and 'I studied the major details of the course but was only examined on trivia and footnotes' are not uncommon. Nor are they necessarily unjustified" (p. 52). It has been noted many times that teacher-made tests are generally of low quality, particularly with respect to their validity and reliability and with respect to the observation that they tend to assess students primarily at low cognitive levels.

AUTHENTIC ASSESSMENT

Serious students of assessment are committed to a review of the entire educational system, and this would certainly involve a close look not only at how we have traditionally evaluated students but also of the effects on students of *how* they have been evaluated. Perhaps the key to understanding the alternative assessment movement is found in a thoughtful consideration of the term *authentic assessment*. The term implies that, by contrast, it should replace assessment that is inauthentic, which means false. So, the idea of authentic assessment is to create evaluation strategies that measure more realistically and accurately those things that students are supposed to be learning. Cangelosi (2000, p. 663) offers the following definition of authentic assessment:

> *Authentic assessment* is the practice of basing formative judgments and summative evaluations of student achievement on measurement results that are *relevant* to stated learning objectives, especially learning objectives that specify reasoning-level cognition (i.e., construct a concept, discover a relationship, comprehension and communication skills, application, and creative thinking), affective, and psychomotor achievement.

One supposes that in order to achieve some level of curricular relevance and coherence, authentic *teaching and learning* ought to accompany any attempts at authentic assessment. To expect less would be to invite sources of invalidity.

Students proceed through their school years being evaluated on daily, weekly, and quarterly bases, taking teacher-made tests, and doing assignments such as directed readings, homework, reports, and projects. For this, they receive semester or yearly marks, many times in the form of letter grades, sometimes supplemented by narrative teacher evaluations. In a seemingly unrelated process, once a year (sometimes less often) they take standardized achievement tests that address basic skills areas as mathematics and reading, as well as content areas including social studies and science. These tests are, at best, variably connected to the curriculum that is actually taught at a given school. It is when the results are disappointing and they get in the newspapers that school people become so discouraged. In fact, a typical defensive reaction by teachers is that their students are learning many wonderful things but that those things are not effectively captured by the tests. Of course, when the results are good we all seem to take them for granted.

In a more perfect educational world (the goal of restructuring), it would be impossible to separate assessment procedures from curriculum content. If we are to do authentic assessment, it stands to reason that we should be assessing what is being taught and, one hopes, what is being learned. So, first, for assessment to be authentic, it should be as closely aligned as possible to the day-to-day experiences of the curriculum. Here there really is little argument between traditionalists and those who would change the assessment paradigm. But good alignment is not enough. It's just a place to start.

Second, it is argued that teaching and learning should be *authentic*. This means that learning should focus on real-life situations. "Let students encounter and master situations that resemble real life" (Cronin, 1993, p. 79). The curricular implications of this view are clearly that school activities and projects should have a real-world cast to them. This argument has been around forever, and it basically represents a philosophic divide between those who espouse an academic-centered curriculum and those who espouse a more society-centered curriculum.

The Center on Organization and Restructuring of Schools at the University of Wisconsin at Madison has developed a framework for "authentic instruction," and "authentic achievement" (Newmann & Wehlage, 1993). Newmann and Wehlage draw a distinction between "achievement that is significant and meaningful, and that which is trivial and useless." They use three criteria to define authentic achievement: "(1) students construct meaning and produce knowledge, (2) students use disciplined inquiry to construct meaning, and (3) students aim their work toward production of discourse, products, and performances that have value or meaning beyond success in school" (p. 8). One might presume that experiences that do not meet these criteria are "trivial and useless."

Not all advocates of alternative assessment procedures have such definitively articulated ideas about achievement, but the essence of their argument is the same: What we teach and what we assess are not what is important for students to learn. All too often, they are removed from the "real world" that students will face when they leave school. Therefore, they argue, it behooves us to rethink our assessment techniques, and therefore our curriculum, to provide and assess learning that is authentic, and not contrived. Such a statement presumes that school is not part of the real world.

The alternative assessment movement is obviously based on two related arguments, one that deals with curriculum and the other with assessment. First, is the ancient, abiding debate over the curriculum, and the relevance of school learning to the real world. The belief in such a dichotomy, of course, can serve as a self-fulfilling prophecy. The question becomes, "Does what students are taught in the schools apply to reality, that is, can they use their knowledge to solve problems, do their jobs, and lead their lives?" Second, "What do traditional evaluation strategies such as paper and pencil tests and standardized tests really measure, and whatever that is, is it important?"

The proponents of alternative assessment strategies have definite and predictable responses to these questions. School learning must be reality-based, and the assessment of that learning must be more natural, a logical outgrowth of the learning experiences themselves. Many of those who hope to restructure education agree and have joined the movement, seeing it as crucial. There appear to be four reasons why alternative assessment is seen as a key to restructuring.

First, alternative assessment strategies are seen as educationally superior to traditional methods. The strategies call for more formative and personalized assessment for the individual student. To do this will provide meaningful feedback to the individual, thus creating the possibilities for more significant, useful learning. The focus shifts naturally to higher level thinking skills and real-life applications that increase student interest and motivation.

A second line of reasoning is that alternative forms of assessment will provide a more adequate representation of what is actually being taught in the schools today. Current standardized tests lack validity as measures of the diverse curricular offerings. It's an interesting argument and one that has a certain elemental appeal, but the idea behind good standardized tests is that they capture students' ability to apply concepts and skills, not their narrowly defined content data knowledge.

A third point is that authentic learning and alternative assessment strategies will facilitate the type of learning that is needed by employees to allow the United States to compete internationally. Here is an example. Students who use alternative assessment procedures are more involved in assessing their own learning and are therefore more aware of their learning. This metacognitive skill (reflecting on the processes of learning) is basic to problem solving, trouble shooting, and to working one's way through difficult, unpatterned situations. Thus, assessment becomes part of the learning experience and not something that is merely tacked on and devoid of context. In the "real world," you don't take periodic paper and pencil tests to measure how well you're doing. You do your job, and that involves assessment that has to do with product quality, customer satisfaction, worker productivity, and so on.

And fourth, alternative assessment strategies and resulting accountability will force intransigent teachers to change the way they teach children. Portfolios, student record keeping, journals, reflective discussions, and other related alternative assessment procedures are themselves metacognitive learning experiences and are therefore shapers of the school day. The amount of student-to-student interaction increases, the amount of time spent in reflective thinking increases, and before teachers and students know it, they have stepped off the conveyor belt that passes for learning and have entered a more seamless world where such things as planning, activity, and assessment flow together. At least that's the argument. Ellis writes, "These are not strategies that culminate in letter grades. These are strategies to be used by those teachers and students who are truly desirous of finding out what is being learned" (Ellis, 1991).

Perhaps at this point an example of authentic performance based assessment will be helpful. Figure 15.1 represents an assessment problem that is reasonably typical of the new paradigm. That is, it contains elements of metacognition, higher-level reasoning, writing about thinking, and justifying one's response as well as merely arriving at one. Take a few minutes to try the assessment yourself. It was designed for performance assessment at the fourth grade level for the state of Washington.

ALTERNATIVE ASSESSMENT STRATEGIES

A number of assessment strategies for teachers (Figure 15.2, p. 241) have emerged from all this. These strategies, or activities, are thought to be useful for measuring and enhancing critical thinking skills and the application of knowledge. With the exception of portfolios, these strategies are not particularly new; good teachers are already using them extensively in their classrooms. What is new, however, is the drive to replace the dominance of standardized tests in the eyes of the public and policy makers with these assessment techniques. At the extreme edges of the argument, enthusiasts wish to replace grades and tests completely with these strategies.

(Text continues on page 242.)

FIGURE 15.1. A REPRESENTATIVE ASSESSMENT PROBLEM

The pictures below show the results when some boxes are placed on a balance.

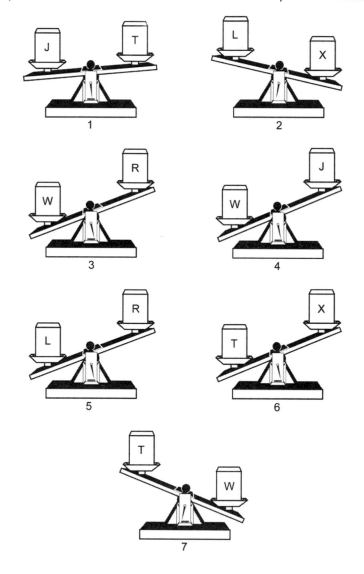

SOURCE: Washington State Department of Education (2000), Olympia, WA.

Do the following:

♦ Name 2 boxes that are heavier than Box X. Write the number of the picture or pictures you used to find each of your answers.

| |
| |
| |
| |

♦ Tell whether Box R is lighter or heavier than Box X. Write the number of the picture or pictures you used to find your answer.

| |
| |
| |
| |

♦ List the 6 boxes in order from heaviest to lightest.

(1)	(4)
(2)	(5)
(3)	(6)

General Scoring Criteria for Extended-Response Mathematical Reasoning Items

4 points—Student's response shows effective interpretations, comparisons, or contrasts of information from sources; effective use of examples, models, facts, patterns, or relationships to validate and support reasoning; insightful conjectures and inferences; or systematic and successful evaluation of effectiveness of procedures and results; with effective support for arguments and results.

3 points—Student's response shows partially effective interpretations, comparisons, or contrasts of information form sources; use of examples, models, facts, patterns, or relationships to validate and support reasoning; expected conjectures and inferences; or mostly successful evaluation of effectiveness of procedures and results; with acceptable support for arguments and results.

2 points—Student's response shows routine interpretations, comparisons, or contrasts of information from sources; examples, models, facts, patterns, or relationships which partially validate and support reasoning; naive conjectures and inferences; or partial evaluation effectiveness of procedures and results with partial support for arguments and results.

1 point—Student's response shows an attempt to interpret, compare, or contrast information from sources; examples, models, facts, patterns, or relationships may not be included to validate or support reasoning; naive conjectures and inferences; or attention to wrong information or persistence with faulty strategy when evaluating effectiveness of procedures and results.

0 points—Student's response shows very little or no evidence of reasoning; or the prompt may simply be recopied, or may indicate "I don't know" or a question mark (?).

FIGURE 15.2. ASSESSMENT ALTERNATIVES

1. **Computer Adaptive Testing**—Any assessment, other than multiple-choice questions or worksheets, that requires the student to respond to the assessment items or task with the aid of a computer.

2. **Enhanced multiple-choice**—Any multiple-choice question that requires more than the selection of one correct response. Most often, the task requires the students to explain their responses.

3. **Extended-response, open-ended**—Any item or task that requires the student to produce an extended written response to an item or task that does not have one right answer (e.g., an essay or laboratory report.)

4. **Group performance assessment**—Any assessment that requires students to perform the assessment task in a group setting.

5. **Individual performance assessment**—Any assessment that requires the student to perform (in a way that can be observed) an assessment task alone.

6. **Interview**—An assessment technique in which the student responds to verbal questions from the assessor.

7. **Nontraditional test items**—Any assessment activity other than a multiple-choice item from which the student selects one response. These items or performances are rated using an agreed-upon set of performance criteria in the form of a scoring guide or a scoring rubric or in comparison to benchmark papers or performances.

8. **Observation**—An assessment technique that requires the student to perform a task while being observed and rated using an agreed-upon set of scoring criteria.

9. **Portfolio**—An accumulation of a student's work over time that demonstrates growth toward the mastery of specific performance criteria against which the tasks included in the portfolio can be judged.

10. **Project, exhibition, or demonstration**—The accomplishment of a complex task over time that requires demonstrating mastery of a variety of desired outcomes, each with its own performance criteria, that can be assessed within the one project, exhibition, or demonstration.

11. **Short-answer, open-ended**—Any item or task that requires the production of a short written response on the part of the

respondent. Most often, there is a single right answer (for example, a fill-in-the-blank or short written response to a question).

SOURCE: Adapted from Council of Chief State School Officers/North Central Regional Educational Laboratory. *The status of state student assessment programs in the United States.* Cited in Caudell, L. S. (1996). High stakes: Innovation meets backlash as states struggle with large-scale assessment. *NW Education*, 2(1), 36.

IS IT WORKING?

The alternative assessment movement proceeded full speed ahead through the first half of the last decade as an integral component of the school restructuring movement. To use Robert Slavin's terms (see Chapter 2), the pendulum had started its swing. The professional literature and conference programs featured advocates who attacked traditional evaluation procedures, often rightly so, touting the reasons for needed changes and offering various alternative assessment remedies. By 1995, the alternative assessment movement had gained wide support throughout the country and alternative assessment procedures were being implemented in nearly every state. Bond and Roeber's research (1995) found that "state assessment remains a significant tool for educational reform in 45 states." They noted that, "students are assessed most often with a combination of traditional and alternative assessments" and that the "use of alternative assessments in conjunction with traditional assessments continues to grow" (p. 9).

As is so often the case in the annals of educational innovation, there were few skeptical articles early on. However, Blaine Worthen (1993), who provided a careful analysis of the issues, sounded a cautionary note. His more salient points are presented in Figure 15.3. Worthen's critique "is a useful primer in what might go wrong. The issues of conceptual clarity, standardization, public acceptance, feasibility, and technical quality, to name a few, are not trivial concerns" (Ellis & Fouts, 1994, p. 174).

FIGURE 15.3. CRITICAL ISSUES FACING ALTERNATIVE ASSESSMENT

- **Conceptual clarity**. As yet, there is too little coherence to the concepts and language being used about alternative assessment, performance assessment, authentic assessment, direct assessment, and practical testing.

- **Mechanisms for self-criticism**. Internal self-criticism is rather scarce among proponents of alternative assessment. If voices of caution are drowned out by the clamor for more rapid adoption of methods of alternative assessment, advocates could easily forget that self-criticism is the only road to continuing improvement.

- **Support from well-informed educators**. The success or failure of the movement will depend on the willingness and competence of the teachers in the classrooms to undertake such tasks. This implies teachers with a higher degree of assessment competencies that differs from what is required now.

- **Technical quality and truthfulness.** What technical specifications and criteria should be used to judge the quality of the assessments, including reliability and validity? The crux of the matter is whether or not the alternative assessment movement will be able to show that its assessments accurately reflect a student's true ability that are relevant to adult life.

- **Standardization of assessment judgments**. How to standardize criteria and performance levels sufficiently to support necessary comparisons without causing them to lose the power and richness of assessment tailored to the student's needs and achievements remains a daunting issue.

- **Ability to assess complex thinking skills.** Do alternative modes of assessment necessarily require the use of more complex processes by students? Proponents cannot assume that students are using such skills just because they are performing a hands-on task.

- **Acceptability to stakeholders.** The public's acceptance of alternative assessments is not a sure thing. They are difficult to use to report learning outcomes for entire classes, school districts, or state systems. Political realities demand such accountability.

- **Appropriateness for high-stakes assessment**. Does alternative assessment provide sufficient standardization to defend high-stakes decisions based on such measures? Will ethnic minorities score better on alternative assessments than on traditional measures—or more poorly, as now appears quite possible? Will the inevitable legal challenges aimed at high-stakes decisions based on alternative assessments be more difficult to defend because of validity and reliability questions?

♦ **Feasibility.** One of the most frequently debated issues is whether or not alternative assessment is feasible for large-scale efforts to assess student performance. Does alternative assessment produce sufficiently greater benefits to justify its increased costs?

SOURCE: Adapted from Worthen, B. (1993). Critical issues that will determine the future of alternative assessment. *Phi Delta Kappan, 74,* 444–454.

Now, several years later, it is worthwhile to examine the status of the movement in relation to these issues. Apropos of this, the following headlines have appeared in recent issues of ASCD's online *Smartbrief* education news service:

Fourth Grade Math Exam Flawed

Mixed Test Results in Two Key Areas

Georgia's New Competency Test Raises Concern

Colorado Schools Feel Pressure of High-Stakes Test

California Teachers Leave Fourth Grade Over Proficiency Tests

Texas Students Take AP Exams in Record Numbers

NYC Report Finds Students Likely to Fail Regents Exam

Indeed, some states that had adopted or attempted to implement statewide alternative assessment systems have begun to temporize. And efforts in other states are bogged down. Bond and Roeber (1995) wrote, "Although there have been some successes, the setbacks in California, Arizona, Indiana, and elsewhere indicate that widespread acceptance of performance assessment is certainly not automatic" (p. 25).

Worthen's analysis of the critical issues facing alternative assessment were right on target. Many of the issues he identified have yet to be resolved, and these problems have been pointed out by a number of writers (Neill, 1996; Caudell, 1996; Olson, 1995; Viadero, 1995; Bond & Roeber, 1995). Specifically, these concerns remain:

♦ There are unresolved technical issues of reliability (basically consistency in scoring across scores and consistency in scoring from school to school or state to state) and validity (i.e., do they really reflect "higher thinking skills," "life skills").

♦ As yet, there is no way to standardize the assessments for "high stakes" purposes (e.g., accountability, program evaluation, and college admission).

♦ There is less than widespread public support among many parent and political groups.

♦ There is insufficient funding or commitment for the needed widespread teacher training that alternative assessment procedures demand.

♦ There is no evidence that alternative assessment procedures are more equitable to certain groups than are traditional assessment procedures.

♦ The estimates of cost of various alternative assessment procedures on a large-scale run from 5 to 30 times the cost of standardized multiple-choice tests, with no evidence that there is a cost benefit to them.

All of these things are embedded in Worthen's earlier critique, and, consequently, on a large-scale basis (state assessments, district assessments) the movement appears to have hit a snag, at least as it applies to school or student accountability. Still, the alternative assessment movement has encouraged many teachers to examine their evaluation or assessment ideas, particularly at the level of formative assessment, and that itself is a very valuable outcome, but one that brings into focus yet another problem.

The problem is basically one of definition, an issue that has plagued more than one educational innovation over the years. Black and William (1998, p. 7) write that there is not "a discourse of formative assessment, and currently the term 'formative assessment' does not have a tightly defined and widely accepted meaning." This is a sticky matter in that most authentic assessment tends to be formative, that is, it is done along the way in order to improve learning rather than render final judgments.

In a very thoughtful article, Morgan and Wyatt-Smith (2000) note the rise of "schooling in which an outcomes-driven assessment agenda is gaining increasing influence....[T]here has been a strong assessment agenda for explicity defined standards and official, public reporting—standardized testing, profiling, benchmarking and national literacy surveys.... Driving this agenda is a concerted move to use assessment in schooling as a means of achieving and measuring educational effectiveness" (p. 124). The authors do a remarkably effective job of pointing out the discrepancies inherent in talking about authentic assessment on the one hand, assessment whose main function is or ought to be teacher/

learner consciousness of what of value ought to be learned, and the often buisness/nationalistic/competitiveness agenda which addresses rather different interests. In a recent speech articulating the need for state standards and assessment, a state director of schools gave as the primary reason for tougher standards the fact that we do not know what jobs will be there for kids in the twenty-first century. It is all too easy to lose track of the notion that schools and learning might also exist for other purposes.

EDUCATIONAL RESEARCH AND ALTERNATIVE ASSESSMENT

Researchers are just beginning to address the questions of whether or not the use of such assessment strategies actually changes teacher behavior, student learning, or the curriculum. Reports from Vermont and Kentucky suggest that the strategies can have a positive effect for changing classroom activities, while reports from Arizona and elsewhere suggest that that is not necessarily so. Research done by Martin-Kniep, Sussman, and Meltzer (1995), for example, has shown that the assessment piece can be a vehicle by which teachers examine the role of the teacher and student in the learning process, but a well-designed staff development program is probably vital to make this happen.

One area of research that does relate alternative assessment to achievement is that of the updated effective schools findings. Effective schools research has been conducted for several decades, and has resulted in a variety of lists of school characteristics that distinguish "more effective" schools from schools that are less so. These characteristics are thought by many to have a cause-and-effect relationship with regard to achievement, but this is a hypothesis that has not been established empirically. Nonetheless, the effective schools characteristics do suggest why some schools may be better than others. A research synthesis by Cotton (1995) identifies the following among a long list of classroom and school attributes:

- ◆ Teachers make use of alternative assessments as well as traditional tests.
- ◆ Administrators and other building leaders develop and use alternative assessments.
- ◆ District leaders and staff support schools' development and use of alternative assessments.

However, these are only 3 of 59 characteristics that describe effective schools. Therefore, it is safe to say that this research in isolation is not adequate evidence to suggest that alternative assessment procedures will lead to greater student achievement.

Whether these procedures do or will actually result in greater learning by students may or may not be the case, but there appears to be no conclusive evidence at this point. If and when researchers focus systematically on this question, methodological problems will arise, namely, the determining of satisfactory educational outcomes and methods of assessing those outcomes. Alternative assessment advocates may balk at the use of standardized test scores as measures of achievement, with the result that no satisfactory way can be agreed upon to compare groups. Thus, the overall effect of this movement on student learning may prove to be highly problematic. Its efficacy would then necessarily be defended based on the belief that it focuses teaching and learning on more purposeful pursuits. One finds some precedent for this in the whole-language movement.

M. E. Gredler (1995) has articulated another note of caution to researchers on the use of alternative assessments by researchers. She examined what research there is on alternative assessment procedures and concluded that, "…at present, portfolio assessments are not recommended as the primary source of evidence about the attainment of program goals in evaluations that compare curricula or programs. The lack of validity and reliability information makes judging a curriculum or program on the scores assigned to student portfolios problematic at best" (p. 435). She states further that, "[t]he use of portfolios for other purposes that differ from fostering individualized student growth or demonstrating the intrinsic value of a program, leads, to no surprise, to problems and unresolved issues" (p. 436).

CONCLUSION

The alternative assessment movement is in many ways a breath of fresh air in an atmosphere gone stale over time. Those teachers and administrators who continue to search for ways to involve students more fully in their own learning toward a heightened state of consciousness of purpose in learning are to be applauded. Traditional tests and measures have so many obvious shortcomings that it is hardly necessary to go back over that ground in the closing moments of this chapter. But even given their obvious weaknesses, they do have value, and it would be most unwise to abandon them in spite of the allure of "authentic" approaches. Both are needed. It is probably true that teachers and students simply do not do enough assessing in school settings. Assessment at its best is the stuff of growth, reflection, metacognition, communication, and moral judgment. We can thank the alternative assessment movement for reminding us of that thought. In fact, the movement may be as much about teaching/learning strategies than about assessment. Or, put another way, the movement has shown us how to bring teaching, learning, and assessment together into a seamless whole.

References

Arter, J. (1995). *Portfolios for assessment and instruction.* Greensboro, NC: ERIC Clearinghouse on Counseling and Student Services.

Black, P., and William, D. (1998). Assessment and classroom learning. *Assessment in education: Principles, policy and practice, 5,* 7–74.

Bond, L., and Roeber, E. (1995). *The status of state student assessment programs in the United States. Annual report.* Washington, DC: Office of Educational Research and Improvement.

Cangelosi, J. (2000). *Assessment strategies for monitoring student learning.* New York: Addison Wesley Longman.

Caudell, L. (1996). High stakes: Innovation meets backlash as states struggle with large-scale assessment. *NW Education* 2(1), 26–28, 35.

Cotton, K. (1995). *Effective schooling practices: A research synthesis 1995 update.* Portland, OR: Northwest Regional Educational Laboratory.

Cronin, J. (1993). Four misconceptions about authentic learning. *Educational Leadership, 50*(7), 78–80.

Darling-Hammond, L. (1994). Setting standards for students: The case for authentic assessment. *Educational Forum, 59*(1), 14–21.

Ellis, A. (1991). Evaluation as problem solving. *Curriculum in Context, 19*(2), 30–31.

Ellis, A. (2001). *Teaching, learning, and assessment together: The reflective classroom.* Larchmont, NY: Eye On Education.

Goleman, D. (1998). *Working with emotional intelligence.* London: Bloomsbury.

Gredler, M. (1995). Implications of portfolio assessment for program evaluation. *Studies in Educational Evaluation, 21*(4), 431–437.

Lehman, N. (1994). Is there a science of success? *The Atlantic Monthly, 273*(2), 83–98.

Marcoulides, G., and Heck, R. (1994). The changing role of educational assessment in the 1990s. *Education and Urban Society, 26*(4), 332–339.

Martin-Kniep, G., Sussman, E., and Meltzer E. (1995). The North Shore Collaborative Inquiry Project: A reflective study of assessment and learning. *Journal of Staff Development* 16(4), 46–51.

McClelland, D. (1973). Testing for competence rather than intelligence. *American Psychologist, 46,* 1973.

Mehrens, W., and Lehmann, I. (1991). *Measurement and evaluation in education and psychology.* Orlando, FL: Holt, Rinehart and Winston.

Neill, M. (1996, February 28). Assessment reform at a crossroads. *Education Week*, 33.

Newmann, F., and Wehlage, G. (1993). Five standards of authentic instruction. *Educational Leadership, 50*(7), 8–12.

Olson, L. (1995, March 22). The new breed of assessments getting scrutiny. *Education Week*, 1.

Rayborn, R. (1992). Alternatives for assessing student achievement: Let me count the ways. In *Assessment: How do we know what they know?* pp. 24–27. Union, WA: Washington State Association for Supervision and Curriculum Development.

Ryan, J., and Miyasaka, J. (1995). Current practices in testing and assessment: What is driving the changes. *NASSP Bulletin, 79*(573), 1–10.

Steinberg, A., Cushman, K., and Riordan, R. (1999). *Schooling for the real world: The essential guide to rigorous and relevant learning.* San Francisco: Jossey-Bass.

Toch, T. (1991). *In the name of excellence: The struggle to reform the nation's schools and why it's failing and what should be done.* New York: Oxford University Press.

Toch, T. (2000). *In the name of excellence: The struggle to reform the nation's schools: Why it's failing and what should be done.* Bridgewater, NJ: Replica Books.

Trice, A. (2000). *A handbook of classroom assessment.* New York: Addison Wesley Longman, Inc.

Viadero, D. (1995, April 5). Even as popularity soars, portfolios encounter roadblocks. *Education Week*, 8.

Worthen, B. (1993). Critical issues that will determine the future of alternative assessment. *Phi Delta Kappan, 74*, 444–448.

EPILOGUE

*Have not the verses of Homer continued twenty-five hundred
years or more without the loss of a syllable or letter; during
which time infinite palaces, temples, castles, cities have been
decayed and demolished.*

Francis Bacon

The spirit of educational reform is endowed with perennial qualities. There seems to be a never-ending quest by educators for better programs, better delivery systems, better ideas about how students learn. Each year new approaches are touted, and thousands of teachers and administrators find themselves in meetings, taking notes while listening to some guru who claims to have at last gotten to the heart of the matter. The claims themselves have an enduring nature, only the topics change.

University of Kentucky professor and writer Thomas Guskey (1996) likened the education profession's infatuation with educational innovations and fads with the infatuations of a young child. Guskey points out that young children are prone to infatuations which are "passionate, totally consuming, and held in staunch resistance to alternative points of view." Young children see only the positive qualities of the object of infatuation, and are blind to the faults no matter how obvious those faults may be to others. And, what imperfections the child does notice are "dismissed as inconsequential and unimportant." Only later with maturity do we realize the short-lived nature of these infatuations, and only with maturity do we develop a "richer understanding more likely to endure the tests of time."

Concerning education, Guskey goes on to say:

> Although professional development in education certainly cannot be considered young and innocent, it still appears to be caught up in infatuations. Ideas, techniques, and innovations are latched on to with innocence and naivete. Devotion to these ideas is passionate and unfettered by criticism. Only positive attributes are perceived, while weakness and flaws pass unnoticed. And as is true in the case of most infatuations, the devotion tends to be short-lived. As a result, earnest but confused education leaders career from trend to trend. Their infatuations compel them to invest in the perspectives and programs

251

that are currently in vogue, even though their use may not be justified by the current state of theory or sound evidence. (p. 34)

Few fields of endeavor are as vulnerable as ours is to miracle cures. After all, we want desperately to be efficient, to provide equality of opportunity for children, and to promote academic excellence. We want our schools to be places of good repute, of best practice. Each of us wants people to talk about our own school with expressions of admiration. We want our students to recall their days with us as times of hope and glory. And why not? Why expect less of ourselves?

O. L. Davis, Jr. (2000), reflecting on this phenomenon, writes:

> Examples of educational best practices litter common memory. From efforts to apply cardinal principles to abandoned teaching machines, from problem-solving techniques to total quality management procedures, invention and advocacy of best practices have advanced like wind-driven prairie fires. Because the practice carried the imprimatur of "best," school officials and citizens alike routinely urged its general use across all school settings, for all pupils and teachers, and for all school offerings. The brilliant spectacle of advocacy, like the prairie fire, dies when the winds calm, as they always to, and the results total significant loss of commitment time, energy, and talent. The wreckage evidences failed crusades.

HOPE SPRINGS ETERNAL

Those teachers and administrators who have toiled in the vineyards of education over time come to know the rhythms of the school year. The hope and the high expectations of a golden September morning when the whole year lies before us and even the most mediocre student in the most mediocre class taught by the most mediocre teacher seems filled with the promise of success. We learn to know the ambiguities of a cold and dark January late afternoon when the kids have left for the day and we're sitting at our desk wondering what's the point and why are we doing this? And we've experienced that day in June when it's over once more and we made it and so did the kids and we're not sure how, and they're saying goodbye to us and where did the year go anyway? And that kid comes up to say goodbye, the one that everybody but us had written off, and hands us a note that simply says, "Thank you."

Maybe there is something more to teaching and learning than the quest for the latest program. Maybe it has more to do with a caring teacher and a group of kids who want to learn something than we are willing to admit in this age of innovation. Maybe the real answers were there all along, and they had more to do with decency, perseverance, character, and plain old high standards than we realized in our quest for the new. Still we look for help because it's a tough job and we want to do it right. How do we know when and whether to invest our time, our energy, the public's money, and the other resources that it takes to innovate?

THE GRAVEYARD OF LOST SHIPS

To paraphrase singer Neil Diamond, there is no way to count or to measure the cost of the energy lost in the annals of educational innovation. Today's flagship is often tomorrow's abandoned shipwreck. There was the incredible new program that everyone talked about, and if you weren't up to speed, well....Now the same people who touted it can barely remember it. Where are they now? All the miracle cures, all the new curriculums and methods that at long last had arrived to rescue us from the depths of mediocrity. All the answers for low test scores, for low self-esteem, for apathy and indifference to learning.

Whatever happened to Values Clarification? Whatever happened to Career Education? Whatever happened to TESA, GESA, and the other ESA's? And what of the New Math? The New Science? Competency-based Education? Behavioral Objectives? Outcome-Based Education? The Hunter Model? Glasser Circles? And the list goes on. It may be difficult to imagine it now, but there was a time when each of these items was the latest trend in educational circles. Some of them sank beneath the waves leaving no wake in their path. Others though were forerunners of later trends and thus contributed to a certain extent to the ongoing search for better schools. Not every innovation is in vain.

BEYOND EMPIRICISM

Much of the space in this book has been devoted to a look at the research base that supports certain educational innovations. The point of this has been that teachers and administrators should demand evidence before plunging ahead into some effort that just may dry up and blow away in time if for no other reason than that it never had a solid empirical basis. But this is not to say that everything we do in the name of learning demands evidence based on carefully controlled studies. Some things that are done, or should be done, in the name of education are not of a nature to be empirically based.

An example of a promising idea that one might assign to this category is *increased involvement by parents* in their children's academic life. Researcher John Goodlad noted that where parents are involved, school tests scores are higher. His conclusion makes good sense, but there is probably no way that one could conduct cause-and-effect experiments to determine the actual driving force in the mix of variables, given the range of rival hypotheses that immediately come to mind. Rather, we must in this case be content with well-established correlations at Level II and try to document positive academic outcomes at Level III, program evaluation. But the supportive evidence should lead building principals and classroom teachers to do everything they can to get parents meaningfully involved in their children's education. It not only is common sense, but it supports a larger societal goal of family togetherness. Two closely related challenges schools should mount include an exponential increase in the amount of reading students are expected to do accompanied by a corresponding decrease in the amount of time they spend watching television. Obviously, both of these quests would require parental support.

These ideas lead to a closing statement that must be considered thoughtfully if we are truly serious about raising achievement levels. Schools are the direct responsibility of those entrusted to their care. We should expect good value from them. But school, it is easy to forget, is really only a subset of that something larger called education. Education is the responsibility of the entire society. The perspectives on the importance of learning, which our young people develop, come from all quarters of society. To the extent that the messages are uplifting, coherent, and supportive of one another, a society will do an honorable job of educating the young. Schools simply cannot do it alone apart from the larger society. A society's cultural, spiritual, and academic vision is communicated to the young through its art, architecture, music, religion, science, media, government, and social and family structures. Inevitably, the better the society, the better its schools.

RESEARCH QUESTIONS TO ASK

Anyone who contemplates educational innovation should ask three basic sets of questions. These questions have been at the heart of the assessments of the programs reviewed in this book. The questions are:

- ♦ What is the theoretical basis of the proposed program? How sound is that theoretical base?
- ♦ What is the nature of the research done to document the validity of the proposed program? What is the quantity and quality of the research done in classroom settings?
- ♦ Is there evidence of large-scale implementation program evaluation? What comparisons were made with "traditional" forms? How realistic was the evaluation? What was the duration? What was the setting?

As you consider any innovation, you must pose these questions seriously. You should especially ask them of the purveyors of innovation. And you probably shouldn't settle for answers such as, "The movement is so new that much of this has not been done at this point." or "We don't have the luxury of time to do the research because we've got to help these kids." Too much is at stake.

CLOSING THOUGHTS AND A FINAL PLEA

We've looked together at a number of highly touted educational innovations in this book. In some instances, the supportive evidence is there. In other instances, well, serious reservations arise, especially where shaky theoretical foundations are concerned, where few or dubious studies have been conducted, and where program evaluation studies are lacking. The point is certainly not to make cynics of you or even suggest that you not *consider* an innovation until it has "proven" itself conclusively.

The watchword is caution, especially where large expenditures of funds and extensive teacher retraining are at stake. That is only prudent. But a certain amount of risk taking in the form of pilot programs and other efforts to transcend the ordinary qualities of school life are all to the good. These efforts should be mounted as Level II investigations. That alone will separate your school or district from the bandwagon-hopping legions that merely think they are doing something innovative while actually practicing self-delusion. The other outcome of a commitment to Level II research is that your school or district really will become a pilot center, one that others begin to look to for leadership. When schools commit to this level of quality, we can look forward to real progress, and perhaps the era of pendulum swings will come to a well-deserved end.

There is always the temptation to think of researchers as university types who possess arcane knowledge of statistical procedures and research design. The average teacher or principal probably seldom thinks of her/himself as a researcher in any sense. But why not become one? This is my plea to you. Consider joining the ranks. After all, you have knowledge and access that "professional" researchers don't have. You have experience, practice, professional judgment, and knowledge of kids that few people could ever hope to possess.

The term "action research" has been around a long time, since Kurt Lewin introduced it in the 1940s. Yet it remains an illusive and mainly undervalued commodity. I suggest that rather than wait for the next innovation to sweep the country, you get involved in your own study of what works with learners. It may involve some partnering with a university or some other research facility. Certainly it should involve some partnering with your fellow staff members. But please do not undervalue your own ability to make sense of life in classrooms. The time has come for the educator/practitioner to become a serious and respected player in the study of education.

As you yourself read research findings, you will find that your experience can and should interact with what the "experts" have to say. You will find that indeed you have something to say, something that informs practice. As you become familiar with the Level I, II, and III findings related to who and what you teach, you will find that the truly missing piece in all this is your perspective. The time has come for you, the reflective practitioner, to join the team. And the next time someone tells you, "the research says…," you will hear yourself replying, "Well, we're working on that very research, and this is what we're finding.…" Best wishes to you and the children we teach.

REFERENCES

Davis, O. (2000). Beyond "best practices" toward wise practices. *Journal of Curriculum & Supervision, 13*(1), 1–5.

Guskey, T. (1996, October 23). To transmit or to construct: The lure of trend infatuation in teacher professional development. *Education Week, 16*(8), 34.

INDEX